GUN
A VISUAL HISTORY

Featuring material from *Weapon*

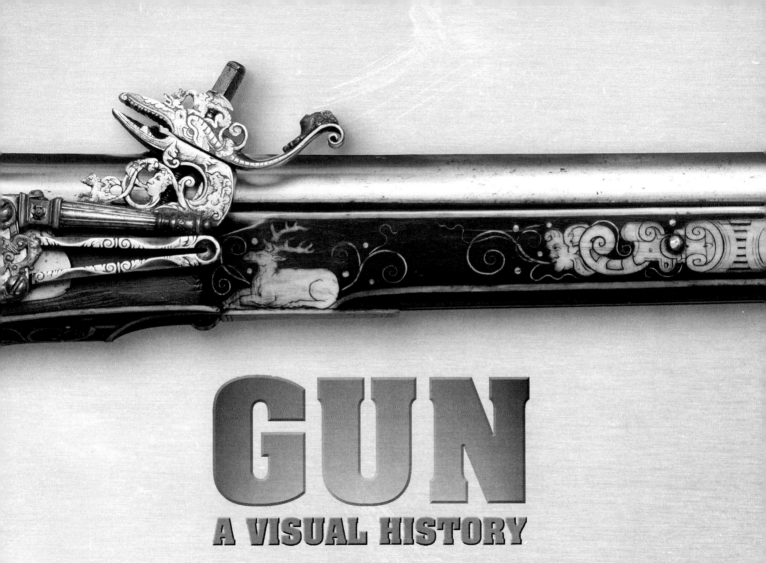

GUN
A VISUAL HISTORY

LONDON, NEW YORK, MELBOURNE,
MUNICH, AND DELHI

DESIGNERS Philip Fitzgerald, Tim Lane, Victoria Clark
EDITOR Chris Stone **DTP DESIGNER** Laragh Kedwell
PRODUCTION CONTROLLER Elizabeth Warman
MANAGING EDITOR Debra Wolter
MANAGING ART EDITOR Karen Self
ART DIRECTOR Bryn Walls **PUBLISHER** Jonathan Metcalf

DK DELHI
DESIGNERS Arunesh Talapatra, Enosh Francis
SENIOR DESIGNER Shefali Upadhyay
DTP CO-ORDINATOR Pankaj Sharma
DTP DESIGNERS Harish Aggarwal, Tarun Sharma
DESIGN ASSISTANCE Preetam Singh, Neeraj Aggarwal

First American Edition, 2007

Published in the United States by
DK Publishing
375 Hudson Street
New York, New York 10014

10 11   10 9 8

021 – GD093 – May/09

Published in Great Britain by
Dorling Kindersley Limited.

A catalog record for this book is available from the
Library of Congress.

ISBN 978-0-7566-2848-2

DK books are available at special discounts when
purchased in bulk for sales promotions, premiums, fund-
raising, or educational use. For details, contact: DK
Publishing Special Markets, 375 Hudson Street, New
York, New York 10014 or SpecialSales@dk.com.

Color reproduction by Wyndeham Icon, London, UK

Printed and bound in China by Hung Hing

Discover more at
www.dk.com

PISTOLS & REVOLVERS

HANDGUNS ARE THE ultimate expression of portable firepower. From their earliest days in the 16th century they were designed to be easily concealed, lightly carried, and operated with one hand. In terms of ballistic performance and accuracy, the sacrifices made by this emphasis on portability are many.

Handgun accuracy, even in today's high-specification weapons, tends to have a ceiling of around 82 ft (25 m), the precision limited by the instability of the grip and the shortness of the barrel. The barrel length, plus the limited ability for a small gun to handle any recoil, also means that range and penetration are steeply curtailed when compared to rifles. Yet such considerations are missing the point about handguns. In pure defense terms, handguns are about close-range reassurance. They can be deployed quickly, carried unobtrusively (one of the principal reasons they are standard police weapons), and, within the limits of their performance, pack a hard punch.

※

The handgun evolution effectively began with the advent of the wheellock system in the early 16th century. Wheellock guns provided pure mechanical ignition, not requiring a smoldering slow match, and so could be tucked into a belt or holster ready for use. They also entered military service as cavalry weapons, part of the mounted tactic known as the caracole.

The caracole seems to have developed around 1540, and involved massed ranks of wheellock-armed cavalry riding to within pistol range, discharging their handguns at the enemy ranks, then wheeling back to their lines to reload.

※

While the pistol was not an ideal weapon for organized battlefield firepower, it was perfect as a soldier's back-up weapon or as a self-defense tool for the civilian or law-enforcement officer. Wheellocks were highly expensive and delicate, so with the introduction of cheaper flint ignition systems handguns came into wider use.

There was also innovation. Multi-barrel "volley" pistols were made, particularly for naval use, and in the early 1800s the "pepperbox" revolving-barrel flintlocks enjoyed some popularity. Flintlock pistols varied in scale, but those most commonly carried were large, heavy items, usually chambered in big calibers of .50 in and above. They were also, by virtue of being muzzle loaders, slow to load.

Handguns stretched to their full potential during the technological revolutions of the 19th century. These came thick and fast. Alexander Forsythe's invention of percussion ignition in 1807 led to the development of the percussion cap in the 1820s. This in turn facilitated Samuel Colt's revolver by 1835, inaugurating the era of the true multi-shot handgun. Then in 1856 Smith & Wesson launched a .22 rimfire revolver with bored-through cylinders to take unitary brass cartridges. Such seminal advances meant that by the end of the 19th century revolvers had become globally common and highly effective. They ranged from small civilian rimfire pocket models in .22 caliber through to large military guns in .44 and .45 calibers.

While revolvers dominated the 19th century, the close of the century saw Austrian inventor Joseph Laumann produce the world's first automatic handgun in 1892, and German Hugo Borchardt design a more commercially successful model at roughly the same time. These first automatics were bulky and hard on the user, but the principles of self-loading pistols using blowback or recoil operation quickly resulted in sophisticated early 20th century models, such as the Colt M1911 and Luger P'08.

Automatics offered certain advantages over revolvers. Ammunition capacity can be far greater—today's standard Glock 17 handgun, for instance, carries 17 rounds of 9 mm Parabellum and the weight of this ammunition is located centrally in the user's grip hand rather than pulling down the gun from the front. No gas is lost between a cylinder and the barrel. For such reasons most military pistols in use today are automatic handguns, and they also dominate law-enforcement use.

———※———

In real terms, revolvers and automatic handguns have changed little since the stage of development reached by the end of WWII. New materials, particularly use of high-impact plastics, have lightened auto handguns, and there are much improved sighting systems. There have been several experiments with unusually powerful handguns, such as the gas-operated Desert Eagle, capable of firing the .50 in Action Express cartridge. Yet the most commercially successful guns are those that fulfill the same purpose as the wheellock back in the 16th century—convenient firepower for the close-range emergency.

PISTOLS & REVOLVERS

WHEELLOCK PISTOLS

The wheellock was a significant step beyond the matchlock, as it did not require a smoldering slow-match to fire the gun. Wheellock mechanisms emerged in Europe around 1507, and hailed as much from the minds of clockmakers as gunsmiths. The wheellock consisted of a metal wheel that was wound up under spring tension (a winding bolt projected from the middle of the wheel and was operated by a key). A metal arm, known as a cock, held a piece of iron pyrites, and this was lowered to sit on the wheel. Pulling the trigger released the wheel from its spring tension, causing it to spin around in contact with the iron pyrites, in turn generating a shower of sparks that ignited the powder in the pan and set off main-charge detonation.

FULL VIEW

Trigger guard

POWDER AND BALL
The size of the ball was expressed in "bore," being the number of balls of a given size that could be cast from 1 lb (0.45 kg) of lead.

Cock spring

GERMAN WHEELLOCK

DATE	1620
ORIGIN	Germany
WEIGHT	3 LB (1.3 KG)
BARREL	17 IN (43 CM)
CALIBER	.573

This pistol was made by Lorenz Herold, who is recorded as working in Nuremburg from 1572 until his death in 1622. However, this model is stamped with the Augsburg control mark. Therefore, Herold was either working in both regions, or buying in Augsburg-made barrels.

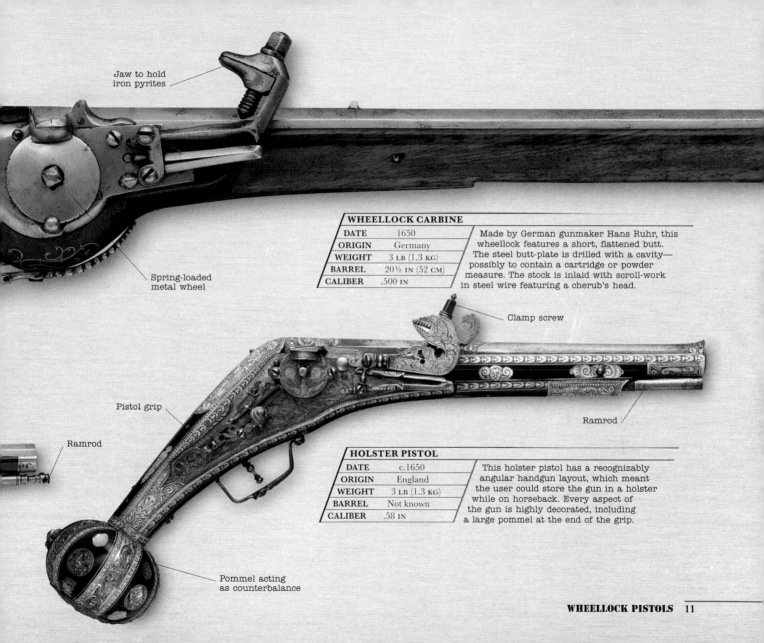

Jaw to hold
iron pyrites

Spring-loaded
metal wheel

WHEELLOCK CARBINE

DATE	1650
ORIGIN	Germany
WEIGHT	3 LB (1.3 KG)
BARREL	20½ IN (52 CM)
CALIBER	.500 IN

Made by German gunmaker Hans Ruhr, this
wheellock features a short, flattened butt.
The steel butt-plate is drilled with a cavity—
possibly to contain a cartridge or powder
measure. The stock is inlaid with scroll-work
in steel wire featuring a cherub's head.

Clamp screw

Pistol grip

Ramrod

Ramrod

HOLSTER PISTOL

DATE	c.1650
ORIGIN	England
WEIGHT	3 LB (1.3 KG)
BARREL	Not known
CALIBER	.58 IN

This holster pistol has a recognizably
angular handgun layout, which meant
the user could store the gun in a holster
while on horseback. Every aspect of
the gun is highly decorated, including
a large pommel at the end of the grip.

Pommel acting
as counterbalance

WHEELLOCK PISTOL, 1635

The idea of the wheellock seems to have originated with Leonardo da Vinci, as an example of this type of mechanism is described in his *Codico Atlantico* of 1508. By around 1517 the first working examples had emerged. The wheellock mechanism was simple but significant to the development of handguns. Once the serrated steel wheel was wound up under spring tension, the gun could be stowed ready for use at a moment's instance. This contrasted with the matchlock, which was impossible to conceal owing to its smoldering slow match.

—✳—

The thought of the new hidden gun obviously alarmed various European authorities, hence in January 1549 Britain's King Edward VI banned the carrying of pistols within a radius of 3 miles (5 km) of his court. His feared assassins were class specific—with more than 30 precision parts in some wheellocks only the rich could afford to buy one.

Lock plate

Trigger guard

ITALIAN WHEELLOCK	
DATE	1635
ORIGIN	Italy
WEIGHT	1¾ LB (0.75 KG)
BARREL	10¼ IN (26 CM)
CALIBER	.525

This wheellock was produced in Brescia, Italy, by the famed gunmaker Giovanni Battista Francino. Francino built his reputation on the high quality of finish, fine balance, and the superb lockwork of his guns, and he often made paired pistols for affluent customers.

WHEELLOCKS PERFORMED WELL, EVEN IN DAMP CONDITIONS.

Cock

Spring holds cock in place

BATTLE OF NASEBY
A Roundhead soldier fires a wheellock pistol at King Charles' Cavalier Army during the Battle of Naseby (1645.) This conflict was the key battle of the English Civil War.

FLINTLOCK PISTOLS 1550–1700

Wheellock pistols were never destined to become mass-market firearms, although they did draw out official concern—the Holy Roman Emperor Maximilian I banned their use in 1517, and several other monarchs followed suit. Yet the process by which they were produced required relatively rare levels of expertise on the part of the gunmaker, hence they were expensive guns to buy. The solution lay in a new lock system that used a struck flint as the means of powder ignition. The Dutch snaphaunce lock, a precursor to the flintlock, emerged in the 1540s. This featured a flint gripped in the jaws of a spring-loaded hammer, which when released struck a steel and directed a shower of sparks into the priming pan. The new system caught hold quickly, and evolved toward the emergence of the true flintlock in the early 1600s.

Jaw-clamp screw

Pan cover

Lock plate

Cock

Feather spring

Trigger guard

Rounded butt

Striker for upper barrel

Cock

Barrel release

Striker for lower barrel

Flattened pommel

Ramrod-retaining thimble

Barrel becomes round toward the muzzle

Forestock cap

Barrel is hexagonal toward the breech

ENGLISH FLINTLOCK PISTOL

DATE	c.1650
ORIGIN	England
WEIGHT	2¼ LB (1 KG)
BARREL	14¼ IN (34.2 CM)
CALIBER	25-bore

English gunmakers did not come into their own until the end of the 18th century. In the middle of the 17th century, when this holster pistol was made, they were still imitating their continental colleagues, and the maker of this piece, which has a French-style lock, was no exception.

EARLY FLINTLOCK PISTOLS WERE HEAVY AND DIFFICULT TO CONTROL, AND WERE WOEFULLY INACCURATE AT ANYTHING OVER 15 M (50 FT).

Side-mounted ramrod

DUTCH DOUBLE-BARRELED FLINTLOCK

DATE	c.1650
ORIGIN	Netherlands
WEIGHT	2½ LB (1.2 KG)
BARREL	19¾ IN (50.3 CM)
CALIBER	36-bore

Early multiple-shot handguns normally had a lock for each barrel. However, by mounting a pair of barrels on an axial pin and providing each with a striker and pan with a secure cover, it was possible to present each in turn to a single lock, reducing the cost considerably.

POWDER AND BALL
To achieve any sort of accuracy, the ball fired from a flintlock had to be spherical and of an exact size.

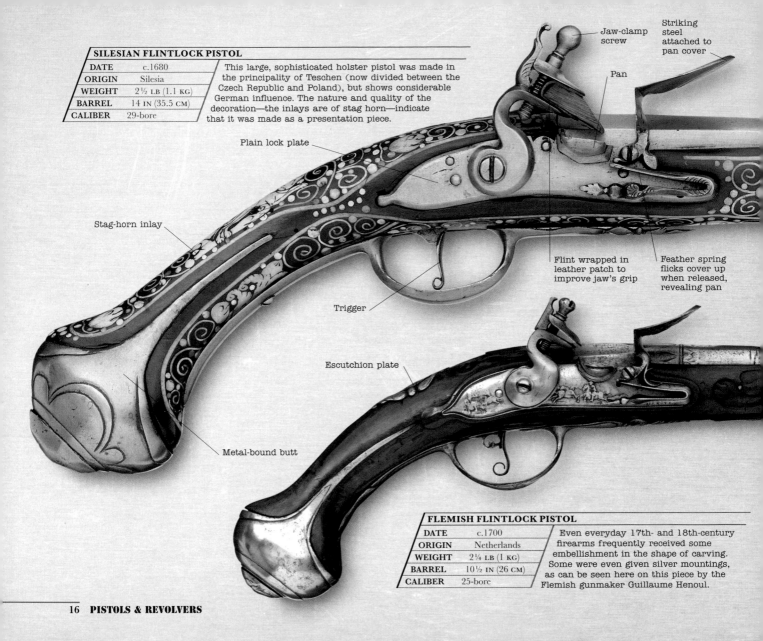

Jaw-clamp
screw

Striking
steel
attached to
pan cover

Pan

SILESIAN FLINTLOCK PISTOL

DATE	c.1680
ORIGIN	Silesia
WEIGHT	2½ LB (1.1 KG)
BARREL	14 IN (35.5 CM)
CALIBER	29-bore

This large, sophisticated holster pistol was made in the principality of Teschen (now divided between the Czech Republic and Poland), but shows considerable German influence. The nature and quality of the decoration—the inlays are of stag horn—indicate that it was made as a presentation piece.

Plain lock plate

Stag-horn inlay

Flint wrapped in
leather patch to
improve jaw's grip

Feather spring
flicks cover up
when released,
revealing pan

Trigger

Metal-bound butt

Escutchion plate

FLEMISH FLINTLOCK PISTOL

DATE	c.1700
ORIGIN	Netherlands
WEIGHT	2¼ LB (1 KG)
BARREL	10½ IN (26 CM)
CALIBER	25-bore

Even everyday 17th- and 18th-century firearms frequently received some embellishment in the shape of carving. Some were even given silver mountings, as can be seen here on this piece by the Flemish gunmaker Guillaume Henoul.

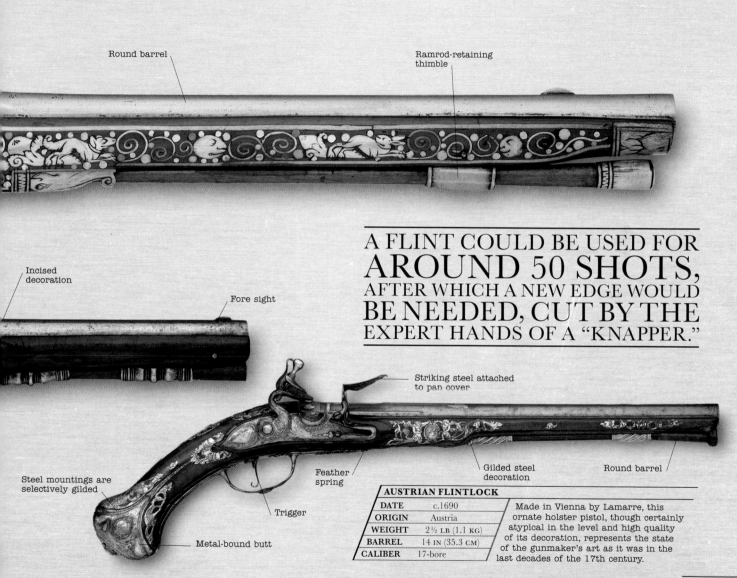

Round barrel

Ramrod-retaining
thimble

Incised
decoration

Fore sight

A FLINT COULD BE USED FOR **AROUND 50 SHOTS,** AFTER WHICH A NEW EDGE WOULD BE NEEDED, CUT BY THE EXPERT HANDS OF A "KNAPPER."

Striking steel attached
to pan cover

Steel mountings are
selectively gilded

Feather
spring

Gilded steel
decoration

Round barrel

Trigger

Metal-bound butt

AUSTRIAN FLINTLOCK		
DATE	c.1690	Made in Vienna by Lamarre, this ornate holster pistol, though certainly atypical in the level and high quality of its decoration, represents the state of the gunmaker's art as it was in the last decades of the 17th century.
ORIGIN	Austria	
WEIGHT	2½ LB (1.1 KG)	
BARREL	14 IN (35.3 CM)	
CALIBER	17-bore	

DICK TURPIN

Born on September 21, 1706 in London Turpin's childhood was immersed in smuggling and crime. In his late teens he was forced to flee into the Essex countryside, northeast of London, after being discovered cattle rustling—a capital offense in 18th century England.

—※—

Shortly thereafter he joined the infamous Gregory Gang, a large group of bandits operating around the Essex and London area. The gang was eventually broken apart in 1735, with several members going to the gallows, but Turpin went into partnership with the highwayman Tom King. Turpin's favored weapon was the flintlock pistol which he was using when he accidentally killed King in a gunfight with constables. After this Turpin fled north to York. His finances eventually unwound, and a spell in debtor's prison led to his discovery. He was hanged on April 7, 1739.

Trigger guard

Butt plate

WILSON PISTOLS	
DATE	c. 1730
ORIGIN	UK
WEIGHT	1¾ LB (0.74 KG)
BARREL	5½ IN (13 CM)
CALIBER	.596

Robert Wilson was a maker of fine pistols during the 18th century. His firearms were sought after collector's pieces and of the sort used by Dick Turpin. Paired pistols were usually either for dueling or came in a boxed collector's set.

Frizzen

Flint-clamping screw

PARTNERS IN CRIME

Dick Turpin shoots at soldiers who had arrested his partner Tom King in 1737. Turpin and King met one night when the former attempted to rob the latter. They quickly established a partnership and set up a base in an extensive cave system within Epping Forest, Essex.

FLINTLOCK PISTOLS 1700–1775

By the early 1700s, the flintlock mechanism was becoming the dominant lock system in European firearms manufacture, steadily replacing the snaphaunce and miquelet systems. The former had a mechanically operated pan cover, which opened via an arm or plunger link when the cock was released, exposing the priming powder to the flint's sparks. Miquelet locks developed in Spain during the early 17th century, had a combined steel and pan cover that was spring activated and driven forward by the impact of the cock. The flintlock, by combining the snaphaunce's internal workings and the miquelet's steel and pan cover arrangement, brought a reliable gun (depending on the quality of production) and an easier process of manufacture that galvanized European firearms ownership.

Ramrod-retaining thimble

Fore sight

Twin cocks

Frizzen (striker) attached to pan cover

Ramrod

Upper barrel

Lock plate

Figured walnut stock

D OLEP LONDINI

Frizzen spring flips up cover, revealing pan

Ramrod-retaining thimble

Trigger for upper barrel

Trigger for lower barrel

Butt is brass-bound

DOUBLE-BARRELED PISTOL

DATE	1700
ORIGIN	England
WEIGHT	3 LB (1.4 KG)
BARREL	13 IN (33 CM)
CALIBER	.5 IN

This is one of a pair of excellent English twin-lock, double-barreled, over-and-under pistols. It was made by the émigré Dutch gunmaker Andrew Dolep in London at the turn of the 17th/18th centuries. The right-hand lock and the forward trigger fire the lower barrel.

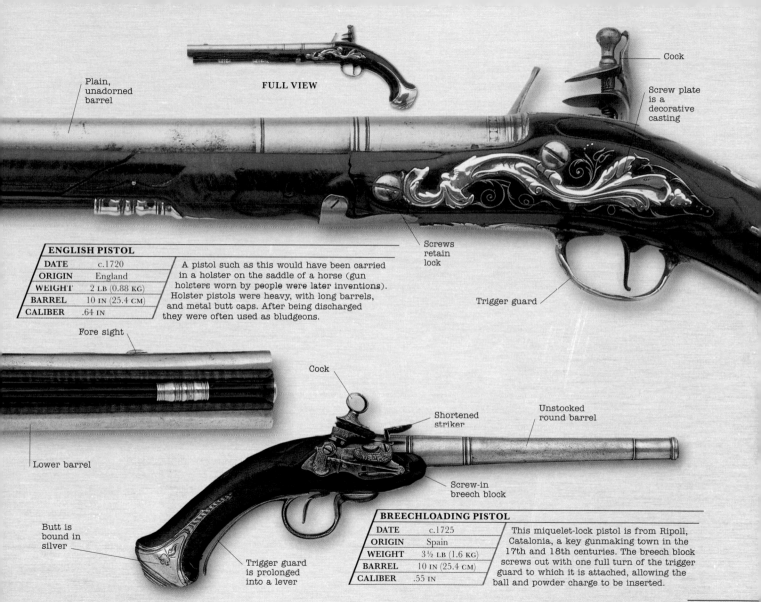

FULL VIEW

Plain,
unadorned
barrel

Cock

Screw plate
is a
decorative
casting

Screws
retain
lock

Trigger guard

ENGLISH PISTOL

DATE	c.1720
ORIGIN	England
WEIGHT	2 LB (0.88 KG)
BARREL	10 IN (25.4 CM)
CALIBER	.64 IN

A pistol such as this would have been carried in a holster on the saddle of a horse (gun holsters worn by people were later inventions). Holster pistols were heavy, with long barrels, and metal butt caps. After being discharged they were often used as bludgeons.

Fore sight

Lower barrel

Cock

Shortened
striker

Unstocked
round barrel

Screw-in
breech block

Butt is
bound in
silver

Trigger guard
is prolonged
into a lever

BREECHLOADING PISTOL

DATE	c.1725
ORIGIN	Spain
WEIGHT	3½ LB (1.6 KG)
BARREL	10 IN (25.4 CM)
CALIBER	.55 IN

This miquelet-lock pistol is from Ripoll, Catalonia, a key gunmaking town in the 17th and 18th centuries. The breech block screws out with one full turn of the trigger guard to which it is attached, allowing the ball and powder charge to be inserted.

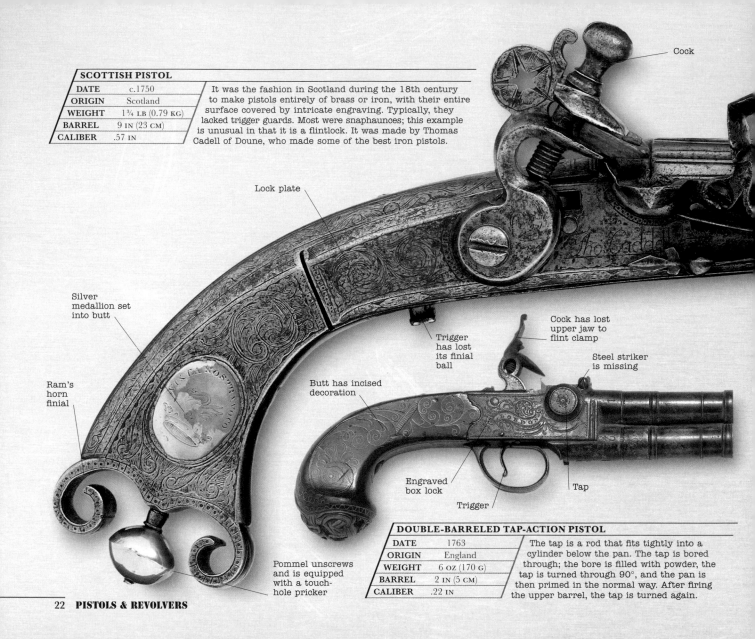

Cock

SCOTTISH PISTOL

DATE	c.1750
ORIGIN	Scotland
WEIGHT	1¾ LB (0.79 KG)
BARREL	9 IN (23 CM)
CALIBER	.57 IN

It was the fashion in Scotland during the 18th century to make pistols entirely of brass or iron, with their entire surface covered by intricate engraving. Typically, they lacked trigger guards. Most were snaphaunces; this example is unusual in that it is a flintlock. It was made by Thomas Cadell of Doune, who made some of the best iron pistols.

Lock plate

Silver medallion set into butt

Ram's horn finial

Trigger has lost its finial ball

Butt has incised decoration

Cock has lost upper jaw to flint clamp

Steel striker is missing

Engraved box lock

Trigger

Tap

Pommel unscrews and is equipped with a touch-hole pricker

DOUBLE-BARRELED TAP-ACTION PISTOL

DATE	1763
ORIGIN	England
WEIGHT	6 OZ (170 G)
BARREL	2 IN (5 CM)
CALIBER	.22 IN

The tap is a rod that fits tightly into a cylinder below the pan. The tap is bored through; the bore is filled with powder, the tap is turned through 90°, and the pan is then primed in the normal way. After firing the upper barrel, the tap is turned again.

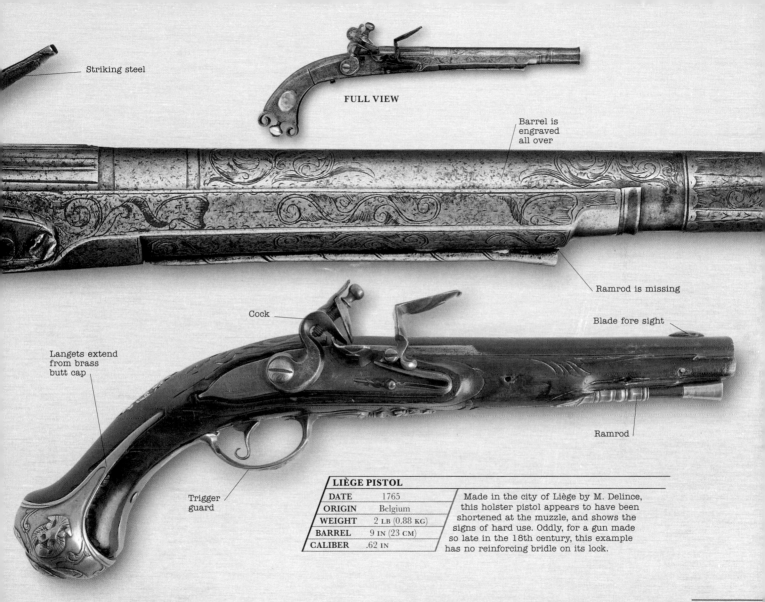

Striking steel

FULL VIEW

Barrel is engraved all over

Ramrod is missing

Cock

Blade fore sight

Langets extend from brass butt cap

Ramrod

Trigger guard

LIÈGE PISTOL		
DATE	1765	
ORIGIN	Belgium	
WEIGHT	2 LB (0.88 KG)	
BARREL	9 IN (23 CM)	
CALIBER	.62 IN	

Made in the city of Liège by M. Delince, this holster pistol appears to have been shortened at the muzzle, and shows the signs of hard use. Oddly, for a gun made so late in the 18th century, this example has no reinforcing bridle on its lock.

OTTOMAN EMPIRE FIREARMS

At the end of the 17th century the Ottoman Empire's occupation of large portions of south-west Europe ensured a steady inflow of modern military technology from the West, as reflected in the high quality of Ottoman handguns (most of these were direct copies of European models). The 18th century produced fine examples of Ottoman snaphaunce, miquelet, and flintlock handguns. Ornate decoration defines many of these pieces, with Persian, Islamic, and even Indian designs apparent in the use of inlaid precious metal and stones, and the sumptuous application of floral and geometric designs.

Butt terminates in lemon-shaped pommel

Feather spring

Engraved, inlaid lock plate

FULL VIEW

FLINTLOCK PISTOL	
DATE	Late 18th century
ORIGIN	Turkey
WEIGHT	Not known
BARREL	Not known
CALIBER	Not known

A pistol such as this—stocked all the way to the muzzle, with its woodwork copiously inlaid, and its lock, barrel, and trigger guard decorated with silver and gold—would have graced any arms cabinet in the Ottoman world. The lock appears to be of European pattern.

Striking steel

Decoration extends to muzzle

FLINTLOCK PISTOL

DATE	18th century
ORIGIN	Turkey
WEIGHT	Not known
BARREL	Not known
CALIBER	Not known

With the gentle fall to the butt and the slim "lemon" pommel, this pistol is reminiscent of European pieces of a century or more earlier. This flintlock also displays the common trademark of Ottoman gunmakers: gilded decoration surrounding the muzzle.

Barrel is blued and inlaid with gold

Gilt appliqué

Barrel is left unblued

Decorated lock plate

Silver inlay

Flared muzzle

Saddle bar

Carved walnut stock

Incised checkering on grip

FLINTLOCK BLUNDERBUSS

DATE	Early 18th century
ORIGIN	Turkey
WEIGHT	Not known
BARREL	13½ IN (34.3 CM)
CALIBER	Not known

Despite its being furnished with a shoulder stock that is incised, carved, and inlaid with silver, this blunderbuss is actually a large horse pistol. The work of "the Dervish Amrullah," according to an engraved inscription, it was clearly made for use by a cavalryman, as it has a bar and ring for suspension from a saddle.

OTTOMAN EMPIRE FIREARMS 25

INDIAN FIREARMS

As in many Asian countries, India remained wedded to the matchlock for far longer than was the case in the West, principally because flints were only available through importation. Furthermore, for indigenous gunsmiths operating out of humbly equipped workshops, matchlocks were straightforward to manufacture. Many of the lockwork designs, however, were of superb quality, and the British were still encountering matchlocks during their colonial expansion in India in the 1800s.

Flint clamp screw

Cock

Pan

Painted decoration

English-style lock plate

Trigger

Trigger guard

Checkered grip

BECAUSE OF THE COST OF FLINTLOCKS AND WHEELLOCKS, MATCHLOCKS WERE COMMON IN INDIA WELL INTO THE 19TH CENTURY.

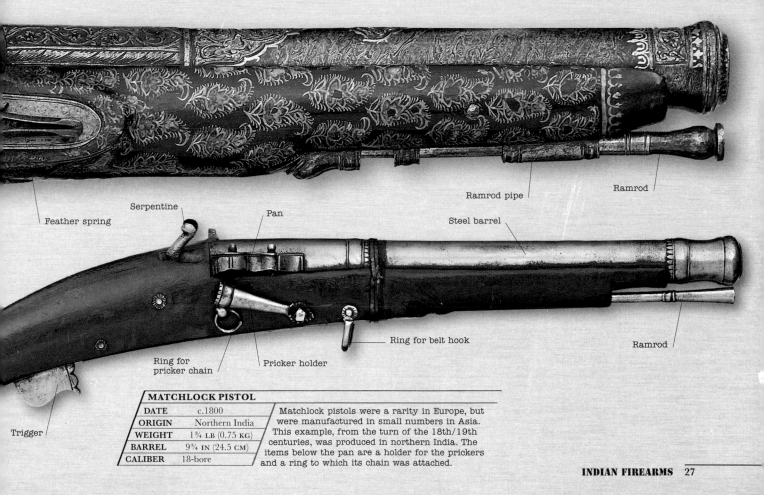

Striking steel

PUNJABI FLINTLOCK PISTOL

DATE	c.1800
ORIGIN	Lahore, India
WEIGHT	2 LB (0.86 KG)
BARREL	8½ IN (21.5 CM)
CALIBER	28-bore

This is one of a pair of superbly decorated pistols made in Lahore (now part of Pakistan) early in the 19th century. By this time, Sikh gunmakers were well able to fashion the components of a flintlock, though most of their energies were devoted to somewhat more workaday muskets known as jazails. This pistol has a "damascened" barrel, formed by coiling strips of steel around a mandrel and then heating and beating them to weld them together.

Ramrod pipe

Ramrod

Feather spring

Serpentine

Pan

Steel barrel

Ramrod

Ring for pricker chain

Pricker holder

Ring for belt hook

Trigger

MATCHLOCK PISTOL

DATE	c.1800
ORIGIN	Northern India
WEIGHT	1¾ LB (0.75 KG)
BARREL	9¾ IN (24.5 CM)
CALIBER	18-bore

Matchlock pistols were a rarity in Europe, but were manufactured in small numbers in Asia. This example, from the turn of the 18th/19th centuries, was produced in northern India. The items below the pan are a holder for the prickers and a ring to which its chain was attached.

BLACKBEARD

Edward Teach, better known to history as the pirate Blackbeard, hailed from the west of England and lived from c.1680 to November 22, 1718. Having been a privateer during the War of the Spanish Succession (1701–13), Teach turned to outright piracy in 1716, becoming the commander of his own pirate vessel the following year. For two years Teach brought a reign of terror to the eastern seas of the Americas and West Indies, building a reputation for merciless violence.

——※——

He was finally brought down by a specially commissioned pirate hunting force headed by British Royal Navy lieutenant Robert Maynard. After a battering encounter between Maynard's sloops and Blackbeard's *Adventure* off North Carolina, a close-quarters battle resulted in Teach being decapitated. His head was hung from Maynard's bows as a warning to others.

Flint-clamping screw

Cock

Feather spring

FLINTLOCK PISTOL	
DATE	c1700
ORIGIN	English
WEIGHT	3 LB (1.3 KG)
BARREL	Not known
CALIBER	.58

This pistol, of the type used by the pirate Blackbeard, features a rounded lockplate with double line engraving. The rammer is missing. It was made by Andrew Dolep, the gunsmith to Prince George of Denmark, the husband of Queen Anne.

BLACKBEARD'S
HEAD WAS HUNG FROM MAYNARD'S
BOWS AS A WARNING
TO OTHER PIRATES.

Holder for
ramrod

BLACKBEARD'S BLOODY END
Edward Teach fell before Robert Maynard's
sword on 22 November, 1718. After an
initial long range confrontation, Blackbeard
boarded Maynard's sloop with ten men
wrongly thinking that the government
vessel was undermanned. However, it
was a trap, and once the pirates were
aboard, Maynard called upon around
30 of his crew (who had been hiding
in the hold). Blackbeard's men were
quickly overrun and killed.

FLINTLOCK PISTOLS 1775-1800

The flintlock pistols of the 18th century served a variety of social purposes. Ownership of expensively made versions gave protection and status symbols to the noble and the wealthy. Early police units used them as standard side arms, as did many in the criminal fraternity, and they were also used in shooting clubs for target competitions. One particularly distinctive form of flintlock gun was the dueling pistol, which came to the fore once swords lost their civilian dress fashionability in the 1760s. Dueling pistols came as an identical boxed pair. Because the consequences of a misfire could be fatal for a duelist, the pistols were manufactured to the highest standards, and had extremely light triggers and heavy barrels to ensure accuracy.

Four barrels mounted side by side in vertical pairs

Flint held in leather patch

Striking steel

Joint between barrel and breech

Barrels unscrew for loading

Bead fore sight

Safety catch was a simple cover over the pan

GRIFFIN & TOW

Engraved plate

Each lock has its own trigger

QUEEN ANNE PISTOL	
DATE	1775
ORIGIN	UK
WEIGHT	1¾ LB (0.8 KG)
BARREL	4½ IN (11.7 CM)
CALIBER	48-bore

The distinctive form of the Queen Anne pistol continued long after the eponymous lady's death in 1714. The tapered "cannon" barrel screwed into a standing breech in which the lock plate, trigger plate, and butt strap were forged in one piece. This double-barreled example is by Griffin and Tow.

Striking steel

Flint held in
leather patch

I·REA

Turning tap
delivers
priming to
lower barrel

Internal, side-by-
side box-locks

Embossed silver
butt plate

FOUR-BARREL TAP-ACTION PISTOL

DATE	1780
ORIGIN	UK
WEIGHT	1½ LB (0.68 KG)
BARREL	2½ IN (6.35 CM)
CALIBER	85-bore

A simpler alternative to the cylinder revolver was to multiply the number of barrels; two, each with their own lock, were quite common, and four—and even six—became feasible with the invention of the tap. The taps, one for each vertical pair, presented priming for the second barrel when turned.

POCKET PISTOL

DATE	1800
ORIGIN	Belgium
WEIGHT	1 LB (0.48 KG)
BARREL	4¼ IN (11 CM)
CALIBER	.59 IN

Short-barreled pistols replaced the sword as the gentleman's weapon of self-defense. Box-locks were preferred to side-locks, because they were less likely to catch in the clothing. Pistols often had a bayonet, which was released by pulling back the trigger guard.

Striking steel

Safety catch locks pan cover in closed position

Octagonal barrel

Jaw clamp screw

Trigger guard retains bayonet in closed position

Striking steel

Rectangular box enclosing lock mechanism

Trigger

Rear "trigger" releases bayonet

Prawl

Cock

Smooth-bore barrel

Fore stock extends to muzzle

Feather spring

Ramrod

Hair trigger

MIQUELET DUELING PISTOL

DATE	1815
ORIGIN	UK
WEIGHT	2¼ LB (1 KG)
BARREL	9 IN (23 CM)
CALIBER	34-bore

Pistols specifically designed for dueling made their first appearance in Britain after 1780. They were invariably sold as a matched pair, cased, with all the accessories necessary for their use. "Saw handle" butts with pronounced prawls and steadying spurs on the trigger guard were later additions.

Catch locks bayonet in open position

Bayonet

Brass barrel

Bell mouth ensures wide spread of shot at close range

Spring-loaded bayonet

BLUNDERBUSS PISTOL

DATE	1785
ORIGIN	UK
WEIGHT	2 LB (0.95 KG)
BARREL	7½ IN (19 CM)
CALIBER	1 IN at muzzle

The blunderbuss (from the Dutch donderbus, or "thunder gun") was a close-range weapon, its bell mouth aiding the loading and dispersal of the shot. This box-lock model was the work of John Waters of Birmingham, England, who held a patent on the pistol bayonet. Officers of the British Royal Navy often used such pistols during boarding operations.

COLT

There are few names in the world of gunmaking as famous as Colt. In 1836 Samuel Colt established the Patent Arms Manufacturing Company in Paterson, New Jersey, to manufacture revolvers and rifles. This company fell into bankruptcy in 1842, but Colt continued his sales efforts, resulting in an army order for 1,000 revolvers in 1846. By 1855 Colt had opened major factories in Hartford, Connecticut, and London, England, and by the next year production was running at about 150 guns a day. Samuel Colt died in 1862, but the Colt name prospered in family hands for the rest of the century. Product lines expanded from revolvers to automatic handguns (such as the M1911) and machine guns, and this diversity bought major war contracts during WWI and

WWII. After a serious post-war slump between 1945 and 1959, Colt's business picked up in the 1960s with US military demand for Colt's M16 rifle. Military/law enforcement M16/M4 orders, plus sales of replica Colt revolvers and new auto handgun series have maintained Colt's strong position ever since.

Fore sight

Double action trigger

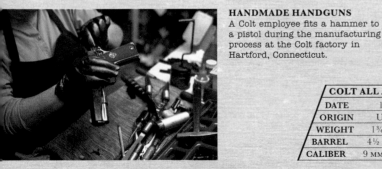

HANDMADE HANDGUNS
A Colt employee fits a hammer to a pistol during the manufacturing process at the Colt factory in Hartford, Connecticut.

COLT ALL AMERICAN 2000	
DATE	1991
ORIGIN	US
WEIGHT	1¾ LB (0.8 KG)
BARREL	4½ IN (11 CM)
CALIBER	9 MM

The All-American emerged from Colt in 1991, the brainchild of Reed Knight, Jr. and Eugene Stoner. It was a short-recoil 9 mm gun with a frame made of either polymer or aluminum, hence it was extremely light. However, the gun suffered from some major malfunction issues.

Hammer

Ejector rod
housing

COLT FRONTIER DOUBLE ACTION 1878

DATE	1878
ORIGIN	US
WEIGHT	2¼ LB (1 KG)
BARREL	5½ IN (14 CM)
CALIBER	.44/45 IN

Colt produced its first double-action pistol in 1877, and the following year developed a double-action version of the Peacemaker/Frontier in .44 and .45 calibers. Contrary to expectations, Colt managed to sell only 51,210 of the Frontier DA by 1905, around a third the number of single-action guns sold.

Six-round
cylinder

AT THE AGE OF 21 SAMUEL COLT PATENTED HIS REVOLVER DESIGN, AND SO LAID THE GROUNDWORK FOR THE FUTURE OF HANDGUNS.

Rammer
lever

Cylinder

COLT CAPS
Percussion caps, as used in the Navy Model 1861, were first introduced in this form in 1822.

COLT NAVY MODEL 1861

DATE	1861
ORIGIN	US
WEIGHT	2½ LB (1.2 KG)
BARREL	5½ IN (19 CM)
CALIBER	.36 IN

Colt was a firm believer in standardization in manufacture. One of the factors that made Colt's pistols so sought-after was the interchangeability of their components, which meant that replacements for broken parts could be bought off the shelf.

FLINTLOCK PISTOLS 1800–1850

The early 19th century continued the movement toward standardization of firearms begun in earnest in the 1700s. Pistols became standard auxiliary weapons to the sword in cavalry forces, resulting in the plain appearance of mass-market firearms—decoration was an unnecessary expense. The quality control in manufacturing common parts, however, was often extremely poor, and there were many inferior pistols available. Typical failures included broken mainsprings and badly constructed steels. High-quality handguns were still available, although these commanded the highest price tags. Only with the development of true mass-production engineering technologies in the mid 19th century did the quality of standardized fire-arms improve.

Jaw-clamp screw

Trigger

Brass trigger guard

Heavy brass butt plate

THE MILITARY FLINTLOCK PISTOLS OF THE 19TH CENTURY WERE OFTEN DESIGNED TO BE FLIPPED AROUND AND USED AS CLUBS, THE BUTTS OFTEN FEATURING HEAD-CRACKING HEAVY BRASS PLATES.

Striker

Striking
steel

HARPER'S FERRY PISTOL

DATE	1805
ORIGIN	US
WEIGHT	2 LB (0.9 KG)
BARREL	10 IN (25.4 CM)
CALIBER	.54 IN

The Model 1805 was the first pistol manufactured at the newly-established Federal Arsenal at Harper's Ferry, in what is now West Virginia. Like all martial handguns of the period, it was robust enough to be reversed and used as a club, should the need arise.

Crown over "GR"
—the mark of all
four King Georges

Feather spring
flicks pan open
as flint falls

Ramrod retainer
swivels so rod
can be turned and
inserted in muzzle

Tower proof mark

Brass forestock cap

Brass-bound
butt

Brass
trigger
guard

NEW LAND-PATTERN PISTOL

DATE	1810
ORIGIN	UK
WEIGHT	1¼ LB (0.5 KG)
BARREL	9 IN (23 CM)
CALIBER	.65 IN

The Land-Pattern Pistol was first introduced in 1756. It was a competent, sturdy design and was to remain in service until flintlocks gave way to percussion in the 1840s. A version with a flat butt and lanyard ring was produced for cavalry, and copies were made—by Ezekiel Baker—for issue to the East India Company's forces.

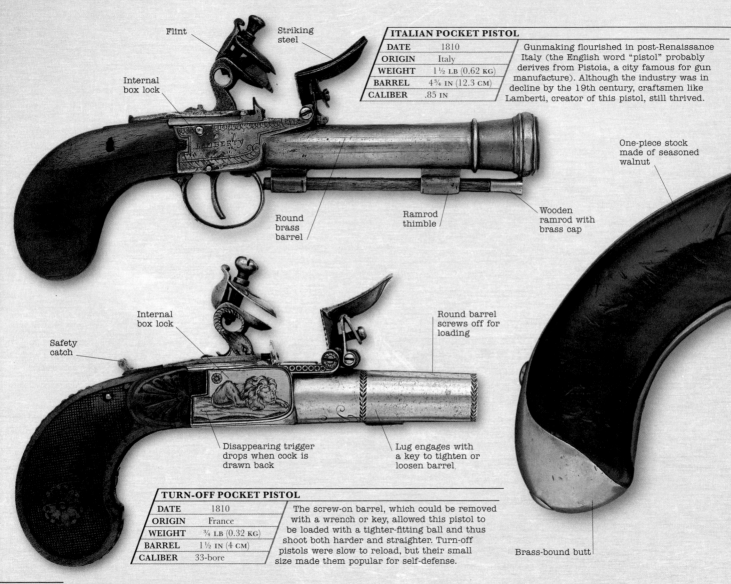

Flint

Striking steel

Internal box lock

ITALIAN POCKET PISTOL

DATE	1810
ORIGIN	Italy
WEIGHT	1 ½ LB (0.62 KG)
BARREL	4¾ IN (12.3 CM)
CALIBER	.85 IN

Gunmaking flourished in post-Renaissance Italy (the English word "pistol" probably derives from Pistoia, a city famous for gun manufacture). Although the industry was in decline by the 19th century, craftsmen like Lamberti, creator of this pistol, still thrived.

One-piece stock made of seasoned walnut

Round brass barrel

Ramrod thimble

Wooden ramrod with brass cap

Internal box lock

Safety catch

Round barrel screws off for loading

Disappearing trigger drops when cock is drawn back

Lug engages with a key to tighten or loosen barrel

Brass-bound butt

TURN-OFF POCKET PISTOL

DATE	1810
ORIGIN	France
WEIGHT	¾ LB (0.32 KG)
BARREL	1 ½ IN (4 CM)
CALIBER	33-bore

The screw-on barrel, which could be removed with a wrench or key, allowed this pistol to be loaded with a tighter-fitting ball and thus shoot both harder and straighter. Turn-off pistols were slow to reload, but their small size made them popular for self-defense.

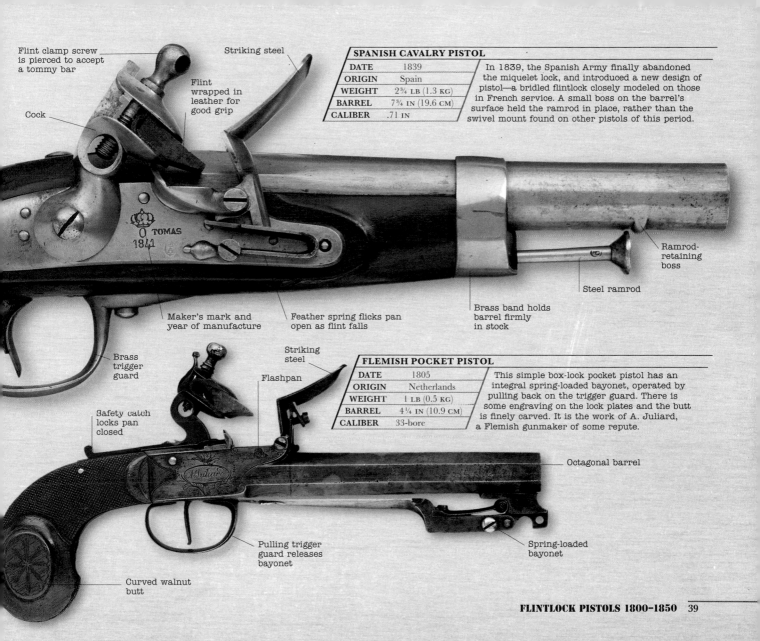

Flint clamp screw is pierced to accept a tommy bar

Striking steel

Flint wrapped in leather for good grip

Cock

DATE	1839
ORIGIN	Spain
WEIGHT	2¾ LB (1.3 KG)
BARREL	7¾ IN (19.6 CM)
CALIBER	.71 IN

In 1839, the Spanish Army finally abandoned the miquelet lock, and introduced a new design of pistol—a bridled flintlock closely modeled on those in French service. A small boss on the barrel's surface held the ramrod in place, rather than the swivel mount found on other pistols of this period.

TOMAS
1841

Maker's mark and year of manufacture

Feather spring flicks pan open as flint falls

Brass band holds barrel firmly in stock

Ramrod-retaining boss

Steel ramrod

Brass trigger guard

Safety catch locks pan closed

Striking steel

Flashpan

DATE	1805
ORIGIN	Netherlands
WEIGHT	1 LB (0.5 KG)
BARREL	4¼ IN (10.9 CM)
CALIBER	33-bore

This simple box-lock pocket pistol has an integral spring-loaded bayonet, operated by pulling back on the trigger guard. There is some engraving on the lock plates and the butt is finely carved. It is the work of A. Juliard, a Flemish gunmaker of some repute.

Octagonal barrel

Pulling trigger guard releases bayonet

Spring-loaded bayonet

Curved walnut butt

PERCUSSION-CAP PISTOLS

The percussion cap revolutionized the history of firearms. Percussion systems used impact-detonated priming powder to ignite the gun's main charge, and by the early 1820s the percussion cap had emerged. This contained the primer in a small copper cylinder (the cap) that was open at one end. The cap was placed on a hollow nipple, essentially an updated version of the touch-hole, under the hammer. When the hammer fell and crushed the cap, the fulminate detonated and the intense flash was directed down the nipple to the chamber. The key advantages of the percussion cap were reliability, as there was no more loose priming powder, and the greatly enhanced lock time—the speed between releasing the hammer and the gun being fired.

Hammer

Engraved lock plate

Butt has incised decoration

Trigger is pre-set to a very light pull

Incised checkering on butt

Incised checkering on butt

Hammer

Cap fits over nipple

Fore sight

Maker's name

Slide secures barrel in lock

Octagonal barrel

Steadying spur

Butt finishes in a pommel

BELGIAN DUELING/TARGET PISTOL	
DATE	1830
ORIGIN	Belgium
WEIGHT	2 LB (0.9 KG)
BARREL	9¼ IN (23.8 CM)
CALIBER	8 MM

Percussion-cap pistols were more reliable than even the best flintlocks, and one of their earliest uses was as dueling pistols. This half-stocked pistol by Folville, one of a matched and boxed pair, is typical of those produced in Liège, in what is now Belgium.

Animal decoration

Ornate octagonal barrel

Barrel-retaining slide

Animal decoration on hammer

Rear sight

FRENCH DUELING/TARGET PISTOL

DATE	1839
ORIGIN	France
WEIGHT	2 LB (0.9 KG)
BARREL	11¼ IN (28.3 CM)
CALIBER	12 MM

Technically, there is little difference between dueling pistols and those used for shooting at paper targets. However, the latter, such as this example by the renowned Parisian gunmaker Gastinne-Renette, were often beautifully decorated.

Octagonal barrel

Ramrod thimble

Trigger

FULL VIEW

Steadying spur

ENGLISH DUELING/TARGET PISTOL

DATE	c.1830
ORIGIN	England
WEIGHT	2½ LB (1.1 KG)
BARREL	9½ IN (24 CM)
CALIBER	44-bore

Despite their lack of overt decoration, dueling pistols were usually produced without regard to cost. This example, one of a pair, was the work of Isaac Riviere of London. Riviere had considerable influence over the design of percussion pistols, and patented his own lock in 1825.

Round barrel

Combined main
spring and hammer

Butt is
planed flat
on the sides

Ring trigger is
characteristic of
Cooper's pistols

COOPER UNDER-HAMMER PISTOL

DATE	1849
ORIGIN	England
WEIGHT	½ LB (0.27 KG)
BARREL	4 IN (10 CM)
CALIBER	.45 IN

Joseph Rock Cooper was a prolific English firearms inventor. One of his patents was for this pistol, which has an under-hammer by a Belgian named Mariette. In effect it is a "double-action" pistol: pulling the trigger lifts and then releases the hammer.

Bar hammer
acts vertically

Side-mounted
hammer

Checkering
on butt

Nipples set
horizontally

Barrels
rotate on
axial pin

Trigger

BAR-HAMMER "PEPPERBOX" PISTOL

DATE	1849
ORIGIN	UK
WEIGHT	2¼ LB (1.01 KG)
BARREL	3½ IN (9.1 CM)
CALIBER	.55 IN

Pepperbox pistols offered the advantage of multi-shot cylinder revolvers without their principle drawback—the leakage of propellant gas between chamber and barrel. Unfortunately, the type was generally inaccurate, except at point-blank range.

Hammer

Nipple

Fore sight

Plain
walnut
stock

Ramrod retainer
swivels to allow
captive rod to be
inserted in barrel

Lock
plate

PATTERN 1842 COASTGUARD PISTOL

DATE	1842
ORIGIN	UK
WEIGHT	2½ LB (1.05 KG)
BARREL	6 IN (15 CM)
CALIBER	24-bore

British pistols used by the coastguard, police, and other security agencies were similar in style to the Land- and Sea-Pattern pistols of the army and navy, but usually lighter and smaller. Revolvers replaced Pattern 1842 pistols in the 1850s.

Breech lever

Fore sight

SHARPS BREECHLOADING PISTOL

DATE	c.1860
ORIGIN	US
WEIGHT	2 LB (0.96 KG)
BARREL	5 IN (12.7 CM)
CALIBER	.34 IN

Christian Sharps was famous for his breech-loading rifles and carbines for military and sport use. He also made pistols based on the same principles as his early rifles. The falling breech cut off the rear of the linen cartridge when it was returned to battery.

FULL VIEW

COLT MODEL 1851

A total of 215,348 Colt 1851 revolvers were sold between 1851 and 1876, making it one of Colt's most influential weapons of the 19th century. It was a .36 caliber handgun that offered more manageable dimensions than the huge 1849 Dragoon, and had an overall length of just under 13 in (32.8 cm) and a weight of 2¾ lb (1.1 kg). The barrel was octagonal, and featured a simple bead foresight.

※

The Model 1851 was known as the "Navy"—Colt felt that the US Army would prefer to use the Dragoon—but most of the 1851s would be bought by US land forces. However, in the UK Colt's successful publicity drive at the London Exhibition in 1851 did indeed result in large Royal Navy orders. Chambered for six rounds, the Model 1851 had a respectable performance, generating a muzzle velocity of around 700 ft/ sec (213 m/sec), and it was heavily used during the American Civil War (1861–65).

Cutaway to facilitate placing of cap

Trigger guard

Hole for locking in armory rack

THE 1851 NAVY MODEL
PUT THE NAME OF SAMUEL COLT
ON THE FIREARMS MAP.

Rammer pivot pin

COLT NAVY MODEL 1851

DATE	1851
ORIGIN	US
WEIGHT	2¾ LB (1.2 KG)
BARREL	7½ IN (19 CM)
CALIBER	.36 IN

In 1851, Colt introduced a lighter pistol, the Navy Model, in .36 in rather than .44 in caliber. This example is one of the guns produced at the Colt factory in London in 1853.

WILD WEST SIDEARM
A US Cavalry soldier uses his Colt 1851 revolver during the Indian Wars of the 1870s. The Navy model was a popular sidearm during the American Civil War and beyond.

US PERCUSSION-CAP REVOLVERS 1850-1900

Samuel Colt did not, arguably, invent the revolver. What he did do, however, was take many of the revolving-cylinder experiments of earlier firearms and synthesize them into a successful working handgun, all at the age of only 21. His UK patent was granted in 1835, the US patent following in 1836. Colt's design utilized a pawl attached to the hammer to rotate the cylinder, the pawl engaging with a ratchet on the rear of the cylinder. To rotate the cylinder from one chamber to the next, the hammer was pulled back and cocked, the pawl simultaneously moving the cylinder the appropriate turn to bring the next chamber, and its exposed percussion cap, into line with both hammer and barrel. A vertical bolt locked the cylinder for firing.

AMMUNITION
The powder and projectile were made into simple cartridges with combustible cases made of fabric, rendered waterproof and rigid by an application of varnish.

Hammer spur

Nipple in recess

Side-mounted hammer

Cylinder-locking screw

Stud trigger

One-piece varnished walnut grips

Walnut grips

Top strap

Cylinder axis pin

Cutaway for loading linen cartridge

Octagonal barrel

Rammer lever

Concealed rammer

COLT MODEL 1855 POCKET PISTOL

DATE	1855
ORIGIN	US
WEIGHT	1 LB (0.5 KG)
BARREL	3 ½ IN (8.9 CM)
CALIBER	.28 IN

Such was the success of the Pocket Pistol that Colt launched another model in 1855, this one to the design of Elisha Root, the Works Superintendent, who did much to modernize manufacture. Root's pistol had a top strap a side-mounted hammer, and a stud trigger.

Notched hammer spur forms rear sight

Cylinder-retaining wedge

Octagonal barrel

Rammer lever

Rammer pivot pin

Rammer

Slot for cylinder-locking bolt

Cutaway allows cap to be placed on nipple

COLT MODEL 1849 POCKET PISTOL

DATE	1850
ORIGIN	US
WEIGHT	1.5 LB (0.69 KG)
BARREL	4 IN (10.2 CM)
CALIBER	.31 IN

Colt introduced a five-shot revolver in 1848 as the Baby Dragoon. The next year he produced a revised version, equipped with a standard compound rammer, a choice of three barrel lengths, and a five- or six-shot cylinder. It proved the company's best-selling percussion revolver.

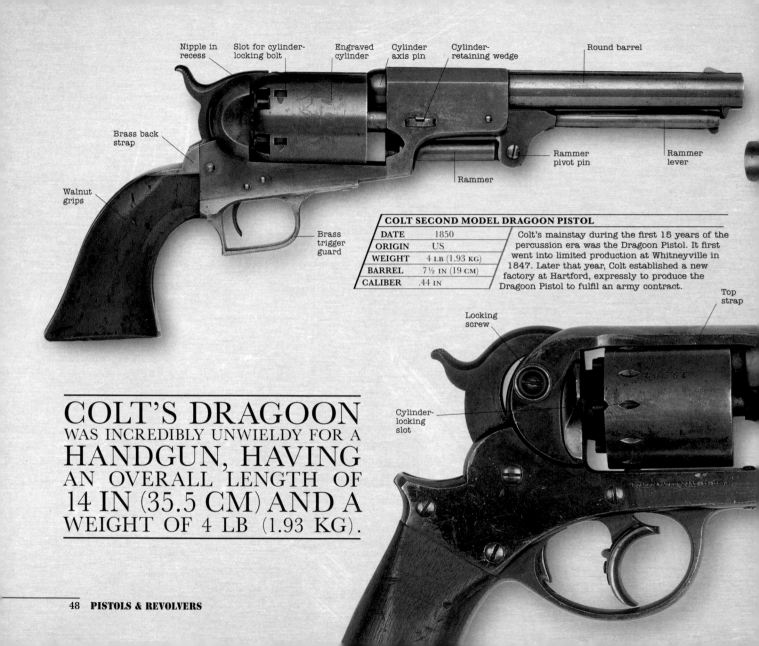

Nipple in recess

Slot for cylinder-locking bolt

Engraved cylinder

Cylinder axis pin

Cylinder-retaining wedge

Round barrel

Brass back strap

Walnut grips

Brass trigger guard

Rammer pivot pin

Rammer

Rammer lever

COLT SECOND MODEL DRAGOON PISTOL

DATE	1850
ORIGIN	US
WEIGHT	4 LB (1.93 KG)
BARREL	7½ IN (19 CM)
CALIBER	.44 IN

Colt's mainstay during the first 15 years of the percussion era was the Dragoon Pistol. It first went into limited production at Whitneyville in 1847. Later that year, Colt established a new factory at Hartford, expressly to produce the Dragoon Pistol to fulfil an army contract.

Locking screw

Top strap

Cylinder-locking slot

COLT'S DRAGOON
WAS INCREDIBLY UNWIELDY FOR A
HANDGUN, HAVING
AN OVERALL LENGTH OF
14 IN (35.5 CM) AND A
WEIGHT OF 4 LB (1.93 KG).

LE MAT PISTOL

DATE	1864
ORIGIN	US
WEIGHT	3½ LB (1.64 KG)
BARREL	7 IN (17.8 CM)
CALIBER	.3 IN and 16-bore

Jean-Alexandre Le Mat's revolver design was produced in both pistol and rifle form. The nine-chambered cylinder revolved around not a pin but a second, unrifled barrel, which was charged from the muzzle with pellets. The hammer had a hinged extension to its nose, which could be angled up or down to fire either barrel.

Hammer nose extension

Rifled barrel and cylinder screw onto smooth-bore barrel

Smooth-bore barrel acts as cylinder axis pin

Round barrel

STARR SINGLE-ACTION ARMY MODEL

DATE	1864
ORIGIN	US
WEIGHT	3 LB (1.35 KG)
BARREL	7½ IN (19.2 CM)
CALIBER	.44 IN

Nathan Starr was a pioneer of the break-open pistol, in which the barrel, top strap, and cylinder were hinged at the front of the frame before the trigger guard. The forked top strap passed over the hammer and was retained by a knurled screw. When broken open, the cylinder could be removed for reloading.

FULL VIEW

WYATT EARP

Wyatt Earp's turbulent life has been so embellished that it is difficult to get at the truth. However, he remains one of the Wild West's most famous lawmen, with several legendary gunfights to his credit, including that at the OK Corral on October 26, 1881 in Tombstone, Arizona. That shoot out, stemming from longstanding tension between the Earp brothers and the Clanton and MacLaury brothers, resulted in three dead and three wounded, Wyatt being the only person to come out unharmed.

—※—

However, much of Wyatt's skill as a gunfighter seems to have come from luck and good publicity rather than talent. His name is often linked with the Colt 1873, although it is possible that he used several weapons during his lifetime. Indeed, in 1876, Wyatt was one of five Dodge City lawmen to be awarded a Colt "Buntline Special" by the dime-novel writer Ned Buntline.

COLT MODEL 1873 SINGLE-ACTION ARMY	
DATE	1873
ORIGIN	US
WEIGHT	2½ LB (1.1 KG)
BARREL	7½ IN (19 CM)
CALIBER	.45 IN

The Colt SAA married the single-action lock of the Dragoon model to a bored-through cylinder in a solid frame, into which the barrel was screwed. It was loaded, and the spent case ejected, by way of the gate on the right of the frame, and a spring-loaded ejector was fitted.

Notched hammer acts as rear sight

Hard rubber-composition grips

OUTSIDE THE OK CORRAL THE GUNFIGHT SAW TWO MEN DEAD AND THREE WOUNDED. ONLY WYATT EARP REMAINED UNHARMED.

Barrel screws
into frame

FULL VIEW

WILD WEST LAWMAN
This is one of the few surviving
photographs of Wyatt Earp. Taken
19 months after the gunfight at
the OK Corral in 1881, this is much
as he would have appeared at the
time, quite possibly wearing the
same suit and hat.

BRITISH PERCUSSION-CAP REVOLVERS 1850–1900

In 1851 Samuel Colt presented his wares at the Great Exhibition in London, generating much publicity. However, by this date Colt's English patent on the revolver had expired (in 1849), and a new breed of English gunmaker was emerging to challenge US dominance. Chief among them was Robert Adams. Adams' first five-shot revolver had a solid frame—the butt, frame, and barrel were forged as one— into which the cylinder was hinged from the side. The gun was also double-action—the hammer was cocked and fired with one pull of the trigger. Although Adams lost the commercial war to Colt, many felt his gun was better in actual combat, and over the second half of the 19th century British pistol-making truly came into its own.

Notched ridge forms rear sight

Engraved plate covers double-action lock

Flash shield

Checkered walnut grips

DOUBLE-ACTION SHOOTING WAS MORE INACCURATE THAN SINGLE-ACTION, BUT ITS RATE OF FIRE WAS FASTER.

DATE	1855
ORIGIN	UK
WEIGHT	3 LB (1.36 KG)
BARREL	6 IN (15.2 CM)
CALIBER	54-bore

Open-framed "transitional" pistols combined elements of both the pepperbox pistols they superseded and the true revolvers. This example is of the type produced by one of the best known proponents, Joseph Lang of London.

Cylinder-locking wedge

Octagonal berrel

Fore sight

Rammer lever

Flash cylinder

Side-mounted hammer

Cylinder axis pin

Recessed nipple

Five-chambered cylinder

Octagonal barrel

Fore sight

Rammer lever

Lock cover plate

KERR DOUBLE-ACTION REVOLVER

DATE	1856
ORIGIN	UK
WEIGHT	2½ LB (1.2 KG)
BARREL	5¾ IN (14.7 CM)
CALIBER	54-bore

To address doubts about the reliability of the revolver, James Kerr fitted his with a simple box-lock and a side-mounted hammer. The lock was retained by two screws, and could be easily removed. Should a component break, any gunsmith would have been able to repair it.

Bar hammer

Engraved plate covers
double-action lock

Grip retaining pin

Fore sight

Flash
guard

Screw secures
barrel to
frame

Octagonal
barrrel

Prawl prevents
pistol from
slipping through
hand

Rammer lever

Trigger guard

Checkered
walnut grip

DEANE-HARDING ARMY MODEL

DATE	1858
ORIGIN	UK
WEIGHT	2½ LB (1.15 KG)
BARREL	5¼ IN (13.5 CM)
CALIBER	40-bore

When Robert Adams broke with his partners
in 1853, the elder Deane, John, set up his
own business. Later he began manufacturing
a revolver designed by William Harding with
a new, simpler type of double-action lock—the
forerunner of modern actions.

Octagonal barrel

DATE	c.1855
ORIGIN	UK
WEIGHT	1¾ LB (0.81 KG)
BARREL	5¼ IN (13.5 CM)
CALIBER	.4 IN

By the late 1850s, there was considerable demand in Britain for cylinder revolvers, but the best of them, by Colt, Deane, or Adams, were very expensive. Cheaper designs such as this example, with a bar hammer derived from a pepperbox revolver, were less satisfactory, with a tendency to discharge two cylinders at once because of the lack of partitions between the nipples.

Octagonal barrel

Cylinder axis pin

Nipple

Spurless hammer

Safety catch

ADAMS REVOLVERS WERE ROBUST FIREARMS, AND SOME AMERICAN OFFICERS PREFERRED OWNING AN ADAMS TO AN INDIGENOUS COLT OR REMINGTON.

ADAMS DOUBLE-ACTION REVOLVER MODEL 1851

DATE	1851
ORIGIN	UK
WEIGHT	2¾ LB (1.27 KG)
BARREL	7½ IN (19 CM)
CALIBER	40-bore

This revolver—Robert Adams' first—is also called the Adams & Deane Model (he was in partnership at the time). The entire frame, barrel, and butt were forged out of a single iron billet, making it extremely strong. Adams' lock was later replaced by a superior design by a young army officer, F.B.E. Beaumont. The Beaumont-Adams was adopted by the British Army in 1855.

BRASS CARTRIDGE REVOLVERS

After Colt's percussion cap revolver, the next big advance in pistol design was powered by Horace Smith and Daniel Wesson. In 1856 they bought a patent from gunsmith Rollin White, who had produced a revolver concept in which the chambers were bored through the whole length of the cylinder to enable breechloading. For Smith and Wesson it was the perfect system to incorporate their new .22 rimfire cartridge (meaning the primer is distributed around the rim of the cartridge base). It transformed handguns, making fast reloading possible—no more fiddling with percussion caps. For the next 13 years, Smith & Wesson had legal control over the breechloading pistol design even as new, more powerful centerfire cartridges (with a percussion cap centrally located in the base) became the norm.

Frame locking catch

Rear sight

Prawl prevents pistol slipping through hand under recoil

Trigger guard with steadying spur

Butt-retaining screw

.44 SMITH & WESSON RUSSIAN
The revolvers S&W supplied to the Russian Army were chambered for a cartridge of different dimensions.

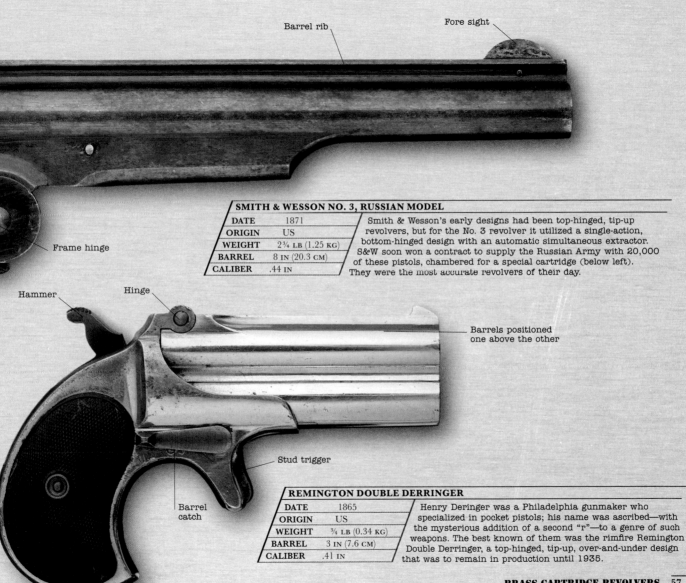

Barrel rib

Fore sight

Frame hinge

Hammer

Hinge

Barrels positioned
one above the other

SMITH & WESSON NO. 3, RUSSIAN MODEL

DATE	1871
ORIGIN	US
WEIGHT	2¾ LB (1.25 KG)
BARREL	8 IN (20.3 CM)
CALIBER	.44 IN

Smith & Wesson's early designs had been top-hinged, tip-up revolvers, but for the No. 3 revolver it utilized a single-action, bottom-hinged design with an automatic simultaneous extractor. S&W soon won a contract to supply the Russian Army with 20,000 of these pistols, chambered for a special cartridge (below left). They were the most accurate revolvers of their day.

Stud trigger

Barrel
catch

REMINGTON DOUBLE DERRINGER

DATE	1865
ORIGIN	US
WEIGHT	¾ LB (0.34 KG)
BARREL	3 IN (7.6 CM)
CALIBER	.41 IN

Henry Deringer was a Philadelphia gunmaker who specialized in pocket pistols; his name was ascribed—with the mysterious addition of a second "r"—to a genre of such weapons. The best known of them was the rimfire Remington Double Derringer, a top-hinged, tip-up, over-and-under design that was to remain in production until 1935.

Loading/
ejection gate

Plain
walnut
grip

Extractor-rod
housing

COLT NAVY CONVERSION	
DATE	1861
ORIGIN	US
WEIGHT	2¾ LB (1.25 KG)
BARREL	7½ IN (19 CM)
CALIBER	.36 IN

Colt replaced its angular 1851 Navy revolver with a new, streamlined version ten years later. This example has been converted to accept brass cartridges after the fashion of the Single-Action Army; many percussion revolvers were adapted in this way.

THE LIGHTNING WAS NOT COLT'S MOST RELIABLE WEAPON, BUT IT FOUND SOME NOTORIOUS USERS, INCLUDING THE RUTHLESS WESTERN KILLER JOHN WESLEY HARDIN.

Round barrel

Extractor rod

Blade fore sight

Hammer

Five-round cylinder

Colt logo

COLT LIGHTNING DOUBLE ACTION

DATE	1877
ORIGIN	US
WEIGHT	2½ LB (1.1 KG)
BARREL	5½ IN (14 CM)
CALIBER	.38 IN

The Lightning was Colt's first double-action handgun. It was a small-frame revolver chambered for .38 cartridges, although Colt also produced an accompanying weapon, the Thunderer, in .44 caliber to cater for those preferring a heavier punch. Although the Lightning had some quality issues, sales were still respectable, and the total production run reached 166,000 guns.

Fore sight

FULL VIEW

MAUSER ZIG ZAG

DATE	1878
ORIGIN	Germany
WEIGHT	2¾ LB (1.2 KG)
BARREL	6½ IN (16.5 CM)
CALIBER	.43 IN

The Zig-Zag is a six-shot .43 revolver, with a top-hinged frame. Diagonal slots cut into the cylinder face were used with a corresponding arm link to rotate the cylinder, but the complexity of this system led to the gun's rejection as a standard sidearm for the German Army.

Frame opening catch

Six-round cylinder

Hinged knife blade

DOLNE APACHE PISTOL

DATE	1890
ORIGIN	Belgium
WEIGHT	Not known
BARREL	Not known
CALIBER	7 MM

Developed in the 1870s by Louis Dolne, a Belgian gunmaker, the Apache pistol was a pure street weapon. It consisted of a barreless pinfire revolver—only of value at point-blank range—to which was attached a hinged knife blade at the lower front edge of the cylinder frame. Its handle doubled as a set of knuckledusters.

Loading/
ejection gate

Ejector rod   Round barrel

LEFAUCHEUX PIN-FIRE REVOLVER

DATE	1853
ORIGIN	France
WEIGHT	2¼ LB (0.95 KG)
BARREL	5¼ IN (13.5 CM)
CALIBER	12 MM

Casimir Lefaucheux invented the pin-fire cartridge in the mid-1830s, and his son Eugène later produced a six-shot, double-action revolver for it in 12 mm caliber. This is a Cavalry model of 1853. An Army model, without a steadying spur, was also produced.

Frame
catch

Hammer

Rib reinforces
barrel

Cylinder
axis pin

Rubber-
composition
grips

Lanyard ring

WEBLEY-PRYSE POCKET PISTOL

DATE	1877
ORIGIN	UK
WEIGHT	2¾ LB (1.3 KG)
BARREL	6¼ IN (16 CM)
CALIBER	.45 IN

In 1876, Charles Pryse designed a tip-down, break-open revolver with a rebounding-hammer action and simultaneous extraction of spent cartridges. This Fourth Model Webley-Pryse, recognizable by its fluted cylinder, was made in calibers ranging from .32 in to .577 in.

SMITH & WESSON

Founded in 1852 by Horace Smith and Daniel B. Wesson, the Smith & Wesson company remains the most famous maker of handguns in the world. Initially based in Norwich, Connecticut, the company first produced the innovative lever-action Volcanic pistol, but following financial troubles had to sell the business to Oliver Winchester in 1855. Smith and Wesson set up a new factory in Springfield, Massachusetts, in 1856 and began producing the gun that put them on the map—the .22 rimfire cartridge Model 1. This gun and subsequent models, plus the demand generated by the American Civil War, pushed S&W

to great success. Subsequent wars would continue the trend—S&W made 1.1 million .38 revolvers in WWII alone—but the company also became respected suppliers to police forces. Despite some setbacks (particularly losing the US Army's competition to replace John Browning's Colt M1911 in the early 1980s), S&W have remained dynamic, constantly bringing out new revolvers and automatic handguns.

PISTOL ENGRAVING
Former Smith & Wesson employee Harry Jarvis engraves revolvers at the company's gunmaking plant at Springfield, Massachusetts.

Frame

Trigger guard

TIFFANY MAGNUM		Smith & Wesson has produced various decorated "Tiffany-style" revolvers. This gun, based on a .44 Magnum Model 29, features a cast decorated grip produced in silver and gold.
DATE	1989	
ORIGIN	US	
WEIGHT	Not known	
BARREL	6 IN (15 CM)	
CALIBER	.44 Magnum	

THE SMITH & WESSON "ZIP-UP"
SYSTEM OF RELOADING WAS AN INSTANT SUCCESS.

Forward sight

.357 MAGNUM
Developed in 1935 this bullet has since been produced in many varieties.

Cylinder

MODEL 27	
DATE	1938
ORIGIN	US
WEIGHT	3 LB (1.4 KG)
BARREL	11¾ IN (30 CM)
CALIBER	.357 Magnum

Smith & Wesson produced a huge variety of pistols chambered for the various Magnum calibers—.357 and .44 are only the most common—on light, intermediate, and heavy frames. The heavy Model 27, in .357 caliber, was the most popular model, and was produced with 4 in (10.2 cm), 6 in (15.2 cm), and 8 in (21.3 cm) barrels.

Hammer spur

Ejector rod

Checkered grip

.410 SHOT PISTOL	
DATE	1970
ORIGIN	US
WEIGHT	Not known
BARREL	Not known
CALIBER	.410

This unconventional six-shot revolver is dated to 1970, but is actually a smoothbore firearm firing small .410 shot cartridges. The rationale behind such a weapon is questionable, but it would be useful for close-range (i.e., around 20 yards/18 meters range) vermin or game shooting.

Lanyard ring

EARLY SELF-LOADING PISTOLS

The first experiments with self-loading pistols occurred back in the 1850s, but only with the development of box magazines in the 1880s did they become viable. Building on principles explored through Hiram Maxim's machine gun, gunsmiths also realized that the force of recoil on firing could be used to operate a pistol's cycle of ejecting the spent case and reloading a fresh round. The first steps were taken in Austria, with the likes of Joseph Laumann and Anton Schonberger producing unsuccessful auto models, before the German Hugo Borchardt, having returned to Germany after 30 years working for US gunmakers, designed a relatively reliable 7.65 mm self-loading pistol. Although Borchardt's gun was not a commercial success, it laid the mechanical groundwork for the infamous Luger handgun and also demonstrated the now almost universal auto-handgun principle of a removable magazine loaded into the pistol grip.

Cylinder-indexing grooves

Cylinder-retaining wedge

Slide

.455 WEBLEY
Webley's first smokeless powder cartridge was more powerful than earlier types.

WEBLEY-FOSBERY	
DATE	1900
ORIGIN	UK
WEIGHT	2½ LB (1.1 KG)
BARREL	7½ IN (19 CM)
CALIBER	.455 IN

In 1899, Colonel George Fosbery designed a self-cocking revolver in which recoil propelled the barrel and cylinder backward within a slide, indexing the cylinder. It proved too fragile for battlefield conditions.

Recoil spring
housing

Steadying grip

MARS
The designer insisted on
a heavy propellant load
for the Mars bullet.

GABBETT-FAIRFAX "MARS"	
DATE	1898
ORIGIN	UK
WEIGHT	3 ½ LB (1.55 KG)
BARREL	11 ½ IN (26.5 CM)
CALIBER	.45 IN

Perhaps inspired by the Mauser's success,
Hugh Gabbett-Fairfax wanted to produce
a super-powerful pistol; the result was
the Mars. Described by users as "a
nightmare," it was complex, awkward,
and unwieldy, with a vicious recoil.

THE MARS PISTOL
PACKED A FEARSOME LEVEL OF POWER, THROWING OUT THE .45 IN BULLET AT AN IMPRESSIVE 1250 FPS (381 MPS).

Butt houses
removable seven-
round magazine

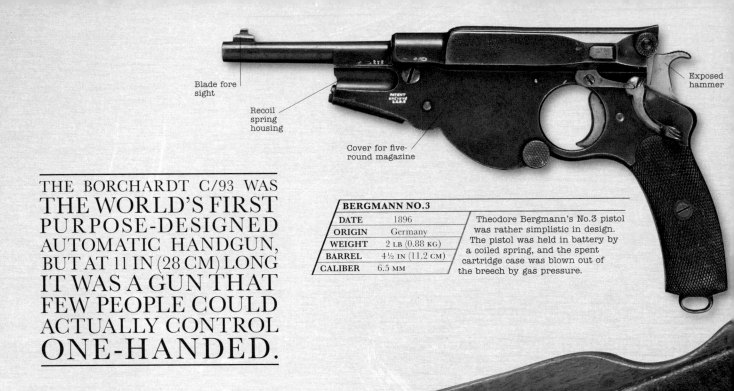

Blade fore sight

Recoil spring housing

Cover for five-round magazine

Exposed hammer

THE BORCHARDT C/93 WAS **THE WORLD'S FIRST PURPOSE-DESIGNED AUTOMATIC HANDGUN, BUT AT 11 IN (28 CM) LONG IT WAS A GUN THAT FEW PEOPLE COULD ACTUALLY CONTROL ONE-HANDED.**

BERGMANN NO.3	
DATE	1896
ORIGIN	Germany
WEIGHT	2 LB (0.88 KG)
BARREL	4 ½ IN (11.2 CM)
CALIBER	6.5 MM

Theodore Bergmann's No.3 pistol was rather simplistic in design. The pistol was held in battery by a coiled spring, and the spent cartridge case was blown out of the breech by gas pressure.

Detachable stock

Leather holster

BORCHARDT C/93

DATE	1894
ORIGIN	Germany
WEIGHT	3¾ LB (1.66 KG)
BARREL	6½ IN (16.5 CM)
CALIBER	7.63 MM

In Borchardt's pioneering design, a toggle joint locks the bolt in place. Recoil forces the toggle to break upward, the bolt travels to the rear against a coil spring, and the spent case is ejected. Rebounding, the bolt picks up a fresh round, chambers it, and leaves the action cocked for the next shot. The gun was a commercial failure; only 3,000 were produced, and it was discontinued in 1898 due to the competition from Mauser.

Rear sight

Toggle joint doubles as cocking piece

Ejection port

SYSTEM BORCHARDT. PATENT.

Recoil spring housing

Butt houses removable eight-round magazine

FULL VIEW

MAUSER C/96

The C/96 was designed by three brothers surnamed Feederle, who all worked for the German gun manufacturer Mauser in the 1890s. It was an automatic design initially chambered for the 7.65 mm Borchardt round, but in 1896, when production actually began, the caliber had changed to the 7.63 mm Mauser.

───※───

The C/96, despite its slightly ungainly appearance, was stable in the hand and shot reliably, and it spawned a wide range of variations until production ended in 1937. In addition to the 7.63 mm Mauser, the C/96 appeared in 7.65 mm Parabellum, 8.15 mm, 9 mm Parabellum, 9 mm Mauser, 9 mm Largo and .45 ACP. The gun was clip loaded via the top of the action, usually into a 10-round box magazine, but 6- and 20-round magazines were also seen. The addition of a shoulder stock made the C/96 into a useful carbine, and this found some service use during trench combat in WWI.

Loading/ejection port

Fixed 10-round box magazine

FULL VIEW

AN UNUSUAL FEATURE OF THE MAUSER WAS THE MAGAZINE BEING FORWARD OF THE TRIGGER.

Blade fore sight

MAUSER C/96	
DATE	1896
ORIGIN	Germany
WEIGHT	2 ½ LB (1.1 KG)
BARREL	5 ½ IN (14 CM)
CALIBER	7.65 MM

The "Broomhandle" Mauser Selbstladepistole soon became popular in military circles thanks to its very powerful ammunition. It remained in manufacture until 1937.

MAUSER ON FILM
British Prime Minister Winston Churchill carried a Mauser C/96 during the battle of Omdurman in 1898, a shoulder injury preventing him from using a saber. Here, Simon Ward plays the title role in the 1972 film *Young Winston*.

SELF-LOADING PISTOLS 1900–1920

The likes of Borchardt, Mauser, and Bergmann had produced serviceable automatic pistols in the late 19th and early 20th centuries, but these tended to be either too expensive or unwieldy for widespead service. Colt's M1911 pistol signaled, alongside the Luger P'08, the true birth of practical automatic handguns. The M1911 held eight rounds of powerful .45 in ammunition in its detachable box magazine, and utilized a new short-recoil system in which the recoil powered a slide along the top of the gun, which in turn powered the cycle of ejection and reloading. This system—much copied ever since—was extremely rugged and reliable. It was not the only one, however, and by the 1920s most major gunmaking nations were embracing workable automatic handgun technologies.

Fore sight

Recoil spring housing

Hold-open catch holds the slide back

COLT M1902	
DATE	1902
ORIGIN	US
WEIGHT	2¼ LB (1.02 KG)
BARREL	6 IN (15.2 CM)
CALIBER	.38 IN ACP

As well as the Model 1900 pocket pistol, Browning designed a series of military self-loading pistols in .38 ACP caliber, with an unsatisfactory double-link locking system that produced a jerky action. That, and the light rounds they fired, disqualified them in the eyes of the US Army.

Butt houses seven-round removable magazine

Rear sight

Hammer

Safety catch

Patent data

Lever holds slide back for stripping

Grip safety

Magazine catch

COLT M1911A1

DATE	1909 onward
ORIGIN	US
WEIGHT	2½ LB (1.1 KG)
BARREL	5 IN (12.7 CM)
CALIBER	.45 IN ACP

Browning designed the Colt M1911 in response to a demand by soldiers fighting Moro rebels in the Philippines. They wanted a pistol firing the heavy .45 round in place of the less-effective .38-caliber revolvers with which they were issued. The example shown here is a later M1911A1.

Butt houses seven-round removable magazine

.45 ACP
The .45 Automatic Colt Pistol round was developed for the John Browning-designed M1911.

Lanyard eye

Fore sight

3941   9 39

Fore sight

Md.1905
WAFFENFABRIK
STEYR

Hammer

Loading/ejector port

Butt houses
ten-round fixed
magazine

STEYR-MANNLICHER M1905

DATE	1905
ORIGIN	Austria-Hungary
WEIGHT	2¼ LB (0.9 KG)
BARREL	6¼ IN (16 CM)
CALIBER	7.63 MM

Produced by Werndl at Steyr, the M1905 was the last in a series of designs executed by Ferdinand von Mannlicher, who was better known for his rifles. It was complicated and expensive to manufacture, and as a consequence, was short-lived.

Barrel locking lug

Ejector port

Loading port

Hammer (or
"hahn")

Safety catch

Butt houses
eight-round fixed
magazine

STEYR "HAHN" M1911

DATE	1911
ORIGIN	Austria
WEIGHT	2¼ LB (0.9 KG)
BARREL	9 IN (12.7 CM)
CALIBER	7.63 MM

Werndl tried for many years to produce a successful military pistol, and succeeded with the M1911. It was similar in concept to the Colt, except that its barrel rotates, rather than tips, to unlock it from the slide.

STEYR 7.63 MM
This popular round has a muzzle velocity of 1000 ft/ sec (312 m/sec.)

4 in (10 cm) barrel, the
longest permitted in
Germany after World
War I

Hold-open
lever

Magazine catch

9MM PARABELLUM
Also known as the Luger, this is
the most common cartridge in
the world. Countless firearms
have been chambered for it.

Butt houses
ten-round
removable
magazine

LUGER P'08	
DATE	1908
ORIGIN	Germany
WEIGHT	2 LB (0.8 KG)
BARREL	4 IN (10 CM)
CALIBER	9 MM Parabellum

One of the best-known guns in the world, with almost iconic status,
the Pistole '08 was designed by Georg Luger in 1900. He copied many
features of Borchardt's gun of seven years earlier, but adopted a leaf
recoil spring and moved it into the butt, improving the overall balance
considerably. Luger also produced improved ammunition for his pistol,
the "Parabellum" round, which was to become the world standard.

Removable
butt stock

Concealed hammer

Fore sight

WEBLEY & SCOTT LTD
LONDON & BIRMINGHAM
'38 AUTOMATIC PISTOL   SAFE

Hold-open
lever

Butt houses
seven-round
removable
magazine

WEBLEY MODEL 1910

DATE	1910
ORIGIN	UK
WEIGHT	2¼ LB (0.9 KG)
BARREL	5 IN (12.7 CM)
CALIBER	9 MM Short

Webley of Birmingham, England, produced a
range of locked-breech self-loading pistols
from about 1904. They were all designed
by J.H. Whiting, who collaborated with
Hugh Gabbett-Fairfax on the Mars, and
were taken up by some police forces.

ASTRA M901

DATE	1920s
ORIGIN	Spain
WEIGHT	4¾ LB (2.1 KG)
BARREL	6¼ IN (16 CM)
CALIBER	7.63 MM Mauser

A direct copy of the Schnellfeuer ("Rapidfire") version of the Mauser C/96, the Astra was produced in Spain. It has an automatic-fire capability, but is impossible to control in that mode.

Rate-of-fire selector

20-round fixed magazine

8 MM NAMBU

The Japanese officer's pistols issued from 1909 onward were the only weapons ever made for this powerful round.

Fore sight

Safety catch

Ejector port

Cocking grip

火 安 十四年式

Magazine catch

Butt houses eight-round removable magazine

NAMBU TAISHO 14

DATE	1920
ORIGIN	Japan
WEIGHT	2¼ LB (0.9 KG)
BARREL	4¾ IN (12 CM)
CALIBER	8 MM Nambu

The first Nambu pistols appeared in 1909. Though they were clearly influenced by the Luger P'08, they have nothing in common with it internally, the unlocking of the bolt from the barrel being achieved by the rotation of a linking block.

SELF-LOADING PISTOLS 1920–1945

During WWI revolvers remained common side arms, and indeed remained dominant among many armies. Some nations, however, introduced automatic handguns as standard equipment for their officers. US soldiers carried the Colt M1911. Austro-Hungary fielded a variety of automatics, including the M1896 and M1905 Mannlichers and the Steyr M12, while German soldiers took the Mauser C/96 and Luger P'08. All proved themselves under the combat conditions of the Western Front, not only with officers but also with trench-raiding parties, who valued portable close-range firepower over an unwieldy long-range rifle. By WWII, the number of different automatic handgun types worldwide had proliferated tremendously, and ranged from the excellent 9 mm Browning HP to the chronically bad Japanese Type 94.

Fore sight

Semi-shrouded hammer

Fore sight

Butt houses eight-round removable magazine

TOKAREV TT MODEL 1933		
DATE	1933	The Tokarev TT was the first self-loading pistol on general issue to the Red Army. In design, it was similar to the Browning GP35, with a single swinging-link locking system. It was simple and could be field-stripped without tools. It lacked a safety catch, but could be put at half-cock.
ORIGIN	USSR	
WEIGHT	1¾ LB (0.85 KG)	
BARREL	4½ IN (11.6 CM)	
CALIBER	7.62 MM	

Polish eagle
proof mark

Data engraved
on slide

Decocking lever

Rear sight

Hammer

Hold-open
lever

RADOM M1935	
DATE	1935
ORIGIN	Poland
WEIGHT	2¼ lb (1.05 kg)
BARREL	4½ in (11.5 cm)
CALIBER	9 mm Parabellum

The Radom was similar in concept to the
Browning High Power, but it was more
compact and had extra security features.
These included a device that dropped the
hammer and retracted the firing pin, allowing
the pistol to be fired safely with one hand.

AUTOMATIC PISTOLS WERE THE PERFECT BACKUP WEAPON IF A RIFLE OR SUBMACHINE GUN JAMMED.

BERETTA

Beretta is not only the world's oldest gunmaker, it is also one of the oldest firms in history to remain in family hands. First evidence of its existence dates back to 1526, when gunmaker Mastro Bartolomeo Beretta was given 296 ducats for 185 arquebus barrels sold to the Arsenal of Venice. The company subsequently produced a variety of long arms and handguns for military and sport gun customers. Beretta's ascent to international dominance began under the directorship of Pietro Beretta (1870–1957), who took over the company in 1903 and upgraded their production process. By 1915 Beretta was also manufacturing automatic pistols, a weapon type for which it would subsequently become famous. Throughout the 20th century Beretta diversified, making assault rifles, shotguns, handguns, machine guns, and submachine guns, all of superb quality and backed by high sales. A crowning achievement came during the 1980s, when the Beretta 92 was selected to become the US Army's official replacement for the Colt M1911.

Trigger guard

ITALIAN CRAFTSMANSHIP
Pistol engraving is a delicate process so the gun needs to be secured by means of a tight-fitting mold or vice.

BERETTA 318	
DATE	1935
ORIGIN	Italy
WEIGHT	1¼ LB (0.5 KG)
BARREL	2¼ IN (5.7 CM)
CALIBER	.25 ACP

The Beretta Modello 318 was produced in Italy from 1935 to 1943. It was one of a developing line of Beretta small-frame pistols in 6.35 mm (.25 ACP) introduced in 1919, and it was exported in decent numbers to the United States, where it sold under the name Bantam or Panther.

Fire
selector

BERETTA 9000S

DATE	2001
ORIGIN	Italy
WEIGHT	2½ LB (1.1 KG)
BARREL	3¼ IN (8 CM)
CALIBER	.4 IN / 9 MM

The Beretta 9000S is a 9 mm or .40 S&W automatic handgun with a polymer frame and a 10-shot magazine. It is both single- and double-action, and has good safety features, such as an automatic firing pin block alongside a manual safety switch.

Magazine

Fore sight

PISTOLA STANDARD MOD.89 - CAL.22 L.R.
PATENTED

Fire selector

Slide catch/
release

BERETTA 89 TARGET

DATE	1989
ORIGIN	Italy
WEIGHT	1¾ LB (0.8 KG)
BARREL	6 IN (15 CM)
CALIBER	.22 LR

The Beretta 89 is an automatic blowback-powered handgun designed for competitive target shooting. Along with the Model 87, the 89 is a single-action gun and is built for high accuracy, with a heavy barrel, an adjustable rear sight, and even the facility for a scope.

Hammer

Recoil spring housing

Hold-open lever holds slide back

Safety catch

Butt houses eight-round removable magazine

Lanyard eye

STAR MODEL M

DATE	1932
ORIGIN	Spain
WEIGHT	2¼ LB (1.07 KG)
BARREL	5 IN (12.5 CM)
CALIBER	9 MM Largo

Manufactured by Echeverria in Eibar, the Star was one of the best of many copies of the Colt M1911, though it lacked the grip safety that the Colt had acquired by the mid-1920s. It was produced in a variety of models and calibers until the mid-1980s.

Fore sight

Data engraved on slide

Grip for pulling slide to rear

Hammer

Recoil spring housing

Safety catch and hold-open lever

Butt houses removable nine-round magazine

Magazine release catch

BERETTA MODEL 1934

DATE	1934
ORIGIN	Italy
WEIGHT	1 LB (0.65 KG)
BARREL	6 IN (15.2 CM)
CALIBER	9 MM Short

Beretta's M1934 was to become the official Italian officer's side-arm during World War II. The design evolved from one executed two decades earlier. Blowback-operated and without any form of locking mechanism, it was restricted to firing a reduced-power round, originally in 7.65 mm caliber.

Data engraved on slide

Hold-open notch

Milled cocking grip

Rear sight

Hammer

Recoil spring housing

Hold-open lever retains slide to rear

Safety catch

Magazine release catch

Butt houses 13-round removable magazine

BROWNING GP35	
DATE	1935
ORIGIN	Belgium
WEIGHT	2¼ LB (0.99 KG)
BARREL	4¾ IN (11.8 CM)
CALIBER	9 MM Parabellum

The High Power model was taken up by the Belgian Army. During World War II, plans for it were smuggled to Britain, and it was put into production in Canada. It was the first self-loading pistol adopted by the British Army, in 1954.

THE BROWNING HIGH POWER BECAME CENTRAL TO THE SAS ARSENAL, A BACK-UP WEAPON IF THE MAIN RIFLE OR SUBMACHINE GUN FAILED.

SELF-LOADING PISTOLS 1945–

By the end of WWII, automatic handguns had reached impressive standards of form and function. The post-war years brought mostly cosmetic, material, and safety improvements, and major expansions in magazine capacity; many modern 9 mm handguns take around 15 rounds in staggered-row box magazines. There were experiments in designing pistols capable of fully automatic fire—such as the Russian Stetchkin APS—but such weapons proved neither practical nor applicable. However, one name in particular emerged as a potent force in future handgun production—Beretta. The oldest gunmaker in the world remained one of the most commercially aggressive, and in the 1980s its Beretta 92 model replaced the Colt M1911 as the US forces service handgun after a controversial series of trials.

Hold-open lever retains slide to rear

Combined safety and rate-of-fire selector

STECHKIN APS	
DATE	1960s
ORIGIN	USSR
WEIGHT	2¼ LB (1.03 KG)
BARREL	5 IN (12.7 CM)
CALIBER	9 MM Makarov

The Stechkin was an unsuccessful attempt to produce a fully-automatic pistol for use by security forces. Like the Makarov, it was an unlocked blowback design based on the American Walther PP. In automatic mode it was practically uncontrollable.

20-round double-column magazine in butt

Rear sight

Hammer

Slide-mounted
safety catch

BERETTA MODEL 92FS

DATE	1976
ORIGIN	Italy
WEIGHT	2¼ LB (0.98 KG)
BARREL	4¼ IN (10.9 CM)
CALIBER	9 MM Parabellum

Chosen as the US Military's official side-arm to replace the Colt M1911A1 in the 1980s, the Beretta 92 was a conventional short-recoil design, its frame forged from aluminum to reduce weight. The slide top was cut away to allow single rounds to be loaded manually.

9 MM PARABELLUM

The word "parabellum" is derived from the Latin meaning "if you seek peace, prepare for war."

Hold-open lever
holds slide to rear

Safety catch

Hammer

Magazine
release catch

Hold-open
lever retains
slide to rear

Butt houses 13-
round magazine

MAKAROV PM

DATE	1950s
ORIGIN	USSR
WEIGHT	1½ LB (0.7 KG)
BARREL	3¾ IN (9.7 CM)
CALIBER	9 MM Makarov

The Tokarev's replacement as the standard Red Army side-arm was a copy of the American Walther PP, with double-action and a two-stage safety device. Its ammunition was about as powerful as could safely be used in a blowback design at that time.

Butt houses removable
eight-round magazine

PLASTIC PISTOLS ARE LIGHT AND TOUGH. THE ONLY METAL PARTS ARE THE BARREL AND THE ACTION ITSELF.

Enclosed hammer

Push-button safety catch

Burst-fire selector

Butt houses 18-round magazine

HECKLER & KOCH VP70M	
DATE	1970s
ORIGIN	Germany
WEIGHT	3½ LB (1.55 KG)
BARREL	4½ IN (11.6 CM)
CALIBER	9 MM Parabellum

The VP70M, the first pistol to make extensive use of plastic, was another attempt to produce a fully automatic handgun. The mechanism that controlled this was housed in the detachable butt stock; when it was removed, the pistol reverted to normal semi-automatic operation.

Frame-mounted
safety catch

Enlarged
trigger guard

Butt houses
ten-round
magazine

HECKLER & KOCH USP

DATE	1993
ORIGIN	Germany
WEIGHT	1¾ LB (0.75 KG)
BARREL	4¼ IN (10.7 CM)
CALIBER	9 MM Parabellum

The Universal Service Pistol was Heckler &
Koch's answer to the Glock, and it, too, was
largely made of plastic and employed the tried-
and-tested Browning locking system. The USP
was designed to facilitate modification, and
could be configured in nine different ways.

Fiber-reinforced
polymer shoulder
stock

GLOCK 17

The Glock 17 is one of Austria's most famous firearms exports, a superb auto handgun that has enjoyed great commercial success. It is a short-recoil operated gun—a single trigger pull first cocks the striker and releases a firing pin lock, then releases the striker.

※

This system, which Glock terms "Safe Action," means that there is no manual safety switch on the gun because the safety systems fully engage between each trigger pull (the striker also goes to half cock after the first shot), and it gives all the advantages of a double-action gun for a relatively light trigger pull. Further advantages of the Glock include a 17-round magazine (in 9 mm Parabellum) and a tough but light construction. Apart from the slide, barrel, and trigger group, all the other parts are made from a high-impact and environmentally stable plastic. Not only is the Glock 17 a standard Austrian Army weapon, it also equips a number of police forces from around the world.

Recoil spring and laser target indicator housing

Enlarged trigger guard for gloved hands

GLOCK 17	
DATE	1982
ORIGIN	Austria
WEIGHT	1¼ LB (0.6 KG)
BARREL	4½ IN (11.4 CM)
CALIBER	9 MM

The Glock 17's frame was fabricated entirely from plastic, with four steel rails to act as guides for the metal parts. It used Browning's single swinging-link/tipping-barrel locking system.

GLOCK CLAIMS ITS PISTOLS ARE USED BY 65% OF THE WORLD'S LAW-ENFORCEMENT AGENCIES.

IN THE LINE OF FIRE
A group of Iraqi police officers fire the Glock 9 mm during firearms training in 2001. The gun's designation derives from it being Gaston Glock's 17th patent, rather than (as is often misreported) its unusually large magazine capacity.

Butt houses
17-round
magazine

Slide

Silencer

BERETTA MODEL 70

DATE	1951
ORIGIN	Israel
WEIGHT	Not known
BARREL	Not known
CALIBER	7.65 MM

The small Beretta is easy to conceal and can be loaded with reduced-charge cartridges in order to increase the effectiveness of the silencer. This adaptation of a Model 70 was issued to members of Israel's Special Operations' assassination teams (known as *kidon*.)

Safety button

Magazine floorplate

THE BERETTA MODEL 70 IS THE FAVORED FIREARM OF ISRAEL'S SPECIAL OPERATIONS UNIT (MOSSAD).

JERICHO 941

DATE	1990
ORIGIN	Israel
WEIGHT	2¼ LB (1 KG)
BARREL	4½ IN (12 CM)
CALIBER	9 MM /.41 AE

The short-recoil operated Jericho 941 entered production with Israeli Military Industries (IMI) in 1990. The "941" designation refers to the way it was originally supplied with interchangeable barrels, magazines, and recoil springs to swap between 9 mm and .41 Action Express cartridges.

Slide

1048782

Data engraving

Slide catch/ release

Maker's mark

HELWAN

DATE	1965
ORIGIN	Egypt
WEIGHT	2 LB (0.87 KG)
BARREL	4½ IN (11 CM)
CALIBER	9 MM

The Helwan is an Egyptian licensed version of the Beretta Model 1951 Brigadier, a single-action 9 mm auto handgun with an eight-round magazine capacity.

THE MASSIVE, SPACE-AGE LOOKING, ISRAELI-MADE, DESERT EAGLE FAST BECAME A FAVORITE OF MOVIE MAKERS.

Interchangeable barrel

Muzzle brake

Adjustable rear sight

GRIZZLY 44 MAG

Extended barrel

Magazine release catch

LAR GRIZZLY MK IV	
DATE	1985
ORIGIN	US
WEIGHT	3 LB (1.35 KG)
BARREL	6½ IN (16.5 CM)
CALIBER	.44 Magnum

The LAR Grizzly handgun was developed as a high-power hunting or silhouette-shooting weapon. It is based upon the classic Colt M1911, most of the differences being related to size and minor external features. The Mk 1 came with caliber conversion kits; the Mk IV, by contrast, is only available in .44 Magnum.

Telescopic sight

2X-6X REDFIELD

Hammer

Identification data

Milled cocking grip

Safety catch

Recurved trigger guard to facilitate two-handed grip

IMI DESERT EAGLE

DATE	1983
ORIGIN	Israel
WEIGHT	5¾ LB (2.66 KG)
BARREL	10 IN (24.5 CM)
CALIBER	.44 Magnum

Unlike almost all other self-loading pistols, the Desert Eagle, made by Israel Military Industries (IMI), was gas operated, and of modular design. Its standard frame was able to accept sets of components for different ammunition, from .357 Magnum to .5 Action Express, and barrels of different lengths.

DIRTY HARRY

Few guns are so identifiable with a single film character as the Smith & Wesson .44 Magnum, forever linked with Clint's Eastwood's "Dirty" Harry Callahan. The specific gun used by Callahan is the Model 29 with an 8 ¼ in (21 cm) barrel (the Model 29 is available in three other barrel lengths, two shorter and one longer).

※

Prior to the filming of the first and eponymous *Dirty Harry* movie, Eastwood looked around for the ideal gun to represent his character's uncompromising personality. He found the Model 29 ideal, even though that version hadn't officially entered production with S&W at that point. The Model 29 appeared in all of the Dirty Harry films, and led to a surge of orders for Smith & Wesson.

Cylinder

Trigger guard

Checkered grip

Introduced in 1955, the Model 29 is one of S&W's N-frame revolvers, specially designed for shooting heavy loads. It came with a variety of barrel lengths, from 4 in (10 cm) up to 10½ in (27 cm), and all featured adjustable rear sights, indicative of the range expectations for the powerful .44 Magnum cartridge.

.44 MAGNUM

Luminous front sight

"I KNOW WHAT YOU'RE THINKING. 'DID HE FIRE SIX SHOTS OR ONLY FIVE?'"

DIRTY HARRY, 1971

"DO YA FEEL LUCKY, PUNK?"

In the denouement of the first film, Callahan goads Scorpio with this immortal line. Callahan's sensational claim that the .44 Magnum was "the most powerful handgun in the world" and "could blow your head clean off" was the best marketing Smith & Wesson could have hoped for.

REVOLVERS 1900–1945

One of the central applications of the revolver was in law enforcement, and during the late 19th and early 20th centuries certain models became standard police issue. In the United States, Colt and Smith & Wesson both made lucrative deals with state police units, most of the guns being sturdy solid-frame designs with swing-out cylinders. Suited for police needs, these guns could be quickly emptied by use of a star extractor, a rod-operated device designed back in the 1800s that pushed all spent (or otherwise) cartridge cases out simultaneously. A big issue to emerge, however, was caliber choice. Some of the early police issue revolvers were felt to have insufficient stopping power, so US gunmakers either stretched the case length (such as with the .38 Special) or opted for heavy calibers like the .455 Eley in the Colt New Service.

Fore sight

Cylinder axis and ejector rod

COLT POLICE POSITIVE

DATE	1905	In 1905 Colt modified its Official Police revolver, fitting the Positive lock with an intercepting safety device. In various forms, the Police Positive stayed in production for well over half a century.
ORIGIN	US	
WEIGHT	1¼ LB (0.6 KG)	
BARREL	4 IN (10.2 CM)	
CALIBER	.38 IN	

Fore sight

Cylinder-retaining catch

Cylinder gate pivot pin

SMITH & WESSON MILITARY & POLICE

DATE	1900	Having championed the hung-frame revolver, Smith & Wesson was obliged to switch to a solid frame with a swing-out cylinder for its Military and Police pistol. This was chambered for the long .38 Special round.
ORIGIN	US	
WEIGHT	1¾ LB (0.85 KG)	
BARREL	5 IN (12.7 CM)	
CALIBER	.38 Special	

Cylinder axis
and ejector rod

Cylinder
holds six
rounds

Trigger guard

Maker's mark

Grip retaining
screw

COLT NEW SERVICE	
DATE	1907
ORIGIN	US
WEIGHT	2 ½ LB (1.15 KG)
BARREL	5 ½ IN (14.4 CM)
CALIBER	.455 Eley

The Colt New Service was the last standard-issue service revolver produced by Colt for the US Army. Unbreakable under normal conditions, it had a solid-frame design with a swing-out cylinder. The British Army also bought them in great numbers, chambered, like this example, for the .455 Eley round.

THE .38 SPECIAL CARTRIDGE WAS
PRACTICALLY THE STANDARD-ISSUE ROUND
IN THE US POLICE FOR 60 YEARS.

Hammer

Ejector rod

Cylinder holds
six .38 Spl-caliber
rounds

Grip-retaining
screw

COLT AGENT	
DATE	1955
ORIGIN	US
WEIGHT	½ LB (0.23 KG)
BARREL	2 IN (5 CM)
CALIBER	.38 Spl

The Colt Agent was a lightweight version of the popular snub-nosed Colt Detective's Special. The Agent had an aluminum frame and an alloy cylinder. The butt was also shortened slightly. All of these features reduced the weight of the gun, but some safety issues hindered its sales and it was eventually discontinued.

Spurless
hammer

Cylinder holds
six .38-caliber rounds

ENFIELD NO.2 MK 1

DATE	1938
ORIGIN	UK
WEIGHT	1 LB (0.76 KG)
BARREL	5 IN (12.7 CM)
CALIBER	.38 IN

After World War I, the British Army decided to adopt a lighter caliber for its service side-arm. The revolver it chose was almost a copy of the Webley Mark VI. The version shown was issued to tank crews, and lacks a hammer spur.

Cylinder holds
six .45 ACP-caliber rounds

Pivot pin
for cylinder gate

SMITH & WESSON M1917

DATE	1917
ORIGIN	US
WEIGHT	2 LB (0.96 KG)
BARREL	5 IN (14.4 CM)
CALIBER	.45 ACP

During World War I, Smith & Wesson was commissioned to produce a revolver that chambered the rimless .45 ACP round. The model was a success, but had extraction problems unless flat half-moon clips, each carrying three rounds, were used.

WEBLEY & SCOTT MKVI

The Mk VI was a classic revolver in the Webley series of revolvers that began with the Mk I back in 1887. It was introduced in 1915, and was a robust .455 in handgun with a hinged frame system for loading. In many ways the Mk VI was essentially the same as many preceding models, particularly the Mk V, although the Mk VI had its barrel lengthened to 6 in (15 cm) and its mechanics simplified to aid faster production.

———※———

The Mk VI was a true war weapon, plunged quickly into the horrifying conditions of the Western Front. There it proved itself to be a thoroughly dependable sidearm, popular among trench raiding parties. The gun could also take a short bayonet, and this proved surprisingly popular, while the optional detachable shoulder stock was less practical. Although the British Army officially switched to a .38 caliber gun in 1932, the Mk VI had thousands of devotees, and so it continued in British Army use until a recall in 1939.

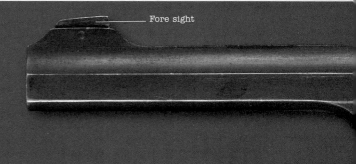
Fore sight

WEBLEY & SCOTT MK VI	
DATE	1915
ORIGIN	UK
WEIGHT	2¼ LB (1 KG)
BARREL	6 IN (15 CM)
CALIBER	.455 Eley

The last in a long line of service revolvers produced by the famous Birmingham partnership, the Mark VI was introduced early in World War I. It retained many of the features of its predecessors, and was renowned for its sturdy reliability.

THE .455 CALIBER WEBLEY WAS THE MOST POWERFUL OF THE TOP-BREAK SERVICE REVOLVERS EVER PRODUCED.

Cylinder-retaining key

Cylinder contains six .455-caliber rounds

WALKING WOUNDED
Wounded British soldiers retreating from the Battle of Mons, Belgium, in August 1914. The soldier on the right is carrying a Webley MkVI, the staple sidearm of British troops during the conflict.

Trigger guard

REVOLVERS 1945–

In the post-war years the advantages of automatic handguns—ease of use, large ammunition capacity—threatened the rationale for handguns. To counteract this trend, however, many revolver manufacturers turned to the production of magnum revolvers. A magnum handgun fires magnum ammunition, that is, cartridges that generate higher-velocities and greater penetration than conventionally cased cartridges of the same caliber. The first magnum revolver round was the .357 Magnum, developed in 1934 as an extension of the .38 Special, with the .44 Magnum following in the 1950s. Such rounds were designed purely for revolvers, as most automatic handguns could not handle the recoil forces. The .357 Magnum in particular sold well to policemen wanting more power in their holsters, the Colt Python being a favorite.

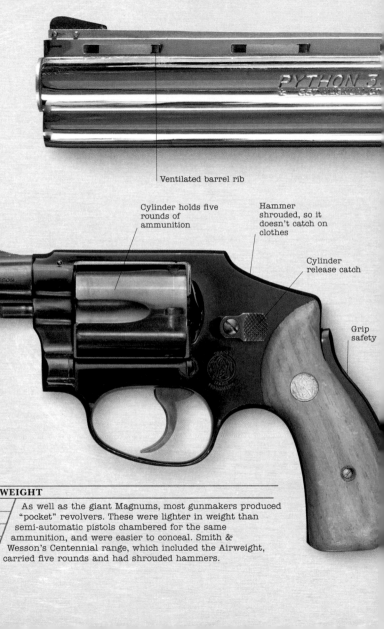

Ventilated barrel rib

Cylinder holds five rounds of ammunition

Hammer shrouded, so it doesn't catch on clothes

Cylinder release catch

Grip safety

Cylinder axis rod

SMITH & WESSON AIRWEIGHT

DATE	1952 onward
ORIGIN	US
WEIGHT	1 LB (.45 KG)
BARREL	2 IN (5 CM)
CALIBER	.38 Special

As well as the giant Magnums, most gunmakers produced "pocket" revolvers. These were lighter in weight than semi-automatic pistols chambered for the same ammunition, and were easier to conceal. Smith & Wesson's Centennial range, which included the Airweight, carried five rounds and had shrouded hammers.

Adjustable
rear sight

Cylinder rotates
clockwise

Cylinder
axis rod

.357 MAGNUM
Developed in 1935, this cartridge
has since been produced in many
varieties. Average muzzle
velocity is around 1,300 fps.

COLT PYTHON	
DATE	1953 onward
ORIGIN	US
WEIGHT	3 LB (1.4 KG)
BARREL	8 IN (20.3 CM)
CALIBER	.357 Magnum

Colt lost no time in producing its own Magnum
pistols, based on the tried-and-tested New Service
and Single-Action Army models, but it was the 1950s
before it produced an all-new purpose-designed
Magnum revolver: the Python. The ventilated barrel
rib has become a feature of these heavy revolvers.

Six-round
cylinder rotates
counterclockwise

Cylinder-
locking bolt
recess

Adjustable
rear sight

RECORY HERE ON SALE RECR. RANGE IS
INSTRUCTION MANUAL AVAILABLE FROM
STURM, RUGER & CO.INC.
SOUTHPORT, CONN. U.S.A.

.357 MAGNUM
The .357 cartridge was created
by Elmer Keith, Phillip Sharpe,
and Smith & Wesson.

Trigger guard

Butt

RUGER GP-100	
DATE	1987
ORIGIN	US
WEIGHT	2½ LB (1.05 KG)
BARREL	4 IN (10.2 CM)
CALIBER	.357 Magnum

Sturm, Ruger & Co. was a latecomer to the
world of gun manufacture, opening for business
in 1949. Initially, the company produced a
range of traditional single-action revolvers, but
later added designs incorporating the full range
of modern ergonomic and safety features.

CHARTER ARMS POLICE BULLDOG

DATE	1971
ORIGIN	US
WEIGHT	1¼ LB (0.6 KG)
BARREL	4 IN (10.1 CM)
CALIBER	.357 Magnum

Built on a heavier frame than the Undercover, the Police Bulldog was also available with a 2 in (5 cm) barrel, chambered for .357 Magnum or .44 Special ammunition. The molded rubber grips helped reduce the "felt" recoil.

Ergonomically designed molded-rubber grips

Five-chambered cylinder revolves clockwise

Cylinder holds five rounds of ammunition

Cylinder axis rod

Cylinder release catch

CHARTER ARMS UNDERCOVER

DATE	1964
ORIGIN	US
WEIGHT	1 LB (.45 KG)
BARREL	2 IN (5 CM)
CALIBER	.38 Special

Charter Arms began trading in 1964, and the Undercover was its first product. It was intended to be easily concealed, and being chambered for .38 Special ammunition it had plenty of stopping power.

JAMES BOND

The legendary character of James Bond, both in literature and film, has a special relationship with his guns. His choice of firearm signals his operational mentality and situation, from the Colt Police Positive slipped beneath his pillow in Ian Fleming's *Casino Royale* (1953) through to the Accuracy International AW sniper rifle used by Pierce Brosnan in the 2002 movie *Die Another Day*.

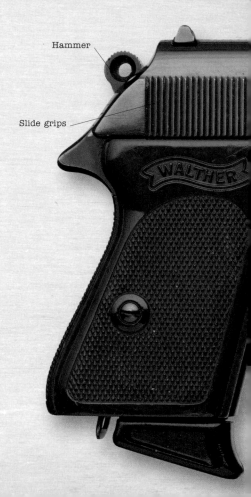

Hammer

Slide grips

Bond is, nevertheless, most closely associated with the Walther PPK, a gun introduced by Fleming in *Dr No* (1958) after Bond's previous handgun, the Beretta 418, fell out of favor with the author. The PPK would persist in Bond literature until the late 1990s when the Walther P99 finally took over. In film, the P99 stepped forward in *Tomorrow Never Dies* (1997). That said, Bond has used an enormous variety of weapons in his appearances—the pistol is often just a trusty fallback. In the movies alone, firearms have included a compressed air speargun, S&W Model 29, Sterling L2A3, CZ58 rifle, Walther WA2000 sniper rifle, several different Kalashnikovs, and the Ingram MAC 10 submachine gun.

WALTHER PPK	
DATE	1931
ORIGIN	Germany
WEIGHT	1¼ LB (0.6 KG)
BARREL	3¼ IN (8.3 CM)
CALIBER	7.65 MM

The Walther PPK was popularized through its cinematic use by James Bond, and it did indeed find its way into many security service hands, mainly on account of its compact dimensions. It was a simple blowback weapon most commonly produced in 7.65 mm (.32 ACP) caliber, and was fed from a seven-round magazine.

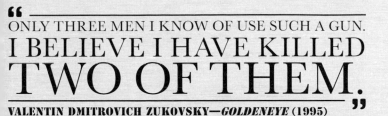

> "ONLY THREE MEN I KNOW OF USE SUCH A GUN. I BELIEVE I HAVE KILLED TWO OF THEM."
>
> **VALENTIN DMITROVICH ZUKOVSKY—*GOLDENEYE* (1995)**

Trigger guard

"THE NAME'S BOND…"
Sean Connery, who played the character of James Bond in a total of six films between 1962 and 1971, is to many fans the quintessential Bond. After a 12-year sabbatical, he returned for *Never Say Never Again* (1983). The movie's title was an allusion to Connery's previous decision to quit the role.

DECORATED HANDGUNS

Although the crudity of the earliest hand-gonnes prohibited decoration, the advent of wheellock and flintlock mechanisms provided more opportunities for artistic flair. Engraving was, and remains, the primary form of decoration, with different styles developing across Europe. Almost all guns up to the percussion era had some form of decoration, from simple scrollwork through to engraved game scenes. For more affluent customers, gun value was further enhanced using inlaid precious stones and metals, particularly around the stock and lock plates. Today, laser engraving means that non-military weapons can receive excellent engraving without prohibitive cost, while hand engraving and more ostentatious decorations still command a premium.

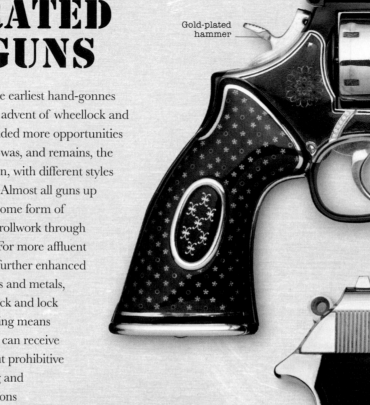

Gold-plated hammer

Gold-plated cylinder

Ejection port

Textured grip— only feature not gold-plated

WALTHER PP	
DATE	Not known
ORIGIN	Germany
WEIGHT	3 LB (1.4 KG)
BARREL	4 IN (10 CM)
CALIBER	9 MM Short

This Walther PP is gold plated to produce an excellent collector's piece. The PP type was one of the first double-action automatic handguns. It became popular with police and military officers, and was issued in two calibers: 7.65 mm Browning or 9 mm Short.

SMITH & WESSON .357 MAGNUM

DATE	Not known
ORIGIN	US
WEIGHT	Not known
BARREL	4¾ IN (12 CM)
CALIBER	.357

This Smith & Wesson revolver has, apart from exquisite grip decoration, a gold-plated cylinder, trigger and hammer. The barrel and much of the frame remain conventional, undecorated S&W parts. As with most S&W special editions, the revolver is fully functional.

Diamond-encrusted slide

Gold-plated trigger

Diamond-edged pistol grip

SiG P220

DATE	Not known
ORIGIN	Switzerland
WEIGHT	3 LB (1.4 KG)
BARREL	4½ IN (11.5 CM)
CALIBER	9 MM

The SiG P220 is one of the post-war period's finest automatic handguns. It is a 9 mm Parabellum short-recoil gun, and was developed as a replacement for the superb, but expensive, SiG P210. This decorated version is encrusted with diamonds.

RIFLES &
MUSKETS

FOR AN INFANTRYMAN the rifle is his principal means of directly influencing the battlefield. Artillery, armor, air power, and other forces may be the elements that are most decisive in terms of tactical and strategic outcomes of a battle, but at some point the soldier must close with the enemy to take ground, and that is where his rifle is most relevant.

Considered more widely, manportable long guns also changed the very nature of warfare and society. The appearance of the arquebus on the battlefields of Europe in the 14th and 15th centuries profoundly destabilized the notion of aristocratic supremacy of arms. A noble knight could possess great skill with horse and sword, yet he could be unseated and killed by a simple peasant armed with little more than a hollow tube and a crude aim.

❧

Muskets and rifles were developed primarily to give the infantryman, or the sportsman in the field, a long-range lethality. Hand in hand with the need for range has been the equal requirement for accuracy over that range. The smoothbore muskets that dominated military and civilian use from the 14th to the 18th centuries were generally inaccurate weapons at anything over 328 ft (100 m), with

some exceptions. Hence, they were applied most effectively in massed ranks, firing simultaneously at close range to provide a battlefield volley of "shock and awe."

❧

Rifled weapons were known to be far more accurate, and were in common sport and some military use by the 16th century. For reasons of expense and slower loading (the ball had to make a tighter fit in the barrel to engage the grooves of the rifling), they did not catch on in common use until the 19th century. However, during the 18th century rifled weapons first made their mark on warfare, principally on the battlefields of the New World.

During the American Revolution (1775–83) colonial marksmen took on the British Army with rifled hunting guns, targeting specific personnel, often at ranges in excess of 656 ft (200 m), rather than firing *en masse* in a general direction. By 1800 the British had learned their lesson, introducing the Baker Rifle into special formations of sharpshooters, before the percussion cap Brunswick rifle took over from the Baker and the Brown Bess in 1837.

The shift to breechloading systems firing unitary cartridges also had a marked effect on rifle range and accuracy, bringing in stable systems of loading uniform, precision rounds. By the turn of the 20th century a Mauser rifle could, in the hands of an experienced marksman, hit a human-size target at 1,968 ft (600 m) and beyond, and since then the development of precision optics has taken ranges out even further. A Canadian sniper in Afghanistan in 2003, for example, achieved a confirmed kill with a McMillan TAC-50 rifle at 7,970 ft (2,430 m).

⌘⌘⌘

Long-range accuracy is only one part of the equation of a successful rifle. Indeed, in military terms it may not be the most important part. German studies in practical combat distance in the 1930s and 40s found that most soldiers (unless snipers) rarely engaged targets more than 984 ft (300 m) away. What was more important for soldiers was the ability to deliver decent volumes of fire.

The advent of breechloading, magazine-fed bolt-action rifles in the late 1800s increased the individual soldier's firepower from a maximum of around four rounds per minute (a solid rate with a muzzle-loading flintlock) to about 15 rounds per minute.

The appearance of semi-automatic rifles in the 1930s, such as the M1 Garand, increased that rate to more than one bullet a second, with pauses for reloading. Yet full-auto rifle fire was not practical (although many would try during the war and after) with the standard long-range rifle rounds because of excessive recoil.

Hence, during WWII the Germans developed the 7.92 x 33 mm Kurz—a shortened cartridge with less recoil but which still retained good performance. The weapon designed for this, the Sturmgewehr 44, was the world's first "assault rifle," designed specifically for intermediate power ammunition and capable of selective fire.

⌘⌘⌘

Today, most of the world's armies are equipped with assault rifles, from the British SA80 to the US M4 Carbine. It is interesting, however, that recently some authorities have called for a return to the old full-power cartridges, arguing that the intermediate rounds do not have the killing power once held by the infantryman.

RIFLES & MUSKETS

EARLIEST FIREARMS

Small-caliber, manportable gunpowder weapons began to emerge as early as the 1340s and 50s. The early hand-gonne consisted of a bronze or iron barrel supported beneath the armpit by either an integral metal extension or, more commonly, by a wooden stave that was attached to the barrel. To fire, powder and ball were first muzzle-loaded, and some powder sprinkled on the touch-hole at the chamber end. The gun was then aimed in the general direction of the target before either the shooter or a third party ignited the touch-hole powder using a smoldering saltpeter-impregnated cord (the "slow match"), producing a dramatic but grossly inaccurate shot.

Hook

Muzzle

Barrel

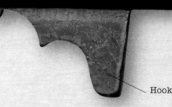

Hook

HAND-GONNE	
DATE	c.1500
ORIGIN	Europe
WEIGHT	Not known
BARREL	Not known
CALIBER	Not known

Although basic, this hand-gonne is very well made, with a strong hexagonal iron barrel, a contoured iron hook and a well-fitted stave. The muzzle is also flared; this feature would protect the end of the barrel from potential damage.

> **AND IN CASE BE THAT ANY SUCH SERVAUNT BE TAKYN SHOTYNG AT ANY FOWL, WYTH ANY CROSS BOWE OR HAND GONNE, THE SAYED OFFENDER SO TAKEN.**
> —STATUTE, 1537

Vent hole

Metal extension serving as a stock

IRON HANDGUN	
DATE	c.1500
ORIGIN	Low Countries
WEIGHT	Not known
BARREL	Not known
CALIBER	Not known

This early hand-gonne does not have a wooden stock, but instead features a long metal extension running out from the rear of the barrel. The weight and awkward shape of the weapon must have made it difficult to handle in the absence of a front support.

Wooden stock

FULL VIEW

ARQUEBUSES & HOOK GUNS

The hand-gonne evolved into the arquebus during the early 15th century, as gunmakers sought to create a more practical battlefield weapon. The name "arquebus" has several derivations, principally the French harquebuse and the German Hakenbüchse, the latter meaning "hook gun." The etymology probably refers to a hook sometimes found under the barrel, used to provide a steadier aim when engaged around a stable object. Central to arquebus development was not only a lengthened barrel and a shoulder stock, but also the use of the pivoting "serpentine." This was an S-shaped piece of metal pivoted in the middle, the bottom acting as the trigger and the top gripping the slow match. This was the first effective gun lock system.

Wooden stave
inserted under armpit

Rear sight

Stock

FULL VIEW

HOOK GUN

DATE	c.1500
ORIGIN	Germany
WEIGHT	10½ LB (4.7 KG)
BARREL	Not known
CALIBER	20-bore

This simplest of firearms consists of little more than an iron barrel fitted to a wooden stave, the stave being held under the armpit to stabilize the gun during firing. The front hook beneath the barrel could be engaged with a stable object to improve accuracy.

Hook for stabilizing barrel

" **THE ARQUEBUS WAS FIRED FROM THE CHEST, SO THAT THE EYE COULD WITH DIFFICULTY BE BROUGHT NEAR ENOUGH TO THE BARREL TO TAKE AIM.** "

J.H. STOCQUELER,
THE MILITARY ENCYCLOPEDIA, 1853

Barrel

HOOK GUN

DATE	c.1560
ORIGIN	Germany
WEIGHT	50 LB (22.5 KG)
BARREL	Not known
CALIBER	5-bore

This match-fired weapon, dating from the 16th century, is fully stocked, giving it the appearance of a more modern firearm. Note also the increased expectations of accuracy indicated by the front and rear sights, although the proportions of the gun (it weighed 50 lb) must have affected accurate handling.

EUROPEAN MUSKETS

The matchlock system, whereby the arm holding the slow match was operated by a trigger, meant accurate fire was more of a possibility—even by the mid 1400s there were firearms fitted with simple "notch and post" sights. Accuracy was further promoted by the development of the snapping matchlock during the 15th century, whereby the match holder was spring powered. With the old matchlock, the shooter could swing off target in the time it took to lower the match holder onto the pan; the snapping matchlock reduced this time significantly. However, despite such improvements, matchlocks were no sniper's weapon, and were best applied militarily as massed volley weapons.

Lock cover is set into the stock

Pan cover

Match holder

Trigger guard shaped to fit the hand

"Fishtail" shoulder stock

Pan cover

Match holder

Lock plate

Small of stock fits in hand

FULL VIEW

Screw secures
barrel in stock

ENGLISH MATCHLOCK MUSKET

DATE	1640
ORIGIN	England
WEIGHT	9¼ LB (4.2 KG)
BARREL	45½ IN (115 CM)
CALIBER	11-bore

Muskets like this featured prominently in the English
Civil War, from the first encounter between Royalists and
Parliamentarians at Edgehill in 1642, to its conclusion at
Worcester in 1651. Because matchlocks took so long to
load, musketeers were extremely vulnerable, particularly
to cavalry, and had to be protected by pikemen.

Barrel is octagonal
for first third of
length, then round

ENGLISH MATCHLOCK MUSKET

DATE	17th century
ORIGIN	England
WEIGHT	10½ LB (4.73 KG)
BARREL	46 IN (117.2 CM)
CALIBER	18 MM

By the end of their period of dominance, the best matchlocks
had acquired a simple sophistication, at least in their finish.
They had also become much lighter, and thus were considerably
easier to handle. A high-quality piece such as this would have
been a prime contender for conversion into a snaphaunce or
flintlock, had it not been preserved in a collection.

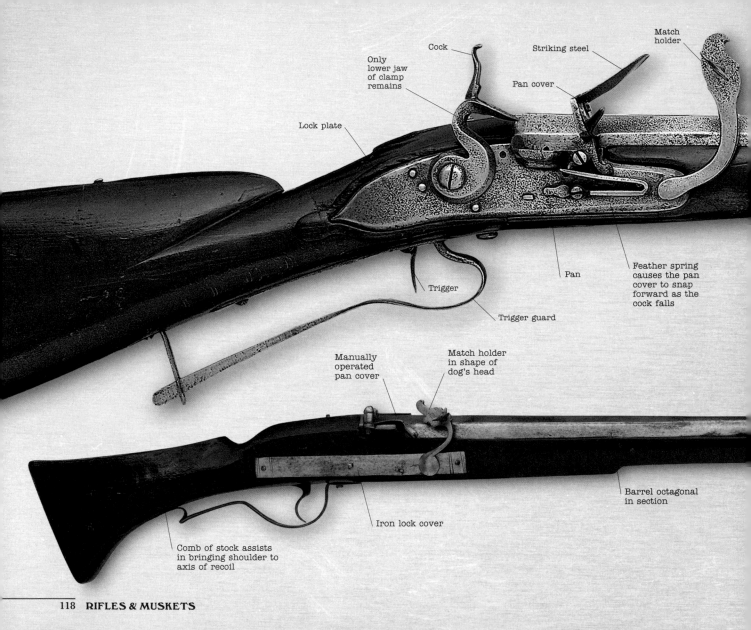

Cock

Striking steel

Match
holder

Only
lower jaw
of clamp
remains

Pan cover

Lock plate

Trigger

Pan

Trigger guard

Feather spring
causes the pan
cover to snap
forward as the
cock falls

Manually
operated
pan cover

Match holder
in shape of
dog's head

Barrel octagonal
in section

Iron lock cover

Comb of stock assists
in bringing shoulder to
axis of recoil

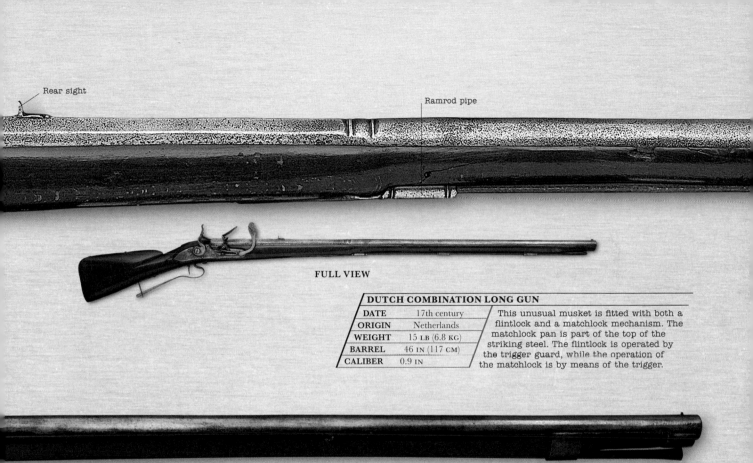

Rear sight

Ramrod pipe

FULL VIEW

DUTCH COMBINATION LONG GUN

DATE	17th century
ORIGIN	Netherlands
WEIGHT	15 LB (6.8 KG)
BARREL	46 IN (117 CM)
CALIBER	0.9 IN

This unusual musket is fitted with both a flintlock and a matchlock mechanism. The matchlock pan is part of the top of the striking steel. The flintlock is operated by the trigger guard, while the operation of the matchlock is by means of the trigger.

MATCHLOCK MUSKET

DATE	mid-17th century
ORIGIN	UK
WEIGHT	13¼ LB (6.05 KG)
BARREL	49½ IN (126 CM)
CALIBER	.75 IN

While the matchlock was a significant improvement over the hand-cannon, it was still a very clumsy weapon. Even in dry weather the match could be extinguished all too easily, and its glowing end was a giveaway at night. However, the best models were suprisingly accurate and were capable of killing a man at a hundred yards or more.

17TH CENTURY MUSKET

The term musket refers generally to any smoothbore long gun that is loaded at the muzzle and designed to be fired from the shoulder. Taken in their broadest sense, muskets include a huge swathe of firearms, over a 300-400 year period, from the matchlock arquebus of the 15th century through to the percussion cap smoothbores found in the 19th century.

However, the term seems to be applied more specifically to the heavier and more powerful infantry long guns that succeeded the arquebus in the early-mid 16th century. Muskets were limited in two primary regards. First, they were slow to load—

a British soldier armed with a Brown Bess, for example, was proficient to fire three rounds per minute, four if he was expert. Second, smoothbore muskets were relatively inaccurate when compared to rifled weapons. The combination of standardized rifling and the inexorable shift to breechloading during the 19th century meant the end of practical use for the musket.

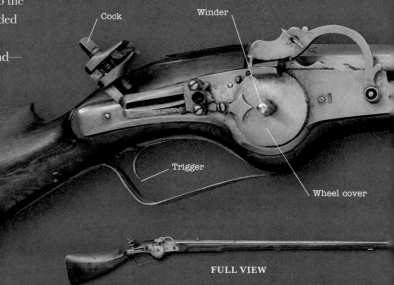

Cock

Winder

Trigger

Wheel cover

FULL VIEW

THE MUSKET WAS THE STAPLE WEAPON OF THE THIRTY YEARS WAR (1618–1648).

COMBINATION WHEELLOCK/MATCHLOCK MUSKET

DATE	1650 (mechanism)
ORIGIN	Germany
WEIGHT	11 ¼ LB (5 KG)
BARREL	44 IN (118 CM)
CALIBER	.70

In this gun, wheellock and matchlock systems are set aside one another on the same lockplate. While the mechanism is German (1650), the stock is from 19th-century Britain.

MUSKET BATTLE
The attack on the French city wall of Boulogne-sur-Mer by English musket-bearing troops in 1550. Muskets were widely used in a number of conflicts from the early 16th century onward, including the Thirty Years War (1618–1648).

ASIAN MATCHLOCKS

In 1543, Portuguese expansion brought the Europeans into contact with the Japanese, and introduced their traders to matchlock weapons. The Japanese readily adopted these and, because of subsequent isolationist policies, matchlocks would be their dominant form of firearm into the 1800s. (The Japanese quickly began manufacturing their own matchlocks, so the expulsion of the Europeans did not cause supply problems.) The classic type of Japanese matchlock was the Tanegashima, an extraordinary weapon with a barrel length of around 40 in (101.6 cm) but also no butt.

Serpentine match holder

Rear sight

Barrel is retained by four pins

Shishi is brass inlay

Hole in butt bordered by elaborate floral washer and eight-bucket waterwheel design

Butt is of the form developed in Sakai

Lock plate

Serpentine match holder

Touch pan

Mainspring

Trigger

JAPANESE TEPPO	
DATE	c.1700
ORIGIN	Japan
WEIGHT	6 LB (2.77 KG)
BARREL	39½ IN (100 CM)
CALIBER	11.4 MM

This early 18th-century matchlock teppo is the work of the Enami family of Sakai, who are widely held to be among the finest Japanese gunmakers of the pre-industrial period. The stock is of red oak, decorated all over with *kara kusa* (vine motifs) scrolls in gold lacquer, with additional inlays of brass and silver.

PAPER CARTRIDGE
Today, thick writing paper is still known as "cartridge paper" owing to this type of charge.

Octagonal barrel

Decorative inlay surrounds barrel pin

JAPANESE MATCHLOCK

DATE	Early 18th century
ORIGIN	Western Japan
WEIGHT	9¼ LB (4.14 KG)
BARREL	40½ IN (103 CM)
CALIBER	13.3 MM

A rather less ornate weapon than that shown below, this matchlock is by Kunitomo Tobei Shigeyasu of Omo, on Japan's west coast. Its red-oak stock is in the style of the Sakai school. Decoration is limited to engraving on the octagonal barrel and some brass inlay; the lock and mainspring are also of brass.

LEAD BULLET
It was not until around 1600 that lead, with its low melting point and high specific gravity, became the universal material for bullets.

Rear sight

Laquerwork *mon* (family badge) is a pine tree in a circle

Octagonal barrel

Gold lacquering over red oak

FULL VIEW

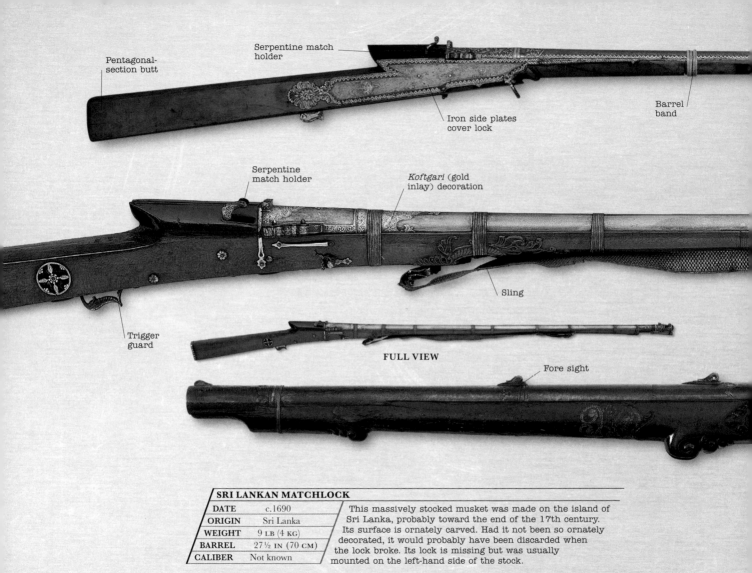

Pentagonal-
section butt

Serpentine match
holder

Barrel
band

Iron side plates
cover lock

Serpentine
match holder

Koftgari (gold
inlay) decoration

Sling

Trigger
guard

FULL VIEW

Fore sight

SRI LANKAN MATCHLOCK	
DATE	c.1690
ORIGIN	Sri Lanka
WEIGHT	9 LB (4 KG)
BARREL	27½ IN (70 CM)
CALIBER	Not known

This massively stocked musket was made on the island of Sri Lanka, probably toward the end of the 17th century. Its surface is ornately carved. Had it not been so ornately decorated, it would probably have been discarded when the lock broke. Its lock is missing but was usually mounted on the left-hand side of the stock.

Gold inlay
on muzzle

INDIAN CARNATIC TORADOR

DATE	18th century
ORIGIN	Southern India
WEIGHT	9 LB (4.05 KG)
BARREL	44½ IN (113 CM)
CALIBER	16 MM

The barrel of this matchlock from Mysore (in what is now Karnataka State, southern India) is exquisitely decorated with incised flowers and foliage, and entirely gilded. The incised side plates are made of iron, and its decoration is in *koftgari*—a method of inlaying gold into steel or iron.

Barrel bands of
leather thongs

Tiger's-head
muzzle

INDIAN MATCHLOCK TORADOR

DATE	19th century
ORIGIN	Central India
WEIGHT	10¾ LB (4.9 KG)
BARREL	49¾ IN (126 CM)
CALIBER	14 MM

This torador has a stock of polished red wood with circular pierced medallions on either side of the butt of iron, with gilding and *koftgari* applied over red velvet. The barrel has an elaborate arabesque decoration in gold *koftgari* at the breech, and the muzzle is fashioned into the shape of a tiger's head.

Stock decorated
with chip-
carving

Trigger

Butt could be held
against the shoulder
or the chest

WHEELLOCK RIFLES

Wheellocks were extremely expensive weapons to produce, so they were bought mainly by the wealthy as hunting pieces. They were also delicate instruments that could be severely compromised by dirt and hard handling, hence they remained civilian rather than military weapons. As hunting guns they had their limitations. The shower of sparks created by the spinning metal wheel could give just enough warning for a bird or rabbit to jink off target before the main charge detonation took place.

Winder

Wheel cover

Cover for serrated striking wheel

Lock plate

Bone inlay

Cheekpiece

Trigger

Squared shaft for winding mechanism

Trigger guard

Barrel fixing pin

Cocking ring

Spring holds
cock firmly
against striking
wheel

ITALIAN WHEELLOCK

DATE	c.1630
ORIGIN	Italy
WEIGHT	4.2 LB (1.9 KG)
BARREL	31½ IN (80 CM)
CALIBER	.45 IN

By the 17th century, the northern cities of Brescia and Bologna had long become the centers for the fabrication of wheellock guns in Italy. This example is by Lazarino Cominazzo of Brescia, who was better known for his pistols.

FULL VIEW

GERMAN WHEELLOCK

DATE	c.1640
ORIGIN	Germany
WEIGHT	8¼ LB (3.8 KG)
BARREL	34 IN (86.4 CM)
CALIBER	.65 IN

The wheellock was invented in Italy, but within half a century, fine specimens were being produced in Germany. This example has its serrated wheel mounted externally, to make it easier to clean, though the rest of the lock-work is protected within the stock.

EARLY FLINTLOCK RIFLES

FLINTLOCK BALLS
To achieve any sort of accuracy, the ball fired from a smoothbore gun had to be spherical and of an exact size.

Flintlock muskets fall into either smoothbore or rifled categories, the latter being far more accurate over range. Rifling—longitudinal lines cut into the bore of a weapon—was first introduced in the 1400s, initially as a method of trapping the fouling of burnt powder. By giving the lines a twist, spin was imparted to the ball, this in turn giving the ball a gyroscopic stability in flight, resulting in improved accuracy and range. One deficiency of the rifled weapons was that they were often harder and slower to muzzle load, as the ball had to be an especially tight fit to engage with the rifling grooves.

Butt is bound with brass

Striking steel attached to pan cover

Barrel band is cut to act as rear sight

Cock holds flint between metal jaws

Small of stock sized to fit in hand

Lock plate stamped with name of armory

Comb of stock puts shoulder in line of recoil

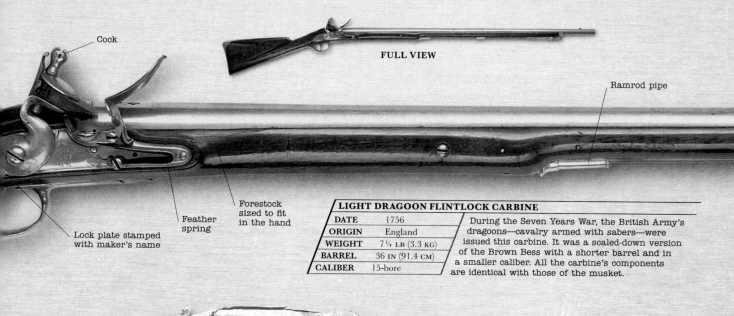

Cock

FULL VIEW

Ramrod pipe

Feather
spring

Forestock
sized to fit
in the hand

Lock plate stamped
with maker's name

LIGHT DRAGOON FLINTLOCK CARBINE

DATE	1756
ORIGIN	England
WEIGHT	7¼ lb (3.3 kg)
BARREL	36 in (91.4 cm)
CALIBER	15-bore

During the Seven Years War, the British Army's dragoons—cavalry armed with sabers—were issued this carbine. It was a scaled-down version of the Brown Bess with a shorter barrel and in a smaller caliber. All the carbine's components are identical with those of the musket.

CARTRIDGE PACK
Combining powder, ball, and paper in one unit negated the need for different pouches.

Blade fore
sight

PRUSSIAN RIFLED FLINTLOCK CARBINE

DATE	1722
ORIGIN	Germany
WEIGHT	7½ lb (3.37 kg)
BARREL	37 in (94 cm)
CALIBER	15-bore

King Frederick William I of Prussia, who came to the throne in 1713, raised a standing army that amounted to four percent of the country's adult male population. He established a state arsenal at Potsdam and among its early products were carbines like this, which were manufactured from 1722 to 1774. Ten men in each squadron of cuirassiers were issued with rifled weapons.

ENGLISH FLINTLOCK

DATE	1791
ORIGIN	England
WEIGHT	7¾ LB (3.5 KG)
BARREL	32 IN (81 CM)
CALIBER	.680

Henry Nock was one of Britain's foremost gunmakers during the 18th century, with many guns made for royalty, and apprentices that included Ezekiel Baker. Here is one of his flintlock weapons, which was in .680 caliber and had nine-groove rifling rather than being smoothbore.

FULL VIEW

Cock

Rear sight

Striking steel

Guard extension

Feather spring

SEA SERVICE GUNS HAD TO BE **CORROSION RESISTANT,** HENCE THE BARRELS WERE OFTEN BLACKENED TO PROTECT THEM AGAINST THE CONSTANT **SALT-WATER SPRAY.**

Ramrod

Sling swivel

Discharger cup

SEA SERVICE MUSKET	
DATE	Mid-18th
ORIGIN	Germany
WEIGHT	Not known
BARREL	Not known
CALIBER	Not known

This Sea Service flintlock is fitted with a discharger cup on the end of the muzzle. Developed in the mid-18th century, the discharger was used for firing cast-iron hand grenades, and was an ideal weapon for close-range boarding actions.

TIMOTHY MURPHY

Timothy Murphy (1751–1818) was one of modern history's true early snipers. His talents as a marksman were employed during the American Revolutionary War (1775–83), when he first enlisted as a rifleman. However, given his ability to hit a seven-inch target from 250 yards, he soon enlisted in the elite Continental Rifle Corps under General Daniel Morgan.

"Morgan's Rifles" were deployed in 1777 to New York State against the British forces under General John Burgoyne, and Murphy and his comrades sniped the British ranks endlessly.

In October 1777 at the Second Battle of Saratoga, Murphy climbed a tree, then shot and killed the British brigadier-general Simon Fraser at 300 yards (274 m), repeating the feat against Sir Frances Clarke, General Burgoyne's chief aide-de-camp. The two killings had powerful, converse effects on British and American morale, and gave Murphy the nickname "Sure Shot Tim." Murphy proved his marksmanship on many subsequent occasions over 200 yards (183 m), and survived the war and a period in Indian captivity.

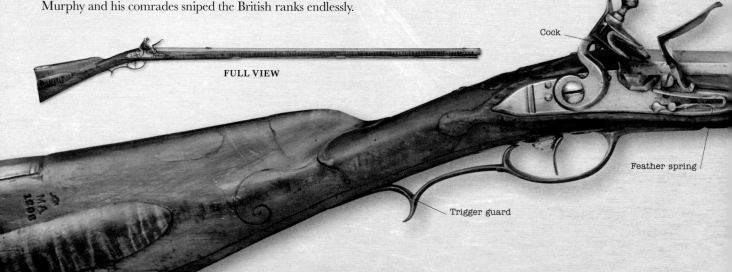

FULL VIEW

Cock

Feather spring

Trigger guard

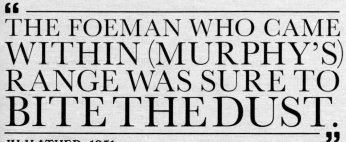

> ## "THE FOEMAN WHO CAME WITHIN (MURPHY'S) RANGE WAS SURE TO BITE THE DUST."
>
> **JH MATHER, 1851**

FLINTLOCK RIFLE	
DATE	1760
ORIGIN	US
WEIGHT	8¼ LB (3.8 KG)
BARREL	45 IN (114 CM)
CALIBER	.45

This flintlock rifle was a forerunner to the famous Kentucky rifle. Based on designs introduced to America by immigrant German gunsmiths, it had accuracy up to 400 yards/365 meters in well-trained hands.

SURE SHOT TIM

On completion of his military service in 1779, Murphy settled in Delaware and, along with several other ex-Army riflemen, he enlisted in the 15th Regiment of Albany County Militia. This painting is the only known depiction of Murphy, although historians disagree as to whether this is an accurate likeness.

FLINTLOCK MUSKETS & RIFLES

The 18th and 19th centuries saw the perfection of the flintlock musket and rifle design. From 1722 to 1838, for example, the redoubtable "Brown Bess"—the Land Pattern Musket—was the British Army's firearm of choice for its infantry. The Charleville musket gave similar service to the French. By the 1800s, however, more forces were beginning to recognize the ballistic advantages of rifled guns. For example, the Baker rifle's barrel length was only 30 in (76 cm), but it featured seven rectangular grooves making a quarter turn along the length of the bore. Accurate shots could be taken at around 150 yards (137 m).

Protective cover for cock and steel

Cock

Flint

Jaw screw

Standard Land-Pattern lock

Pan

Armory mark

Brass cheek plate

Feather spring

Trigger

Brass trigger guard

Leather sling

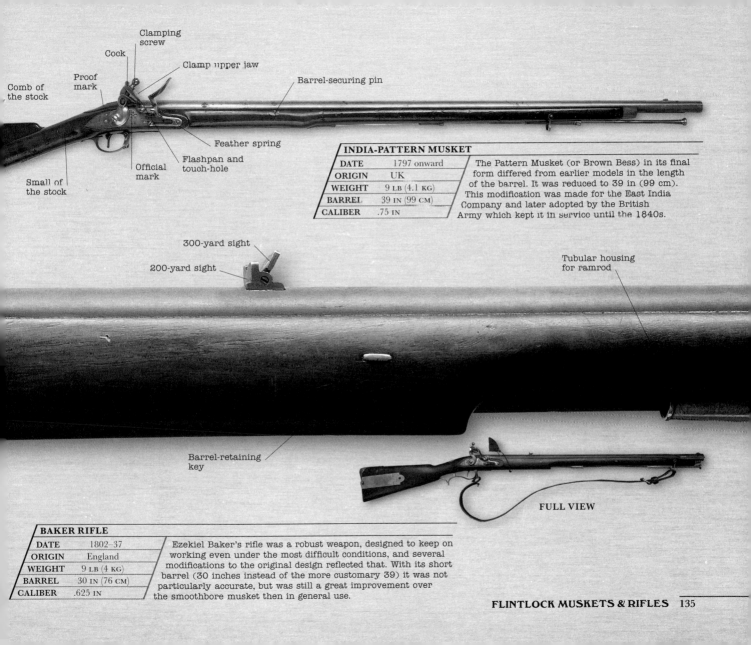

Comb of
the stock

Proof
mark

Cock

Clamping
screw

Clamp upper jaw

Barrel-securing pin

Small of
the stock

Official
mark

Feather spring

Flashpan and
touch-hole

INDIA-PATTERN MUSKET

DATE	1797 onward
ORIGIN	UK
WEIGHT	9 LB (4.1 KG)
BARREL	39 IN (99 CM)
CALIBER	.75 IN

The Pattern Musket (or Brown Bess) in its final form differed from earlier models in the length of the barrel. It was reduced to 39 in (99 cm). This modification was made for the East India Company and later adopted by the British Army which kept it in service until the 1840s.

300-yard sight

200-yard sight

Tubular housing
for ramrod

Barrel-retaining
key

FULL VIEW

BAKER RIFLE

DATE	1802–37
ORIGIN	England
WEIGHT	9 LB (4 KG)
BARREL	30 IN (76 CM)
CALIBER	.625 IN

Ezekiel Baker's rifle was a robust weapon, designed to keep on working even under the most difficult conditions, and several modifications to the original design reflected that. With its short barrel (30 inches instead of the more customary 39) it was not particularly accurate, but was still a great improvement over the smoothbore musket then in general use.

DOUBLE-BARRELED FLINTLOCK WITH BAYONET

DATE	c.1800
ORIGIN	UK
WEIGHT	Not known
BARREL	Not known
CALIBER	Not known

The blunderbuss-type muzzle of this double-barreled weapon features an attached folding spike bayonet. Guns such as these were often used by naval crews, who appreciated the short-range firepower backed by a stabbing weapon for hand-to-hand action.

Striking steel

Flint clamping screw

Cock

Double trigger

Breech-block is hinged at the forward end and tips up through 30° for loading

Breech block release catch

Lock cover

Grip extension

FULL VIEW

Folding spike bayonet

Flared muzzle

MUSKET BALL
The size of the ball was expressed in "bore," being the number of balls of a given size that could be cast from 1 lb (0.45 kg) of lead.

Barrel band

Forward sling swivel

HALL RIFLE	
DATE	1819
ORIGIN	US
WEIGHT	10½ LB (4.68 KG)
BARREL	32½ IN (82.5 CM)
CALIBER	.54 IN

John Hancock Hall's rifle, designed in 1811 and introduced into service in 1819, was the first regulation American rifle to incorporate an opening breech; hinged at the front, it tipped up at a 30-degree angle for loading. Hall rifles and carbines were eventually produced in percussion form, too, when the entire breech unit could be removed and used as a pistol.

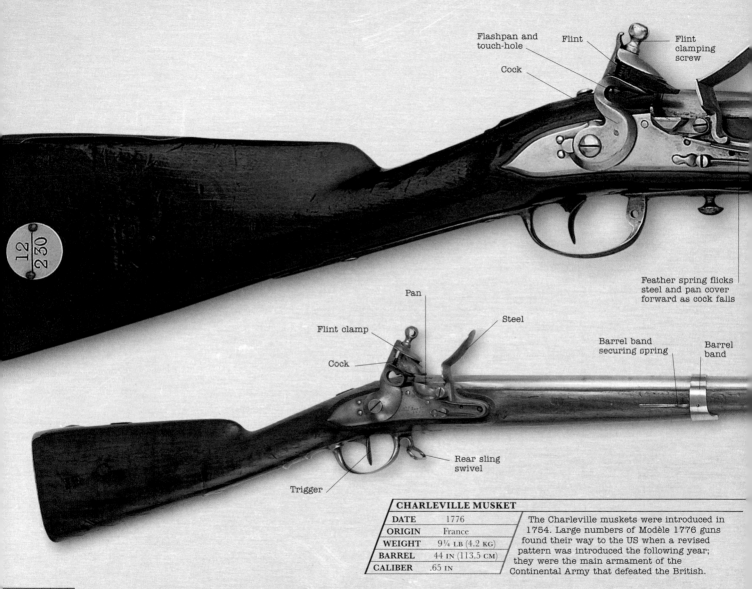

Flashpan and touch-hole

Flint

Flint clamping screw

Cock

Feather spring flicks steel and pan cover forward as cock falls

Pan

Steel

Flint clamp

Cock

Barrel band securing spring

Barrel band

Trigger

Rear sling swivel

CHARLEVILLE MUSKET

DATE	1776
ORIGIN	France
WEIGHT	9¼ LB (4.2 KG)
BARREL	44 IN (113.5 CM)
CALIBER	.65 IN

The Charleville muskets were introduced in 1754. Large numbers of Modèle 1776 guns found their way to the US when a revised pattern was introduced the following year; they were the main armament of the Continental Army that defeated the British.

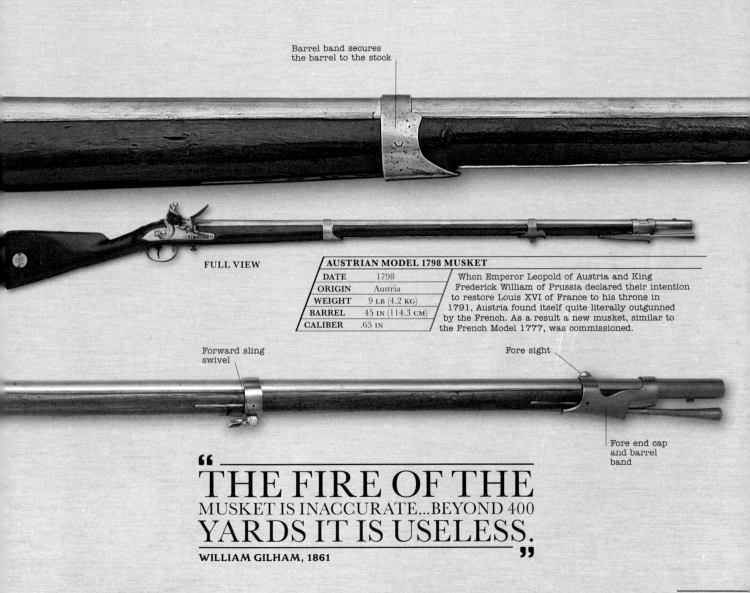

Barrel band secures
the barrel to the stock

FULL VIEW

AUSTRIAN MODEL 1798 MUSKET	
DATE	1798
ORIGIN	Austria
WEIGHT	9 LB (4.2 KG)
BARREL	45 IN (114.3 CM)
CALIBER	.65 IN

When Emperor Leopold of Austria and King
Frederick William of Prussia declared their intention
to restore Louis XVI of France to his throne in
1791, Austria found itself quite literally outgunned
by the French. As a result a new musket, similar to
the French Model 1777, was commissioned.

Forward sling
swivel

Fore sight

Fore end cap
and barrel
band

" THE FIRE OF THE
MUSKET IS INACCURATE...BEYOND 400
YARDS IT IS USELESS. "
WILLIAM GILHAM, 1861

Flint clamp

LEMMERS FLINTLOCK BLUNDERBUSS

DATE	1810
ORIGIN	UK
WEIGHT	Not known
BARREL	Not known
CALIBER	Not known

This blunderbuss had a short effective range of around 30 yards, depending on the shot type. The flared muzzle would have increased the spread of shot, but recent experiments have shown that in blunderbusses the spread did not match the flare of the muzzle.

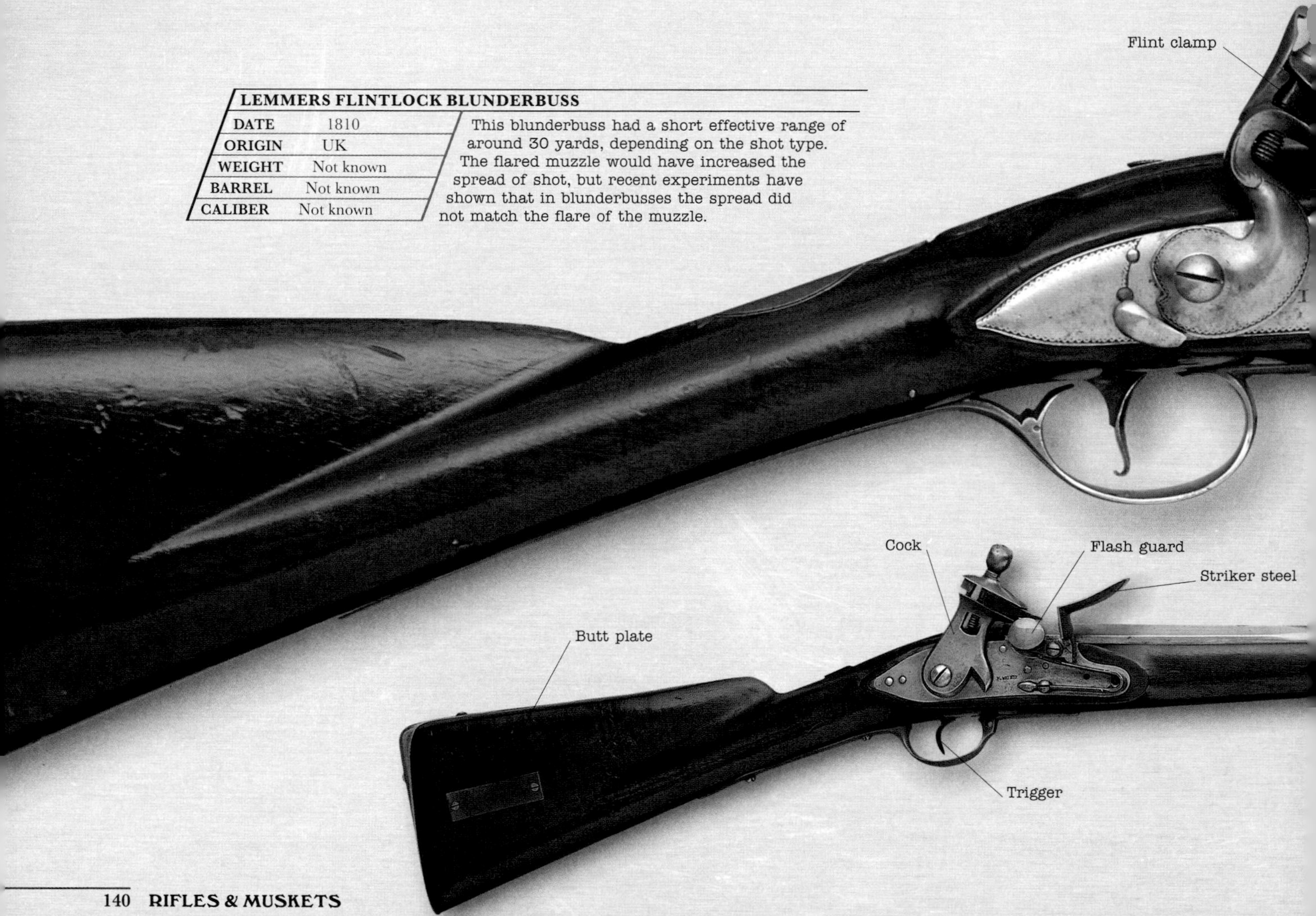

Cock

Flash guard

Striker steel

Butt plate

Trigger

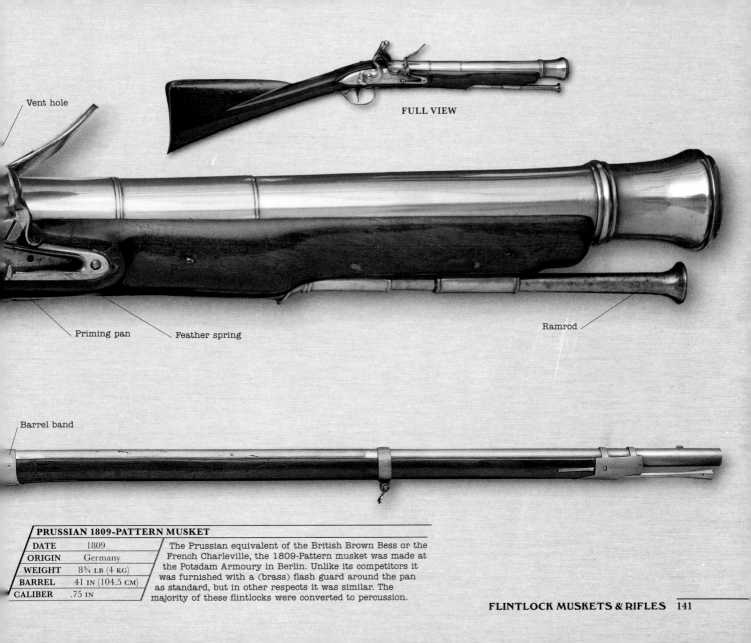

Vent hole

FULL VIEW

Priming pan Feather spring

Ramrod

Barrel band

PRUSSIAN 1809-PATTERN MUSKET	
DATE	1809
ORIGIN	Germany
WEIGHT	8¾ LB (4 KG)
BARREL	41 IN (104.5 CM)
CALIBER	.75 IN

The Prussian equivalent of the British Brown Bess or the French Charleville, the 1809-Pattern musket was made at the Potsdam Armoury in Berlin. Unlike its competitors it was furnished with a (brass) flash guard around the pan as standard, but in other respects it was similar. The majority of these flintlocks were converted to percussion.

BROWN BESS

The British Land Pattern Musket—more commonly known among the ranks as the Brown Bess—dominated the ranks of the British Army for more than 100 years. The first version was the Long Land Pattern of 1722, a flintlock .75 in musket which was 62 in (157 cm) long with a 46 in (117 cm) barrel.

❧

Although the length of the gun gave some advantage in a fixed bayonets clash, the barrel was subsequently shortened to improve handling and to lighten the load of the British soldier (part of the 1768 Clothing Warrant), resulting in the Short Land Pattern of 1768 with 42 in (106 cm) barrels. A further shortening came in the mid 1790s with the India Pattern, so

called because it was developed for use by the East India Company. In this version the barrel dropped to just below 39 in (99 cm), and the British Army adopted it for general use in 1797. The Brown Bess had weaknesses, notably in the trigger group, but millions were made (over 3 million of the India Pattern alone) and it aided Britain's colonial expansion during the 19th century.

Cock

Lock plate stamped with maker's name

Sling swivel

FULL VIEW

"...TAKE THE BROWN BESS ON YOUR SHOULDER AND MARCH,"

CONNECTICUT COURANT, APRIL 1771

BROWN BESS MUSKET	
DATE	1742
ORIGIN	UK
WEIGHT	10¼ LB (4.7 KG)
BARREL	46 IN (117 CM)
CALIBER	10-bore

This modified version of the Land-Pattern Musket by Tippin was a "sealed pattern," meaning that it was retained in the Tower of London Armory as a model for other gunmakers to follow.

Fore stock

WHAT'S IN A NAME?

Brown Bess-wielding British troops at the Battle of Bunker Hill in 1775 during the American Revolutionary War. The origins of the name Brown Bess are unknown, but it probably derives from the German words "braun buss" meaning "strong gun." This argument is further supported by the fact that King George I, who commissioned the gun's use, was from Germany.

OTTOMAN FIREARMS

The Ottoman military forces were among the first in the world to introduce muskets into warfare, with evidence suggesting formal gun use in combat during the 1440s. By the 18th and 19th centuries, however, their advantage in warfare was lost. When faced with the new European or Russian armies, which were based on mass conscription, the Turkish infantry demonstrated little ability to respond with tactical lines or columns. These were essential structures for troops wishing to concentrate their firepower or maneuver their muskets. Furthermore, the Ottomans rejected the use of the bayonet—an "infidel weapon"—despite seeing how devastating these could be in trained hands.

Cast and chiseled decoration on stock

Cock

Striking steel integral with pan cover

Exposed mainspring

Trigger

Cock

Pan

Striking steel

Inlaid decoration

Prawl prevents hand from slipping

Shoulder stock is pentagonal in section

Trigger

Inlaid decoration

Shoulder stock is inlaid with brass and precious stones

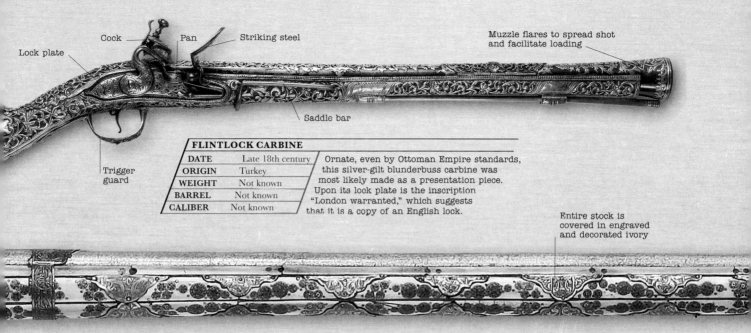

Cock — Pan — Striking steel

Lock plate

Muzzle flares to spread shot
and facilitate loading

Trigger
guard

Saddle bar

Entire stock is
covered in engraved
and decorated ivory

FLINTLOCK CARBINE

DATE	Late 18th century	Ornate, even by Ottoman Empire standards, this silver-gilt blunderbuss carbine was most likely made as a presentation piece. Upon its lock plate is the inscription "London warranted," which suggests that it is a copy of an English lock.
ORIGIN	Turkey	
WEIGHT	Not known	
BARREL	Not known	
CALIBER	Not known	

FULL VIEW

Octagonal
barrel

Barrel bands
made of twine

BALKAN MIQUELET TÜFENK

DATE	Early 19th century	This early 19th-century piece is reminiscent of Indian muskets. The stock is entirely covered in ivory and further embellished with inlays of precious stones and brass. The miquelet lock, common in Spain and Italy, is thought to have made its way to the Ottoman Empire via Africa.
ORIGIN	Turkey	
WEIGHT	Not known	
BARREL	45 in (114.3 cm)	
CALIBER	Not known	

SNAPHAUNCE TÜFENK

DATE	Late 18th century	This smoothbore musket, or tüfenk, is very similar both in overall form and the manner of its decoration to muskets produced in northern India. The pentagonal-section butt stock terminates at the breech in a pronounced prawl. The barrel is octagonal in section, and the lock is a snaphaunce, which had become obsolete in the West by the early 17th century.
ORIGIN	Turkey	
WEIGHT	Not known	
BARREL	28½ in (72.4 cm)	
CALIBER	Not known	

INDIAN FIREARMS

Although India's matchlocks lagged behind Europe in terms of their historical lineage, they were often superbly built, and could feature some exquisite levels of decoration using inlaid ivory, gold, silver, or bone. Nor were they just decorative pieces. The 19th century jezail matchlock was accurate and generally reliable, especially during the dry seasons when there was no climatic interference with powder and smoldering match. In the early 19th century Indian gunsmiths also explored some mechanical sophistications seen occasionally in the Western flintlock, such as using revolving cylinders to create a multi-shot weapon. Only with the steady progress of colonization of India by the British did flintlock, then percussion cap, technologies start to take over from the matchlock.

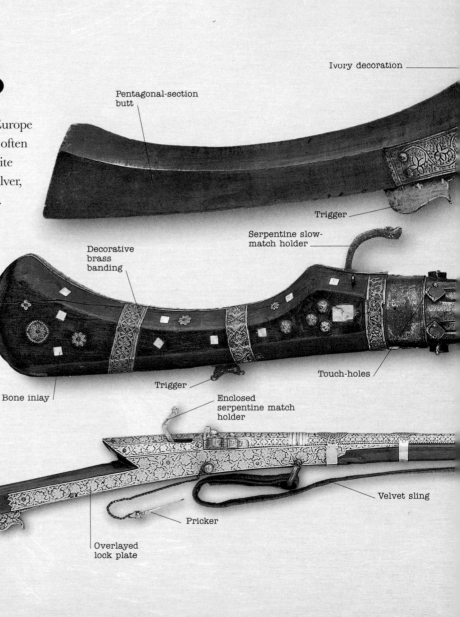

Ivory decoration

Pentagonal-section butt

Trigger

Serpentine slow-match holder

Decorative brass banding

Bone inlay

Trigger

Touch-holes

Enclosed serpentine match holder

Gilded butt

Velvet sling

Pricker

Trigger

Overlayed lock plate

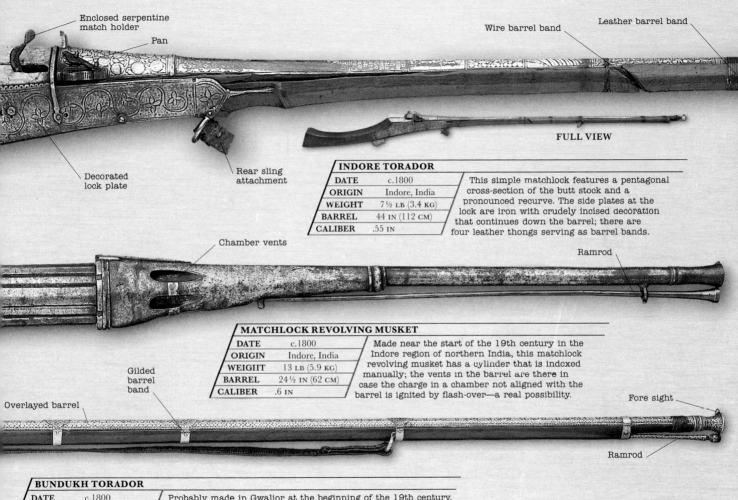

Enclosed serpentine match holder

Pan

Wire barrel band

Leather barrel band

Decorated lock plate

Rear sling attachment

FULL VIEW

INDORE TORADOR

DATE	c.1800
ORIGIN	Indore, India
WEIGHT	7 ½ LB (3.4 KG)
BARREL	44 IN (112 CM)
CALIBER	.55 IN

This simple matchlock features a pentagonal cross-section of the butt stock and a pronounced recurve. The side plates at the lock are iron with crudely incised decoration that continues down the barrel; there are four leather thongs serving as barrel bands.

Chamber vents

Ramrod

MATCHLOCK REVOLVING MUSKET

DATE	c.1800
ORIGIN	Indore, India
WEIGHT	13 LB (5.9 KG)
BARREL	24 ½ IN (62 CM)
CALIBER	.6 IN

Made near the start of the 19th century in the Indore region of northern India, this matchlock revolving musket has a cylinder that is indexed manually; the vents in the barrel are there in case the charge in a chamber not aligned with the barrel is ignited by flash-over—a real possibility.

Gilded barrel band

Overlayed barrel

Fore sight

Ramrod

BUNDUKH TORADOR

DATE	c.1800
ORIGIN	Gwalior, India
WEIGHT	6 ½ LB (3 KG)
BARREL	45 ¼ IN (115 CM)
CALIBER	.55 IN

Probably made in Gwalior at the beginning of the 19th century, this extremely ornate matchlock was almost certainly a presentation piece. Like all matchlocks, it was supplied with a touch-hole pricker, though since this, too, is gilded, it can hardly be considered to be entirely functional. Guns of this type were normally held beneath the arm, not against the shoulder.

OTHER ASIAN FIREARMS

Although the Japanese remained wedded to the matchlock for far longer than most countries, they took matchlock design and style to extremely high standards. Some Japanese matchlocks were plain, functional pieces issued *en masse* to their armies, while others had exquisite inlaid metalwork along the stock and fore-end, and floral patterns running along the full length of the woodwork, enhanced under a coat of rich lacquer. There were also mechanical innovations. Examples of revolving matchlock rifles exist, with a horizontal drum on top containing six chambers, this being rotated to present each chamber to the barrel in turn. For cavalry, carbine matchlocks were used—shortened versions of rifles that could even be fired with one hand if necessary.

Hammer

Lock plate

Pan

Trigger

Hand guard

Stock made of red oak

Touch-hole

Red-oak stock

Brass plate where lock should be

LARGE-BORE JAPANESE MATCHLOCK

DATE	c.1850
ORIGIN	Japan
WEIGHT	9 LB (4.12 KG)
BARREL	27¼ IN (69.3 CM)
CALIBER	18.3 MM

This type of matchlock firearm was sometimes used to launch a primitive incendiary device, the fire arrow. It dates from toward the end of the Tokugawa shogunate, 1603–1867, as evinced by the *mon* that decorate the barrel. The lock and trigger are missing—the former has been replaced by a plain brass plate.

Inlaid mon (family
badge)

JAPANESE PILL-LOCK CARBINE

DATE	c.1850
ORIGIN	Japan
WEIGHT	8 LB (3.64 KG)
BARREL	26½ IN (67 CM)
CALIBER	12.5 MM

Though Japan's doors were closed to foreigners for more than
200 years, there were occasional illicit contacts, and it was
probably through these that pill-lock technology, which had a
brief currency in Europe around 1820, arrived in Japan. This
carbine has a device that dispenses a fresh primer "pill"
from a small magazine when the pan cover is lifted.

Tokugawa mon, or
identifying cartouche

Square fore stock is
rounded here to
accommodate the
hand

Intermediate
sight

Fore sight

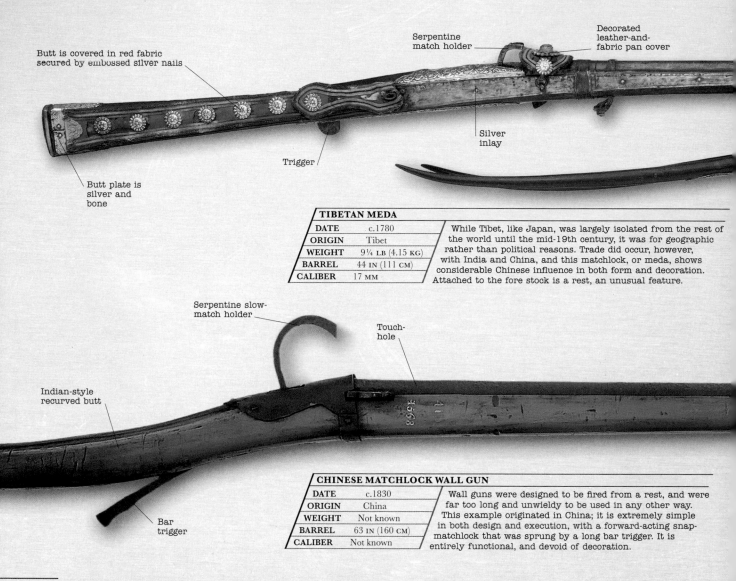

Butt is covered in red fabric secured by embossed silver nails

Serpentine match holder

Decorated leather-and-fabric pan cover

Silver inlay

Butt plate is silver and bone

Trigger

TIBETAN MEDA

DATE	c.1780
ORIGIN	Tibet
WEIGHT	9¼ LB (4.15 KG)
BARREL	44 IN (111 CM)
CALIBER	17 MM

While Tibet, like Japan, was largely isolated from the rest of the world until the mid-19th century, it was for geographic rather than political reasons. Trade did occur, however, with India and China, and this matchlock, or meda, shows considerable Chinese influence in both form and decoration. Attached to the fore stock is a rest, an unusual feature.

Serpentine slow-match holder

Touch-hole

Indian-style recurved butt

Bar trigger

CHINESE MATCHLOCK WALL GUN

DATE	c.1830
ORIGIN	China
WEIGHT	Not known
BARREL	63 IN (160 CM)
CALIBER	Not known

Wall guns were designed to be fired from a rest, and were far too long and unwieldy to be used in any other way. This example originated in China; it is extremely simple in both design and execution, with a forward-acting snap-matchlock that was sprung by a long bar trigger. It is entirely functional, and devoid of decoration.

Damascened barrel

Rest terminates in
forked antelope horn

Ramrod is a modern
replacement

AT THE BATTLE OF NAGASHINO, UP TO 3,000 MATCHLOCK-ARMED GUNNERS DESTROYED THE CAVALRY CHARGES OF TAKEDA KATSUYORI WITH CONTROLLED VOLLEY FIRE.

FULL VIEW

ENFIELD RIFLE MUSKET

The 1853 Pattern Enfield Rifle musket equipped the British infantryman with greater long-range accuracy. Its bore featured three-groove rifling that made a turn every 78 in (198 cm).

❧

The Enfield (as it was called by its users) saw broad service, its firepower being delivered on battlefields ranging from India (where controversy over its cartridges helped ignite the Indian Mutiny in 1857) to Civil War America. It was prized for its robust construction—instead of the barrel being secured to the stock by pins, it was attached by rigid bands that passed around both barrel and woodwork—and the percussion cap lock was reliable in both operation and ignition. Compared to many other muskets and rifles of the period, the Enfield was a lightweight service weapon, a popular feature among infantry who covered all distances on foot. The Enfield's accuracy was reflected in its adjustable ladder backsight, which was graduated at 100 yards (91 m), 200 yards (183 m), 300 yards (274 m) and 400 yards (366 m), although by raising the ladder to the vertical position further ranges could be attempted.

Hammer

Trigger

Attachment for sling

FULL VIEW

THE ENFIELD WAS THE SECOND MOST WIDELY USED WEAPON IN THE AMERICAN CIVIL WAR.

PATTERN 1853 RIFLE MUSKET

DATE	1853
ORIGIN	UK
WEIGHT	9 LB (4 KG)
BARREL	33 IN (84 CM)
CALIBER	.577 IN

The rifle musket was a highly successful weapon. In the hands of a competent infantryman it was effective beyond its sighted distance (2,700 ft/820 m), and at 300 ft (90 m) the bullet could pass through a dozen ½ in (1.5 cm) planks.

Rear sight graduated to 2,700 ft

Barrel

BATTLE OF THE ALMA
Scots Fusilier Guards at the Battle of the Alma, September 20, 1854. Enfield rifle muskets were in regular field use until 1867 after which many were replaced with the cartridge-loaded Snider Enfield.

PERCUSSION-CAP RIFLES

During the US Civil War (1861–65), smoothbore and rifled muskets fought side by side, the latter given superior performance through the development of new ammunition types. Back in 1823, the British Army officer Captain John Norton had designed a conical-shaped ammunition. The problem Norton faced was that when loading bullets into rifled weapons, the bullet had to be a tight fit for it to engage with the rifling, and this made it difficult to muzzle load. Norton made his bullet a comfortable fit, but hollowed out the base to allow the bullet to expand on firing under the gas pressure to grip the rifling. This system was perfected in the Minié bullet of 1847, developed by Claude Étienne Minié.

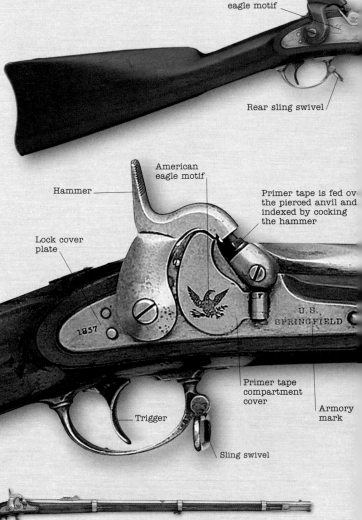

American eagle motif

Hammer

Rear sling swivel

Hammer

American eagle motif

Primer tape is fed ov the pierced anvil and indexed by cocking the hammer

Lock cover plate

Small of stock

1857

U.S. SPRINGFIELD

Primer tape compartment cover

Armory mark

Trigger

Sling swivel

FULL VIEW

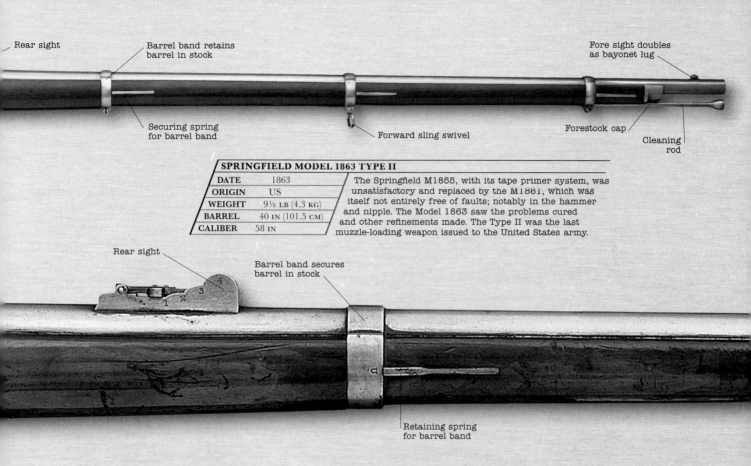

Rear sight

Barrel band retains barrel in stock

Fore sight doubles as bayonet lug

Securing spring for barrel band

Forward sling swivel

Forestock cap

Cleaning rod

SPRINGFIELD MODEL 1863 TYPE II

DATE	1863
ORIGIN	US
WEIGHT	9½ LB (4.3 KG)
BARREL	40 IN (101.5 CM)
CALIBER	58 IN

The Springfield M1855, with its tape primer system, was unsatisfactory and replaced by the M1861, which was itself not entirely free of faults; notably in the hammer and nipple. The Model 1863 saw the problems cured and other refinements made. The Type II was the last muzzle-loading weapon issued to the United States army.

Rear sight

Barrel band secures barrel in stock

Retaining spring for barrel band

SPRINGFIELD MODEL 1855

DATE	1855
ORIGIN	US
WEIGHT	9½ LB (4.2 KG)
BARREL	40 IN (101.5 CM)
CALIBER	14.7 MM

The first regulation American percussion rifle was the Model 1841 Mississippi Rifle, with a 33-in (83.8-cm) barrel. It was later given a longer barrel and modified to use Maynard's patent tape primer fed from a roll housed inside the receiver (instead of individual copper caps placed over the nipple) and became the Model 1855.

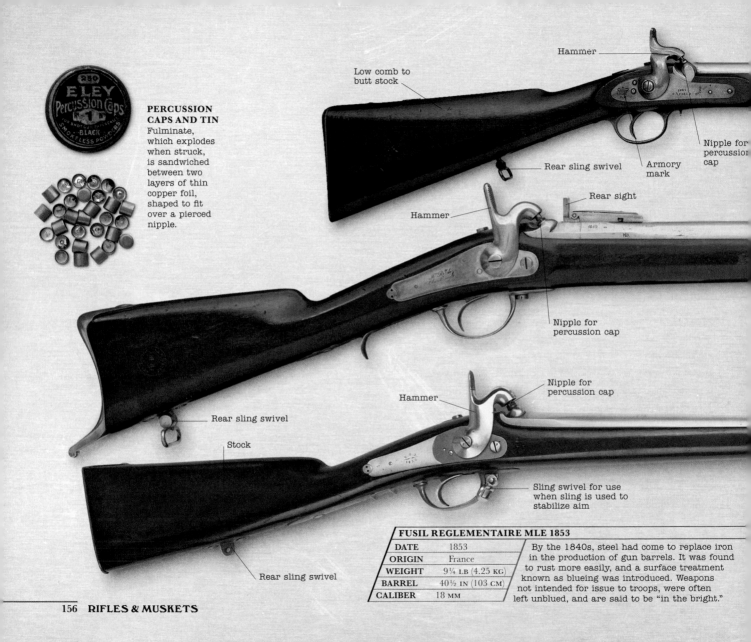

PERCUSSION CAPS AND TIN
Fulminate, which explodes when struck, is sandwiched between two layers of thin copper foil, shaped to fit over a pierced nipple.

Hammer

Low comb to butt stock

Rear sling swivel

Armory mark

Nipple for percussion cap

Rear sight

Hammer

Nipple for percussion cap

Rear sling swivel

Stock

Hammer

Nipple for percussion cap

Sling swivel for use when sling is used to stabilize aim

Rear sling swivel

FUSIL REGLEMENTAIRE MLE 1853	
DATE	1853
ORIGIN	France
WEIGHT	9¼ LB (4.25 KG)
BARREL	40½ IN (103 CM)
CALIBER	18 MM

By the 1840s, steel had come to replace iron in the production of gun barrels. It was found to rust more easily, and a surface treatment known as blueing was introduced. Weapons not intended for issue to troops, were often left unblued, and are said to be "in the bright."

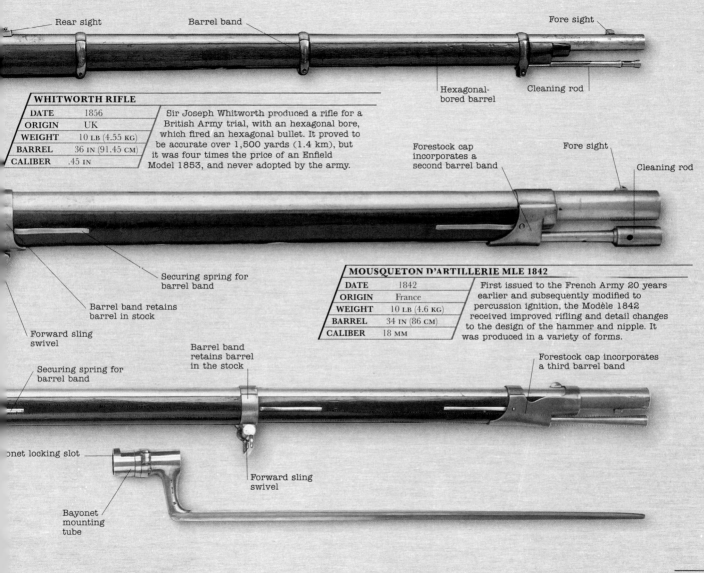

Rear sight

Barrel band

Fore sight

Hexagonal-
bored barrel

Cleaning rod

WHITWORTH RIFLE

DATE	1856
ORIGIN	UK
WEIGHT	10 LB (4.55 KG)
BARREL	36 IN (91.45 CM)
CALIBER	.45 IN

Sir Joseph Whitworth produced a rifle for a British Army trial, with an hexagonal bore, which fired an hexagonal bullet. It proved to be accurate over 1,500 yards (1.4 km), but it was four times the price of an Enfield Model 1853, and never adopted by the army.

Forestock cap
incorporates a
second barrel band

Fore sight

Cleaning rod

Securing spring for
barrel band

Barrel band retains
barrel in stock

Forward sling
swivel

MOUSQUETON D'ARTILLERIE MLE 1842

DATE	1842
ORIGIN	France
WEIGHT	10 LB (4.6 KG)
BARREL	34 IN (86 CM)
CALIBER	18 MM

First issued to the French Army 20 years earlier and subsequently modified to percussion ignition, the Modèle 1842 received improved rifling and detail changes to the design of the hammer and nipple. It was produced in a variety of forms.

Securing spring for
barrel band

Barrel band
retains barrel
in the stock

Forestock cap incorporates
a third barrel band

onet locking slot

Forward sling
swivel

Bayonet
mounting
tube

PERCUSSION-CAP BREECHLOADERS

The 1860s and 70s were a transitional period in rifle development, as the shift toward breechloading guns began. These were already in gestation. A breechloading flintlock had been designed by Major Patrick Ferguson back in the late 1700s. In 1823 Swiss gunmaker Johannes Pauly created a rifle with a hinged barrel that, when tilted, allowed a paper powder-and-ball cartridge to be loaded into the chamber. Another major leap came in the 1830s as unitary brass cartridges (cartridges containing all the ignition components and bullet in one unit) began to emerge, which made breechloading a far easier option. In 1836 Prussian gunsmith Johann Nikolas von Dreyse invented the first rotating bolt rifle. The excellent performance of this weapon in the 1860s resulted in many armies scrambling to either design breechloaders, or adapt existing rifles to the new principle.

Hammer

Nipple for
percussion cap

Bolt

Trigger

Lock cover

FULL VIEW

"Monkey Tail" breech lever — Hammer — Cleaning rod

WESTLEY RICHARDS "MONKEY TAIL" CARBINE

DATE	1866
ORIGIN	UK
WEIGHT	6½ LB (3 KG)
BARREL	19 IN (45.5 CM)
CALIBER	45 IN

Eminent Birmingham gunmakers, Westley Richards & Co. produced two types of carbine for the British Army. One had a falling-block action, the other (illustrated) had a front-hinged tilting breech with a long, curved actuating lever, which gave the weapon its nickname. Westley Richards' carbines required the percussion cap to be located at the mid-point of the cartridge.

Rear sight — Barrel band

TERRY BOLT-ACTION CARBINE

DATE	1861
ORIGIN	UK
WEIGHT	7 LB (3.21 KG)
BARREL	20 IN (51 CM)
CALIBER	.54 IN

The Terry carbine was the first bolt-action weapon adopted by the British Army. Its paper cartridge included a greased felt wad, which remained in the breech after firing and was pushed into the barrel by the insertion of the next round, lubricating and cleaning the bore when it was fired. In a trial, one carbine fired 1,800 rounds without requiring additional cleaning.

SHARPS CARBINE

Percussion-cap breechloaders—also commonly known as capping breechloaders—were a brief family of weapons that appeared in the mid 19th century. They were an early attempt to unite a breechloading system with percussion-cap ignition, and their development was particularly concentrated in the United States and Britain during this time.

In the US, the principal types were the Sharps and Green carbines. The Sharps used a vertical sliding breech block to load a combustible cartridge, which was in turn ignited by

either a percussion cap or tape primer. The problem with the Sharps—and the challenge for all capping breechloaders—was the leakage of gas from the breech (the paper or linen cartridge did not form a gas-tight seal). The Green's Carbine, which had a side-swinging breech, more successfully handled this problem, but ammunition problems limited its use.

FULL VIEW

Hammer

Tape primer compartment

Breech-opening lever

SHARPS' RIFLE
WAS TO STAND THE TESTS OF A
FIRST-CLASS WEAPON.
EDWARD FREEDLEY, AUTHOR, 1858

SHARPS CARBINE	
DATE	1852
ORIGIN	US
WEIGHT	7¾ LB (3.5 KG)
BARREL	18 IN (45 CM)
CALIBER	.52 IN

Christian Sharps devised his breech-loading system in 1848. During the American Civil War, the Union Army bought over 80,000 Sharps' carbines for its cavalry regiments. This rare slant-breech version from 1852 uses a Maynard tape primer.

Rear sight

SHARPS CARTRIDGE
s case is made of
n. Its base was cut off
he breech-block when
action was closed.

SHARPS SHOOTER
Confederate soldiers fire on Union forces at the Battle of Kenneshaw Mountain on June 27, 1864. Christian Sharps' carbine saw heavy use during the US Civil War.

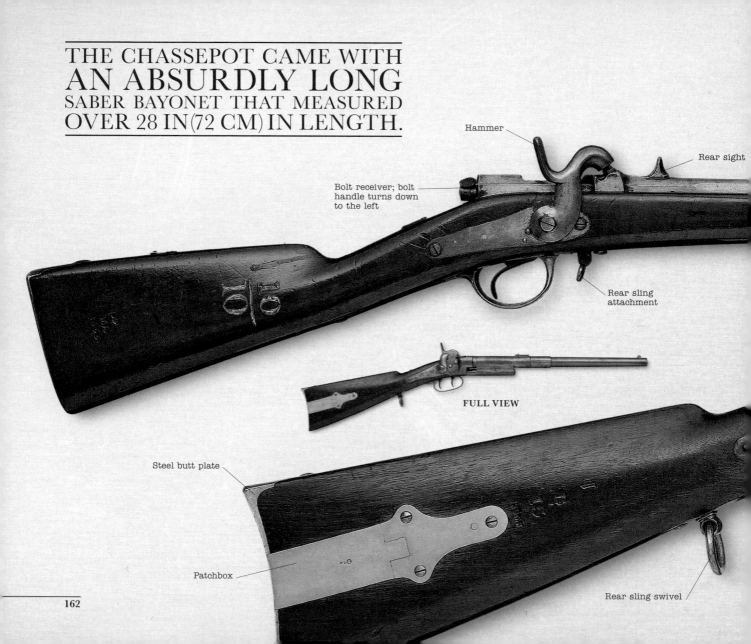

THE CHASSEPOT CAME WITH AN ABSURDLY LONG SABER BAYONET THAT MEASURED OVER 28 IN (72 CM) IN LENGTH.

Hammer

Rear sight

Bolt receiver; bolt handle turns down to the left

Rear sling attachment

FULL VIEW

Steel butt plate

Patchbox

Rear sling swivel

CHASSEPOT CARTRIDGE
After the Franco-Prussian War, the cartridge developed for the Mauser M/71 rifle was adapted for the Chassepot.

CHASSEPOT PERCUSSION CARBINE	
DATE	1858
ORIGIN	France
WEIGHT	6¾ LB (3.03 KG)
BARREL	28 IN (72 CM)
CALIBER	13.5 MM

In the mid-1850s, Alphonse Chassepot produced a breechloading design using a rubber washer to seal the breech. He then replaced the hammer with a needle striker within the bolt, which was accepted for use by the French Army as the Modèle 1866.

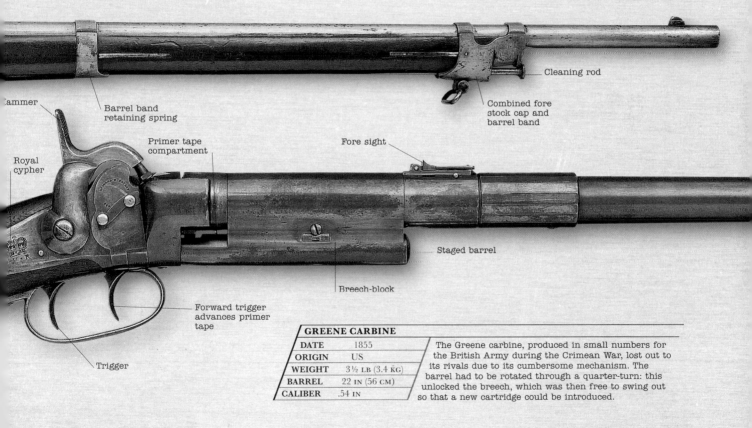

Cleaning rod

Combined fore stock cap and barrel band

Hammer

Barrel band retaining spring

Primer tape compartment

Royal cypher

Fore sight

Staged barrel

Breech-block

Forward trigger advances primer tape

Trigger

GREENE CARBINE	
DATE	1855
ORIGIN	US
WEIGHT	3½ LB (3.4 KG)
BARREL	22 IN (56 CM)
CALIBER	.54 IN

The Greene carbine, produced in small numbers for the British Army during the Crimean War, lost out to its rivals due to its cumbersome mechanism. The barrel had to be rotated through a quarter-turn: this unlocked the breech, which was then free to swing out so that a new cartridge could be introduced.

SINGLE-SHOT BREECHLOADERS

The rush to develop breechloaders in the 1860s and 70s resulted in a number of different operating systems, all attempting to make the most effective use of unitary cartridges. New Yorker Jacob Snider modified the Enfield 1853 Pattern rifle musket by inserting a hinged breechblock through which a cartridge could be inserted. Erskine Allin of Springfield adopted a similar "trapdoor" principle for the Springfield Model 1860 and 1863 rifles. Remington took a different approach, the "rolling block," whereby the action of cocking the hammer allowed the breech to be opened to take a cartridge. The British Army eventually settled on a lever-action "falling-block" system, embodied in the Martini-Henry rifle. However, it would be the bolt-action, being perfected by the likes of Mauser, that would dominate the future of breechloading weapons.

Bolt handle

Rear sling swivel

Hammer

"Trapdoor" breech cover incorporates firing pin

Rear sight

Breech cover hinge

FULL VIEW

Fore sight

Rear sight

Front sling swivel

Cleaning rod

MAUSER M/71

DATE	1872 onward
ORIGIN	Germany
WEIGHT	10 LB (4.5 KG)
BARREL	32½ IN (83 CM)
CALIBER	11 MM

Waffenfabrik Mauser began modifying Dreyse guns to accept brass cartridges, but Peter Paul Mauser produced a new design, strong enough to handle much more powerful ammunition and effective out to a range of 0.5 miles (800 m). The Infanteriegewehr M/71 established Mauser's pre-eminence among suppliers of military rifles.

COMBINATION TOOL
This tool included everything needed to care for a rifle in the field —from screwdrivers and spanners, to a pricker for the nipple.

.45 SPRINGFIELD
The cartridge devised for the Springfield was loaded with 70 grains of powder and a 405-grain bullet.

SPRINGFIELD TRAPDOOR

DATE	1874
ORIGIN	US
WEIGHT	10 LB (4.5 KG)
BARREL	32½ IN (83 CM)
CALIBER	.45 IN

The perfection of the unitary cartridge left the world's armies with a dilemma: what to do with their millions of redundant muzzle-loaders. The US Army modified their rifled muskets by milling out the top of the barrel, creating a chamber for the cartridge, and installing a front-hinged breech cover incorporating a firing pin.

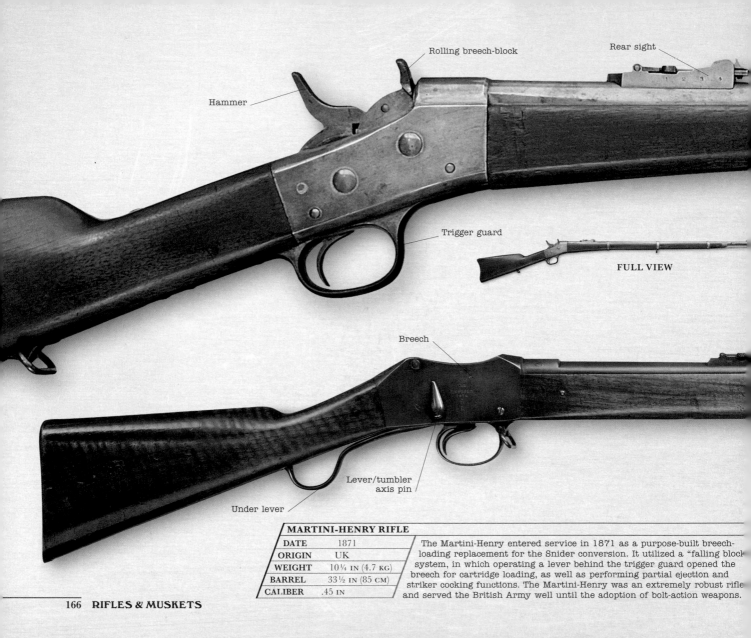

Rolling breech-block

Rear sight

Hammer

Trigger guard

FULL VIEW

Breech

Lever/tumbler
axis pin

Under lever

MARTINI-HENRY RIFLE	
DATE	1871
ORIGIN	UK
WEIGHT	10¼ in (4.7 kg)
BARREL	33½ in (85 cm)
CALIBER	.45 in

The Martini-Henry entered service in 1871 as a purpose-built breech-loading replacement for the Snider conversion. It utilized a "falling block system, in which operating a lever behind the trigger guard opened the breech for cartridge loading, as well as performing partial ejection and striker cocking functions. The Martini-Henry was an extremely robust rifle and served the British Army well until the adoption of bolt-action weapons.

REMINGTON ROLLING BLOCK

DATE	c.1890
ORIGIN	Egypt
WEIGHT	9 LB (4 KG)
BARREL	35¼ IN (90 CM)
CALIBER	.45 IN

Remington's purpose-designed breechloader was declared the best rifle in the world at the 1868 Imperial Exposition in Paris. However, the rifle's rolling-block action, first introduced in 1863, was not as smooth in use as the falling breech-block of the Martini-Henry.

.45 MARTINI-HENRY
The Martini-Henry rifle's cartridge was loaded with 85 grains of black powder. The bullet weighted 480 grains.

Cleaning rod

BAYONET
A socket bayonet, with its triangular-section blade, protuded almost 18 in (46 cm) beyond the muzzle.

DREYSE NEEDLE GUN

Johann von Dreyse's Needle Gun was the first true rotating-bolt-action rifle. Dreyse, alongside Swiss gunmaker Johannes Pauly (one of the inventors of the self-contained cartridge), developed a prototype bolt-action gun in the 1820s. After much trial and error the Needle Gun went into production in 1845, the Prussian army accepting it into service three years later. To load the Needle Gun, the bolt was opened by rotating it out of engagement with a forward locking lug. A cartridge was inserted, and this consisted of a bullet with a percussion cap at its base, the whole structure being attached to a paper tube containing the propellant. The bolt was then locked again. When the gun was fired, a needle-like firing pin pierced the bottom of the cartridge and drove through to strike the percussion cap.

Bolt handle

Shoulder stock

Trigger guard

DREYSE NEEDLE GUN, MODEL 1841	
DATE	1841
ORIGIN	Prussia
WEIGHT	10 LB (4.5 KG)
BARREL	27 IN (70 CM)
CALIBER	13.6 MM

Dreyse produced a rifle with a simple turn-down bolt, terminating in a needle that penetrated the length of a (linen) cartridge to detonate a percussion cap in the base of a Minié bullet. The advent of the brass cartridge made the rifle obsolete, but still the Prussians used it to defeat the French in the Franco-Prussian War in 1871.

PRUSSIA'S USE OF THE DREYSE NEEDLE GUN WAS THE KEY TO THEM WINNING THE AUSTRO-PRUSSIAN WAR (1866) AND FRANCO-PRUSSIAN WAR (1870–71).

FULL VIEW

Rear sight

Barrel band retaining springs

THE BATTLE OF KÖNIGGRÄTZ
At the battle of Königgrätz (Sadowa), on July 3, 1866, thanks largely to the superior firepower of its Dreyse Needle Guns over the muzzle-loaders of the rival Austrians, Prussia was victorious, and went on to become the dominant force in Central Europe in the ensuing years.

MANUAL REPEATER RIFLES 1775–1880

The first major step on the journey toward the repeating, multi-shot rifle was taken by inventor Walter Hunt of Brooklyn in 1849. Hunt patented a weapon known as the "Volitional Repeater," which housed several odd caseless rounds in an underbarrel magazine, the feed being operated by an underlever. This principle underwent a circuitous journey through several illustrious hands, including Smith & Wesson and Oliver Winchester, before Benjamin Tyler Henry produced the now legendary Henry Model 60, a .44 rimfire weapon containing 15 rounds in its magazine. With proper reloading technique, a shooter could send out up to 28 rounds in a minute.

Hammer

847

Locking catch
for cocking
lever

Trigger guard
and cocking
lever

FULL VIEW

Rear sight

Magazine holds
15 rounds

Magazine follower

HENRY MODEL 1860

DATE	1862
ORIGIN	US
WEIGHT	9 LB (4 KG)
BARREL	20 IN (51 CM)
CALIBER	.44 IN Rimfire

When Oliver Winchester set up the New Haven Arms Co., he brought in Tyler Henry to run it. Henry's first act was to design a repeating rifle worked by an underlever that ejected the spent round, chambered a new one, and left the action cocked. To lock the action, he used a two-piece bolt joined by a toggle-joint. This same method was later used by Maxim in his machine gun, and by Borchardt and Luger in their pistols.

Cylinder
axis rod

Hammer

Cylinder has
five chambers

Rear sight

Fore sight

Barrel band

Side-mounted
hammer

COLT REVOLVING RIFLE

DATE	1855
ORIGIN	US
WEIGHT	7½ LB (3.45 KG)
BARREL	27 IN (68.2 CM)
CALIBER	.56 IN

The third model of Colt's revolving rifles made a considerable impact, even though the loading procedure was cumbersome. The cylinder was removed, powder packed into the five chambers, a bullet packed on top, and the chambers sealed with wax. The cylinder was then covered with grease in order to protect against the possibility of loose powder igniting all the chambers at once.

SPENCER RIFLE

DATE	1863
ORIGIN	US
WEIGHT	10 LB (4.55 KG)
BARREL	28¼ IN (72 CM)
CALIBER	.52 IN

Christopher Spencer's rifle was to become the world's first practical military repeater. Its tubular magazine was located in the butt stock; a lever that formed the trigger guard opened the rolling breech and extracted the spent cartridge.

Rear sight

Hammer

Lock plate

Butt contains tubular magazine, holding seven rounds

Trigger guard and breech-operating

Hammer

Rear sling swivel

SPENCER CARTRIDGE
This is the rimfire black-powder round for which the Civil War-era Spencer carbine was chambered.

Small of the stock

Comb

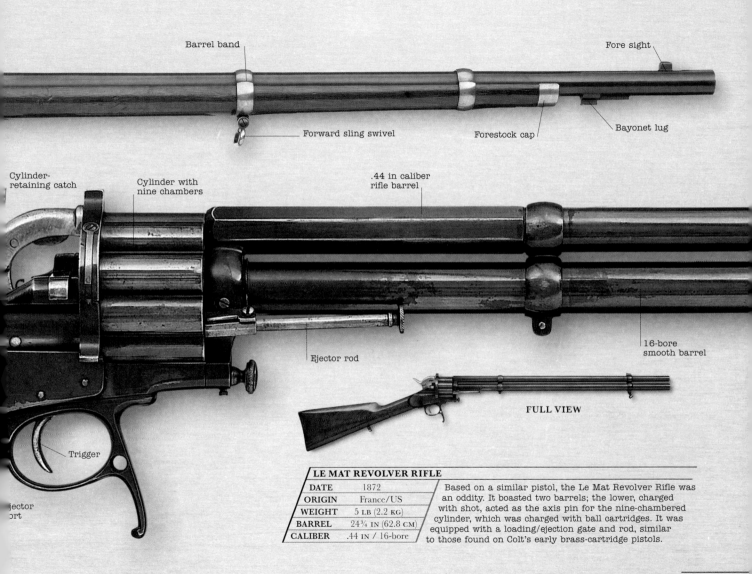

Barrel band

Fore sight

Forward sling swivel

Forestock cap

Bayonet lug

Cylinder-retaining catch

Cylinder with nine chambers

.44 in caliber rifle barrel

16-bore smooth barrel

Ejector rod

Trigger

jector ort

FULL VIEW

LE MAT REVOLVER RIFLE	
DATE	1872
ORIGIN	France/US
WEIGHT	5 LB (2.2 KG)
BARREL	24¾ IN (62.8 CM)
CALIBER	.44 IN / 16-bore

Based on a similar pistol, the Le Mat Revolver Rifle was an oddity. It boasted two barrels; the lower, charged with shot, acted as the axis pin for the nine-chambered cylinder, which was charged with ball cartridges. It was equipped with a loading/ejection gate and rod, similar to those found on Colt's early brass-cartridge pistols.

WINCHESTER

The Winchester Repeating Arms Company is a landmark name in US gunmaking. Oliver Winchester founded the company in 1866. In that year it brought out its first lever-action rifle, and so began a family of guns that, like the Colt Peacemaker, virtually defined the Wild West era. The early 20th century saw Winchester bring out new self-loading rifle and shotgun designs, and during and between the two world wars Winchester was central to the production or development of the BAR, the Browning .50 BMG cartridge, the M1 rifle and carbine, and the M14. In 1931, Winchester was also bought by the Olin Corporation, which in 1981 sold off the firearms-making business (but not the rights to the Winchester brand), this becoming the US Repeating Arms Company. However, in January 2006 the famous New Haven plant in Connecticut was closed, threatening the future of many of the company's great civilian lines, such as the Model 94 and Model 1300 shotgun. At the time of writing, however, Browning has stepped forward to take over the manufacture and sale of Winchester firearms (both are part of the Herstal Group).

Stock

PRODUCTION LINE
Women at the Winchester factory in New Haven, Connecticut, in 1946, perform various stages of gun assembly, including attaching the stock to the barrel and inserting the rifles' sights.

WINCHESTER MODEL 1866 CARBINE		
DATE	1866	The principle shortcoming of Benjamin Tyler Henry's underlever rifle lay in the way its tubular magazine was charged. In 1866, Nelson King introduced an improvement that allowed reloading via a port on the receiver. This doubled the rifle's rate of fire to 30 rounds a minute.
ORIGIN	US	
WEIGHT	9¼ LB (4.2 KG)	
BARREL	23 IN (58.5 CM)	
CALIBER	.44 Rimfire	

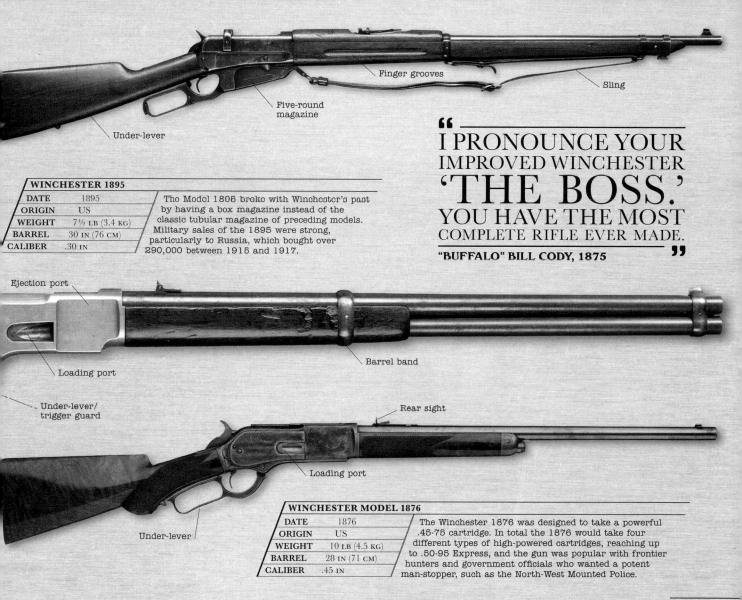

Finger grooves

Sling

Five-round
magazine

Under-lever

WINCHESTER 1895

DATE	1895
ORIGIN	US
WEIGHT	7½ LB (3.4 KG)
BARREL	30 IN (76 CM)
CALIBER	.30 IN

The Model 1895 broke with Winchester's past by having a box magazine instead of the classic tubular magazine of preceding models. Military sales of the 1895 were strong, particularly to Russia, which bought over 290,000 between 1915 and 1917.

> " I PRONOUNCE YOUR IMPROVED WINCHESTER 'THE BOSS.' YOU HAVE THE MOST COMPLETE RIFLE EVER MADE. "
>
> **"BUFFALO" BILL CODY, 1875**

Ejection port

Loading port

Barrel band

Under-lever/
trigger guard

Rear sight

Loading port

Under-lever

WINCHESTER MODEL 1876

DATE	1876
ORIGIN	US
WEIGHT	10 LB (4.5 KG)
BARREL	28 IN (71 CM)
CALIBER	.45 IN

The Winchester 1876 was designed to take a powerful .45-75 cartridge. In total the 1876 would take four different types of high-powered cartridges, reaching up to .50-95 Express, and the gun was popular with frontier hunters and government officials who wanted a potent man-stopper, such as the North-West Mounted Police.

MANUAL REPEATER RIFLES 1880–1890

During the 1870s bolt-action rifles began to ally themselves with magazine feeds. In 1871 Paul Mauser took his bolt-action rifle and connected it to an eight-round underbarrel magazine, a new round being fed with every operation of the bolt. However, tubular magazines had major deficiencies. Their springs were prone to weakening, the gun's center of balance changed as the magazine emptied, and there was always the danger of magazine explosions. Scottish-born American James Lee found the solution in the late 1870s. He relocated the cartridges in a spring-loaded box magazine that sat directly beneath the bolt.

Bolt

Rear sling swivel

Bolt handle

Straight-through stock

Integral six-round box magazine

CAVALRY CARBINE MODELLO 1891 TS	
DATE	1891
ORIGIN	Italy
WEIGHT	6½ LB (3 KG)
BARREL	17¾ IN (45 CM)
CALIBER	6.5 MM x 52

Often known as the Mannlicher-Carcano, it used a modified version of the bolt-action Mauser developed for the M1889. It continued, in modified form, in Italian service until after World War II, and many were sold to dealers in the US; one found its way to Lee Harvey Oswald, who probably used it to kill President John F. Kennedy in 1963.

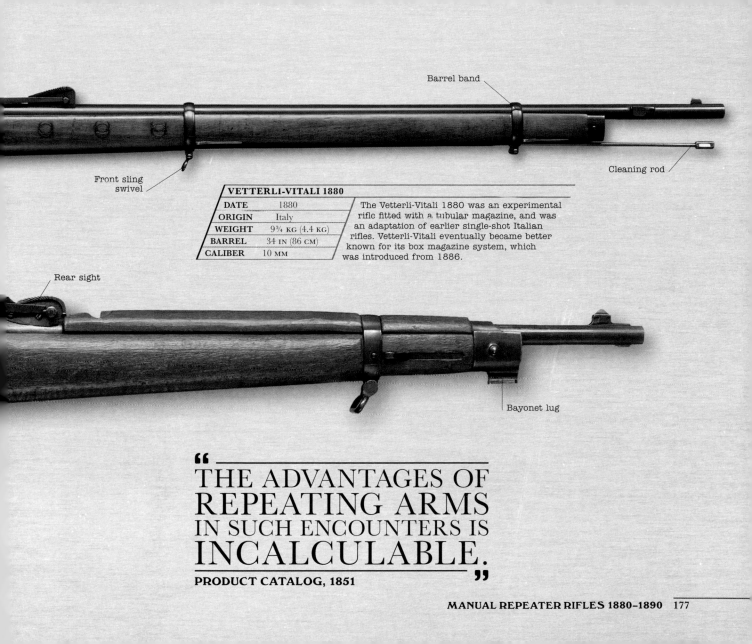

Barrel band

Cleaning rod

Front sling
swivel

VETTERLI-VITALI 1880

DATE	1880
ORIGIN	Italy
WEIGHT	9¾ KG (4.4 KG)
BARREL	34 IN (86 CM)
CALIBER	10 MM

The Vetterli-Vitali 1880 was an experimental rifle fitted with a tubular magazine, and was an adaptation of earlier single-shot Italian rifles. Vetterli-Vitali eventually became better known for its box magazine system, which was introduced from 1886.

Rear sight

Bayonet lug

"
THE ADVANTAGES OF REPEATING ARMS IN SUCH ENCOUNTERS IS INCALCULABLE.

"

PRODUCT CATALOG, 1851

AT EVERY HALT WE TOOK ADVANTAGE
OF THE COVER... THE TREES, OF COURSE,
FURNISHED NO PROTECTION
FROM THE MAUSER BULLETS.

**THEODORE ROOSEVELT, ON THE
SPANISH/AMERICAN WAR, 1899**

Bolt is
locked at
the rear

Bolt handle

Straight-through stock

Bolt handle

Bolt is
locked at
the rear

Rear sight

Straight-through stock

Integral five-round
box magazine

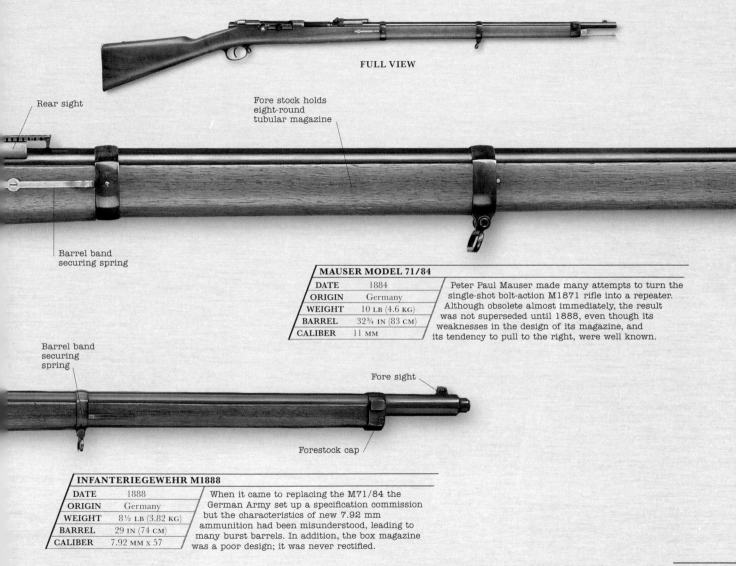

FULL VIEW

Rear sight

Fore stock holds
eight-round
tubular magazine

Barrel band
securing spring

Barrel band
securing
spring

Fore sight

Forestock cap

MAUSER MODEL 71/84

DATE	1884
ORIGIN	Germany
WEIGHT	10 LB (4.6 KG)
BARREL	32¾ IN (83 CM)
CALIBER	11 MM

Peter Paul Mauser made many attempts to turn the
single-shot bolt-action M1871 rifle into a repeater.
Although obsolete almost immediately, the result
was not superseded until 1888, even though its
weaknesses in the design of its magazine, and
its tendency to pull to the right, were well known.

INFANTERIEGEWEHR M1888

DATE	1888
ORIGIN	Germany
WEIGHT	8½ LB (3.82 KG)
BARREL	29 IN (74 CM)
CALIBER	7.92 MM x 57

When it came to replacing the M71/84 the
German Army set up a specification commission
but the characteristics of new 7.92 mm
ammunition had been misunderstood, leading to
many burst barrels. In addition, the box magazine
was a poor design; it was never rectified.

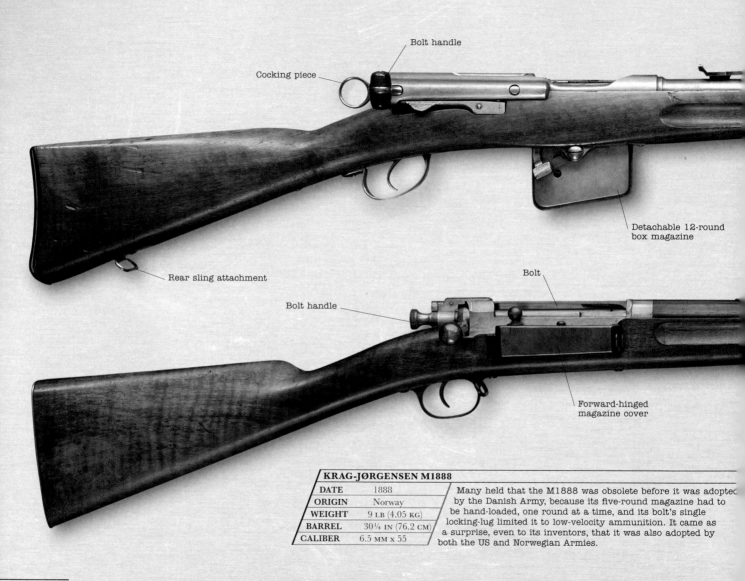

Bolt handle

Cocking piece

Bolt handle

Rear sling attachment

Bolt

Detachable 12-round box magazine

Forward-hinged magazine cover

KRAG-JØRGENSEN M1888

DATE	1888
ORIGIN	Norway
WEIGHT	9 LB (4.05 KG)
BARREL	30¼ IN (76.2 CM)
CALIBER	6.5 MM x 55

Many held that the M1888 was obsolete before it was adopted by the Danish Army, because its five-round magazine had to be hand-loaded, one round at a time, and its bolt's single locking-lug limited it to low-velocity ammunition. It came as a surprise, even to its inventors, that it was also adopted by both the US and Norwegian Armies.

Rear sight   Barrel band   Fore sight

Bayonet lug   Cleaning rod

Rear sight

SCHMIDT-RUBIN M1889

DATE	1889
ORIGIN	Switzerland
WEIGHT	9.8 lb (4.45 kg)
BARREL	30.75 in (78 cm)
CALIBER	7.5 mm

In 1889 Colonel Rudolf Schmidt of the Swiss Army developed a straight-pull bolt-action rifle with a 12-round box magazine. It was accepted as the regulation rifle, and remained in service, only slightly modified, until 1931, when its bolt action was rejigged to operate in half the length. The modified version was only discarded in the late 1950s, and a sniper's version was in use until 1987.

ALTHOUGH PRACTICAL COMBAT
RANGE IS AROUND 300 YARDS (275 M),
MILITARY BOLT ACTION
RIFLES COULD KILL
AT OVER 1000 YARDS (915 M).

.303 CALIBER AMMUNITION
Until the 1890s, rifle bullets were
blunt-nosed. The British Army's
Lee-Metfords and Lee-Enfields were
chambered for the one shown.

Bolt cover

Cocking piece

Bolt handle

Trigger

Eight-round
detachable box
magazine

Magazine
connector

Magazine
release catch

Rear sight

LEE-METFORD PATTERN RIFLE

DATE	1888
ORIGIN	UK
WEIGHT	9 LB (4.05 KG)
BARREL	30 IN (76.2 CM)
CALIBER	.303 IN

The British Army opened a competition to find a replacement for the single-shot Martini-Henry rifle in 1879; 11 years later, it adopted the .303 in rifle, Magazine, Mark I (the name was changed in 1891 to include those of its designers). It had an enclosed bolt action and a box magazine, the work of James Lee, and had anti-fouling rifling developed by William Metford.

Finger groove

FULL VIEW

LEE-METFORD

DATE	1890
ORIGIN	UK
WEIGHT	9¾ LB (4.37 KG)
BARREL	30¼ IN (76.9 CM)
CALIBER	.303 IN

The Lee-Metford began a prestigious lineage of British bolt-action rifles. The name derives from the inventor of its action, James Lee, and the designer of the rifled barrel, William Metford. It featured an eight-round box magazine and was chambered for the powerful .303 in cartridge. The rifle also had a set of "Extreme Range Sights" on the side of the gun, optimistically graduated out to 3500 yards (3199 m).

ANNIE OAKLEY

Annie Oakley (1860–1926) was a legend of the West, and like many legends has attracted her fair share of historical myth and error. She was born Phoebe Ann Mosey in Ohio and by the age of nine was an expert game shot; the death of her father necessitated that she shoot to help support the family.

After winning a shooting competition in Cincinnati in 1881, beating her future husband and manager Francis E. Butler, she adopted the Oakley stage name and in 1885 she and her husband joined the *Buffalo Bill Wild West Show*. Oakley was undoubtedly a phenomenal shot, whether with handguns or with a .22 Marlin rifle. She could hit a dime thrown into the air from 90 ft (27 m), and could hit an edge-on playing card from the same distance. She performed in front of international royalty, including Queen Victoria and the future Kaiser Wilhelm II (she shot the ash off his cigarette). Oakley eventually left the Buffalo Bill show, but kept performing into her 60s.

Hammer

Loading port

Operating lever

FULL VIEW

SHE COULD SPLIT AN EDGE-ON
PLAYING CARD WITH A
.22 CALIBER RIFLE AT 90 FT(27 M).

MARLIN MODEL 1893	
DATE	1893
ORIGIN	US
WEIGHT	Not known
BARREL	Not known
CALIBER	.25-36 IN

The Marlin Model 1893 was a lever-action rifle in several different calibers (the gun here is .25-36) that was produced between 1893 and 1936. It was distinctive by having side ejection, rather than the top ejection of the Winchester rifles.

Adjustable rear sight

ANNIE GET YOUR GUN
Annie Oakley depicted in a poster promoting the *Buffalo Bill Wild West Show*. A renowned sharp-shooter, in 1901 she was awarded a medal by King Edward VII who called her "the greatest rifle shot in the world."

MANUAL REPEATER RIFLES 1890–1900

By the 1890s the bolt-action rifle had been refined and improved to a state of near perfection. During this decade, many armies adopted rifles that would see them through the coming world war and beyond. In Germany, Mauser produced the Gewehr 98, a 7.92 x 57 mm rifle with an excellent bolt-action (known particularly for its robust extraction) and fed from a five-round integral box magazine. Great Britain had the .303 Lee-Metford rifles, which in turn developed into the Lee-Enfield Mark I and began one of the world's most successful series of bolt-action weapons.

Magazine catch

Bolt handle

Bolt

Cocking piece

Integral five-round box magazine

Wooden butt

"3-LINE" RIFLE M1891	
DATE	1891
ORIGIN	Russia
WEIGHT	9¾ LB (4.43 KG)
BARREL	31½ IN (80.2 CM)
CALIBER	7.62 MM x 54R

The M1891 is usually known as the Mosin-Nagant, after its designers. It was Imperial Russia's first repeater rifle, and its first in a "modern" caliber (a "line" was a measure approximating to one-tenth of an inch, and refers to its caliber). It was issued in a variety of forms, including a semi-carbine and a true carbine, and was still in service as a sniper rifle with the Red Army until the 1960s.

Sight range
graduations

Blade front sight

Cleaning rod

MOSIN-NAGANT M1891 REMINGTON

DATE	1891
ORIGIN	US
WEIGHT	9¾ LB (4.43 KG)
BARREL	31½ IN (80.2 CM)
CALIBER	7.62 MM x 54R

During WWI, Russian production levels could not meet the demands for rifles. Consequently, the US gunmakers Remington Arms and New England Westinghouse were commissioned to make up the shortfall. Between them the two companies produced over 1.5 million M1891 rifles between 1915 and 1917, and nearly 300,000 were used in the US for training.

Rear sight

Barrel band
secures the barrel
in the stock

FULL VIEW

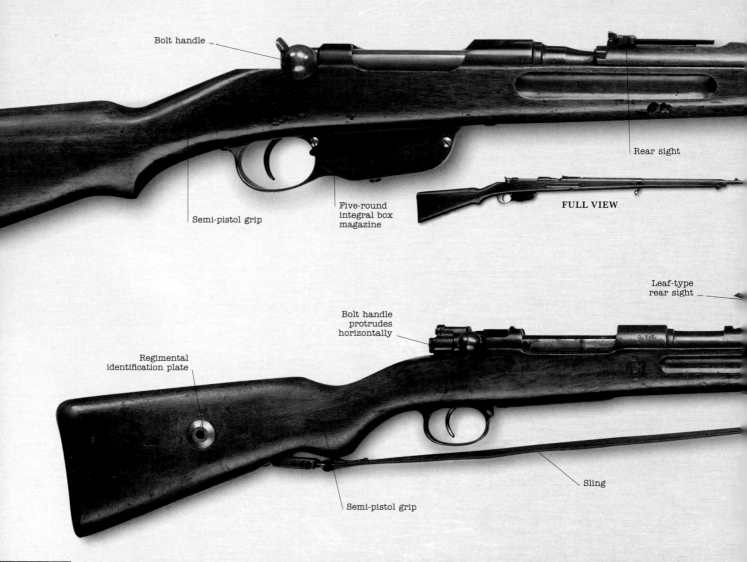

Bolt handle

Rear sight

Semi-pistol grip

Five-round
integral box
magazine

FULL VIEW

Leaf-type
rear sight

Bolt handle
protrudes
horizontally

Regimental
identification plate

Sling

Semi-pistol grip

Bayonet lug

MANNLICHER M1895

DATE	1895
ORIGIN	Austria
WEIGHT	8½ LB (3.78 KG)
BARREL	30 IN (76.5 CM)
CALIBER	8 MM x 50R

The straight-pull bolt-action M1895 was the work of Ferdinand von Mannlicher, and used a rotating locking lug turned in a camming (spiraled) groove. Ammunition was fed from a fixed box magazine that Mannlicher also designed. It was used widely throughout the Austro-Hungarian empire.

Bayonet lug

MAUSER INFANTERIEGEWEHR 98

DATE	1898
ORIGIN	Germany
WEIGHT	9¼ LB (4.15 KG)
BARREL	29¼ IN (74 CM)
CALIBER	7.92 MM x 57

By the time of the Gew98, Mauser had solved virtually every problem known to beset the bolt-action magazine rifle. It added a third rear-locking lug to reinforce the two forward-mounted lugs, as well as improving gas sealing and refining the magazine.

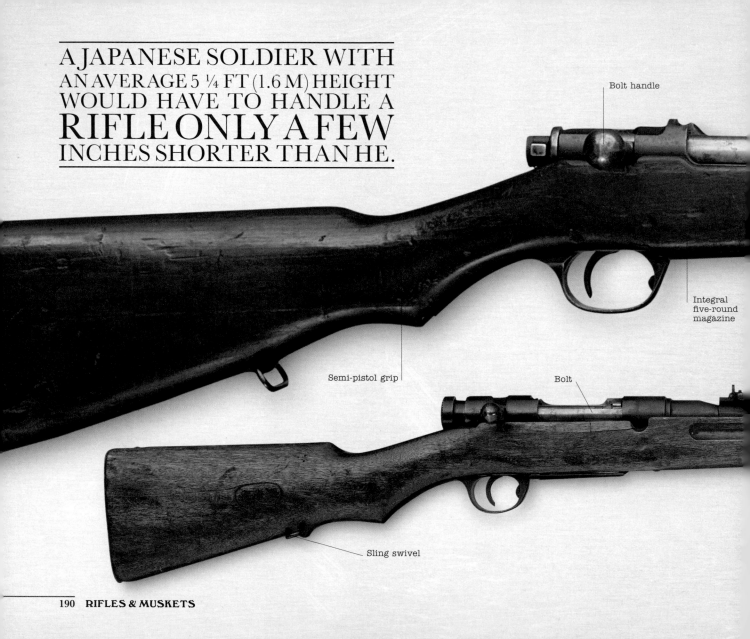

A JAPANESE SOLDIER WITH AN AVERAGE 5 ¼ FT (1.6 M) HEIGHT WOULD HAVE TO HANDLE A RIFLE ONLY A FEW INCHES SHORTER THAN HE.

Bolt handle

Integral five-round magazine

Semi-pistol grip

Bolt

Sling swivel

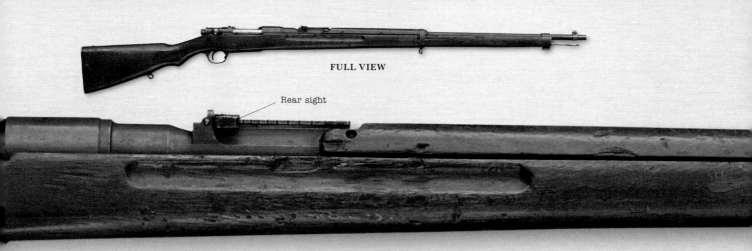

FULL VIEW

Rear sight

ARISAKA MEIJI 30

DATE	1897
ORIGIN	Japan
WEIGHT	9½ LB (4.3 KG)
BARREL	31½ IN (80 CM)
CALIBER	6.5 MM x 50SR

At the conclusion of its war with China in 1895, the Japanese Army decided to adopt a modern weapon in a small caliber. This gun, designed by Arisaka, chambered for a 6.5 mm semi-rimmed round, with an enclosed five-round box magazine, was adopted. It used a turning bolt of the Mauser pattern with forward-locking lugs. It came into service in the 30th year of the Emperor Meiji.

Finger groove
(one on each side)

ARISAKA TYPE 99

DATE	1939
ORIGIN	Japan
WEIGHT	8¾ LB (4 KG)
BARREL	25¾ IN (65.5 CM)
CALIBER	7.7 MM

Japanese war experience showed that the 6.5 mm round used in the 38th Year rifle was inadequately powered. The Type 99, introduced into service in 1939, used the more potent 7.7 mm round. It was available in two versions, a short carbine (specifications left) and a standard version that was 6 in (15.2 cm) longer. An oddity of the Type 99 was a folding metal monopod support beneath the fore-end, although this was not rigid enough for its purpose.

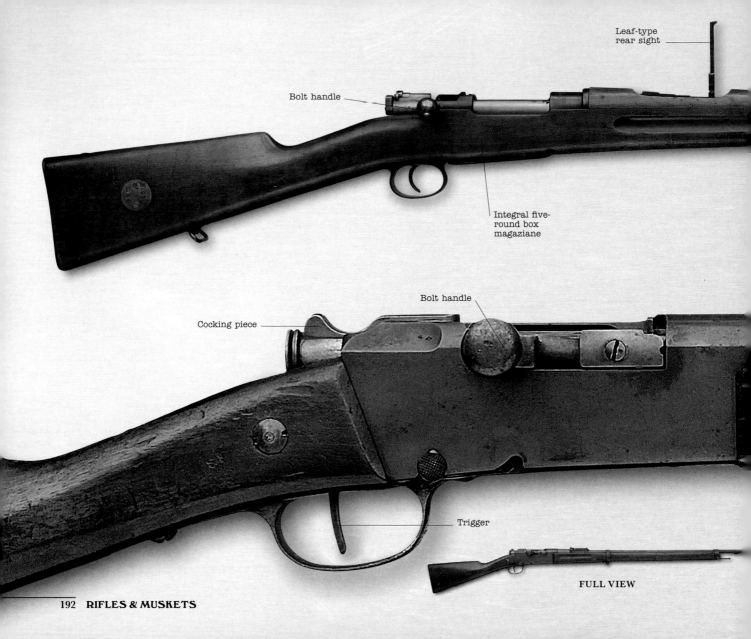

Leaf-type
rear sight

Bolt handle

Integral five-
round box
magaziane

Cocking piece

Bolt handle

Trigger

FULL VIEW

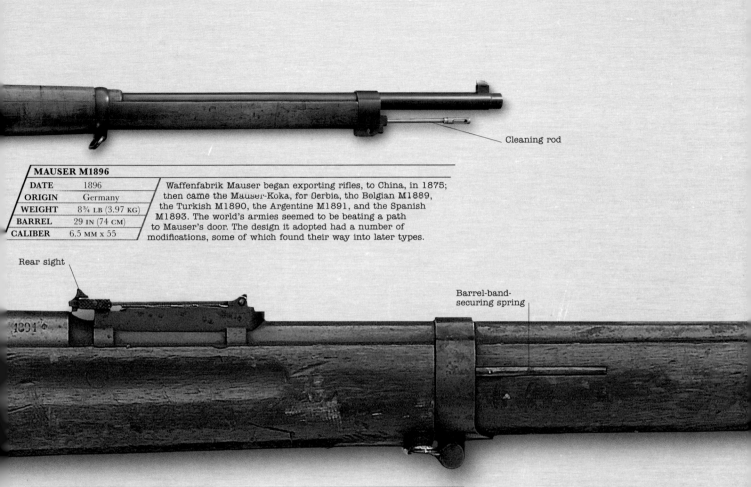

Cleaning rod

MAUSER M1896

DATE	1896
ORIGIN	Germany
WEIGHT	8¾ LB (3.97 KG)
BARREL	29 IN (74 CM)
CALIBER	6.5 MM x 55

Waffenfabrik Mauser began exporting rifles, to China, in 1875; then came the Mauser-Koka, for Serbia, the Belgian M1889, the Turkish M1890, the Argentine M1891, and the Spanish M1893. The world's armies seemed to be beating a path to Mauser's door. The design it adopted had a number of modifications, some of which found their way into later types.

Rear sight

Barrel-band-securing spring

LEBEL MLE 1886/93

DATE	1893
ORIGIN	France
WEIGHT	9½ LB (4.3 KG)
BARREL	31½ IN (80 CM)
CALIBER	8 MM x 50R

In 1885 Boulanger was appointed to the Ministry of War in Paris. One of his first priorities was to introduce a modern rifle. The result was the first rifle firing a small-caliber, jacketed bullet propelled by smokeless powder (invented by Meille in 1884/5); despite being mechanically unsophisticated, it rendered every other rifle in the world obsolete. This modified version followed in 1893.

LEE ENFIELD NO.4 MK I

Alongside the Short Magazine Lee-Enfield the Rifle No.4 was the perfect expression of the Lee-Enfield bolt-action design. It was developed in order to simplify rifle production, and it emerged into service in November 1939.

The No.4 rifle's principal differences from the SMLE Mk III were in the front and rear sights (the rear sight was now a two-stage flip-up type) and the exposed muzzle, and with the Mk 1 model the receiver was altered to improve the speed of manufacture. The No. 4 rifle went through several different subtle modifications, but all were workhorse rifles that served the British Army well beyond the war into the 1950s. (It was replaced by the 7.62 mm SLR, but was kept on for cadet training for many years.) The gun was also an accurate one, and fitted with a detachable stock comb and a No.32 telescopic sight it was also used as a sniper weapon.

FULL VIEW

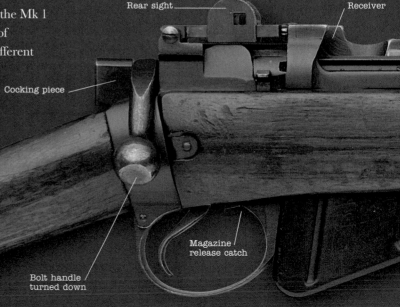

Rear sight

Receiver

Cocking piece

Bolt handle turned down

Magazine release catch

SUCH IS ITS RELIABILITY, THE LEE-ENFIELD NO.4 IS STILL APPEARING IN THE HANDS OF AFGHAN INSURGENTS TODAY.

LEE-ENFIELD RIFLE NUMBER 4 MARK 1

DATE	1939
ORIGIN	UK
WEIGHT	9 LB (4 KG)
LENGTH	25 IN (64 CM)
CALIBER	.303 IN

The new Lee-Enfield differed very little from the model it replaced. The bolt and receiver were modified; the rear sight was a new design, and was placed on the receiver; the fore stock was shortened, and its cap was redesigned.

FIGHT FOR FREEDOM
Two British soldiers try to avoid detection by German forces in the Arnhem area of Holland, December 1944. The soldier on the right is carrying a Sten submachine gun, while the soldier on the left is armed with the Lee-Enfield No.4—the most common rifle used by British forces during WWII.

MANUAL REPEATER RIFLES 1900–1945

Due to the combat limitations of late 19th century rifles, early 20th century gun designers began to shorten the barrels of rifles to produce "carbine" models. The German Mauser Gewehr 98, for example, went from a 33¾ in (74 cm) barrel to a 23½ in (60 cm) barrel to form the KAR98K. The shortening of the barrel in no way compromised practical combat performance, as most of the bolt-action rifles remained capable of killing at ranges beyond 650 yards (600 m), but it improved handling by bringing down the overall gun length.

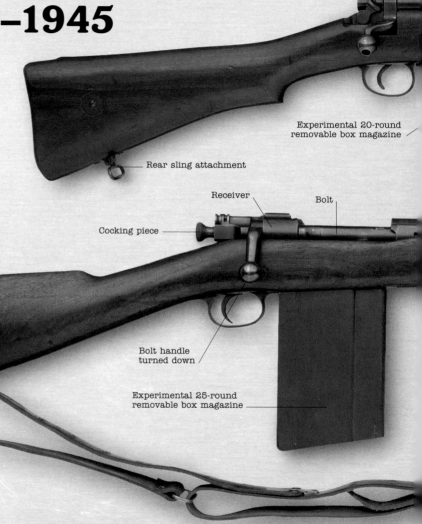

Experimental 20-round removable box magazine

Rear sling attachment

Cocking piece

Receiver

Bolt

Bolt handle turned down

Experimental 25-round removable box magazine

Barrel band

Bayonet lug

Fore sight is mounted
between protective blades

PATTERN 1914

DATE	1914
ORIGIN	UK
WEIGHT	8½ LB (4 KG)
BARREL	26 IN (66 CM)
CALIBER	7 MM Mauser

At the start of World War I, manufacturing problems with the new Pattern 1913 rifle resulted in a change of caliber from .276 in to the standard .303 in chambering, and the weapon's redesignation as the Pattern 1914. The Model 1917, a .30 in-caliber version of the Pattern 1914, was later adopted by the US Army.

Rear sight

Two-part sling

SPRINGFIELD M1903

DATE	1903
ORIGIN	US
WEIGHT	8½ LB (4 KG)
BARREL	24 IN (61 CM)
CALIBER	.30-03

Impressed by the Mauser rifles US troops encountered during the war against Spain in 1898, the United States Ordnance Department looked to replace its Krag rifles. Negotiating a license to build a Mauser design of its own, the result was the .30 in Rifle, Magazine, M1903. The example shown here has an experimental 25-round magazine.

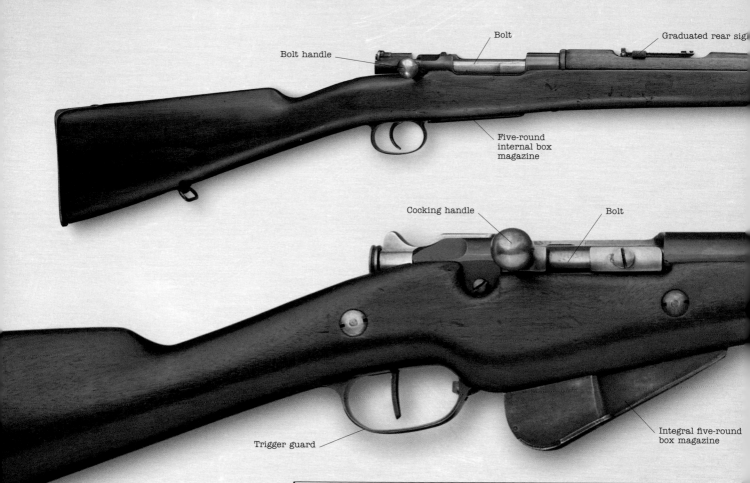

Bolt handle

Bolt

Graduated rear sigh[t]

Five-round
internal box
magazine

Cocking handle

Bolt

Trigger guard

Integral five-round
box magazine

BERTHIER MLE 1916	
DATE	1916
ORIGIN	France
WEIGHT	9 LB (4.15 KG)
BARREL	31¼ IN (79.8 CM)
CALIBER	8 MM x 50R

The shortcomings of the Lebel rifle (see page 192) led to this revised
design being issued to French colonial troops in 1902. Though it
continued to use the bolt action of the Lebel, and was outmoded in
appearance (due to the length of its barrel), The Berthier's only
serious defect lay in its magazine capacity—just three rounds. A
modified version with a five-round magazine was issued from 1916.

Cleaning rod

MAUSER 1893

DATE	1900
ORIGIN	Spain
WEIGHT	8¾ LB (3.95 KG)
BARREL	29 IN (74 CM)
CALIBER	7 x 57 MM

The Mauser 1893 was the seminal Spanish Mauser rifle of the late 1800s. Such was its effectiveness during the Spanish-American War that it pushed the US toward development of the Springfield rifle. The 1893 was fed from a five-round integral box magazine.

FULL VIEW

IN WWI MASS RIFLE FIRE
WAS SOMETIMES CONFUSED WITH
MACHINE-GUN FIRE,
EACH RIFLEMAN SHOOTING UP TO
15 ROUNDS PER MINUTE.

OVER 10 MILLION
KAR98K RIFLES WERE MADE,
AND WERE USED IN
CONFLICTS RANGING FROM
WWII TO THE CIVIL WAR
IN YUGOSLAVIA IN THE 1990s.

Regimental identifying plate

Rear sling attachment

Steel-bound butt

Bolt handle protrudes horizontally

Cocking piece

Integral five-round magazine

Integral five-
round magazine

Fore stock cap

MAUSER KAR98K

DATE	1935
ORIGIN	Germany
WEIGHT	8½ LB (3.9 KG)
BARREL	23½ IN (60 CM)
CALIBER	7.92 MM x 57

The "Karabiner" 98K embodied improvements to the Mauser Gewehr 98 rifle, and became the standard German service rifle of World War II. More than 14 million were manufactured between 1935 and 1945. A number of variations were produced, including those for mountain troops, paratroops, and snipers. During the war, the original design was simplified to speed up production.

Fore sight in
protective shroud

Folding
cruciform
bayonet

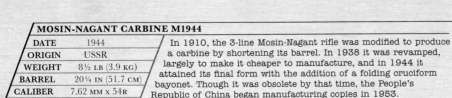

FULL VIEW

MOSIN-NAGANT CARBINE M1944

DATE	1944
ORIGIN	USSR
WEIGHT	8½ LB (3.9 KG)
BARREL	20¼ IN (51.7 CM)
CALIBER	7.62 MM x 54R

In 1910, the 3-line Mosin-Nagant rifle was modified to produce a carbine by shortening its barrel. In 1938 it was revamped, largely to make it cheaper to manufacture, and in 1944 it attained its final form with the addition of a folding cruciform bayonet. Though it was obsolete by that time, the People's Republic of China began manufacturing copies in 1953.

SNIPER RIFLES

Sniping developed rapidly as a military art during the two world wars, providing several important military roles from inflicting attrition on enemy officers through to holding up enemy advances. In the first half of the 20th century most standard-issue bolt-action rifles had the range and accuracy to handle sniper work if properly sighted. As the science of both sniping and ballistics was refined in the post-war period, new breeds of sniper weapons emerged that were purpose-designed for high-accuracy, long-range shooting. Stocks and furniture come with fully adjustable parts, to make an exact, comfortable fit to the sniper's body dimensions. The classic sniper round has remained fairly constant with the 7.62 mm, but heavy anti-material sniper weapons also emerged, particularly those firing the powerful .50 in BMG (Browning Machine Gun).

Busch Visar telescope sight

Eyepiece

Safety catch

Bolt handle

Optical sight

Raised stock comb

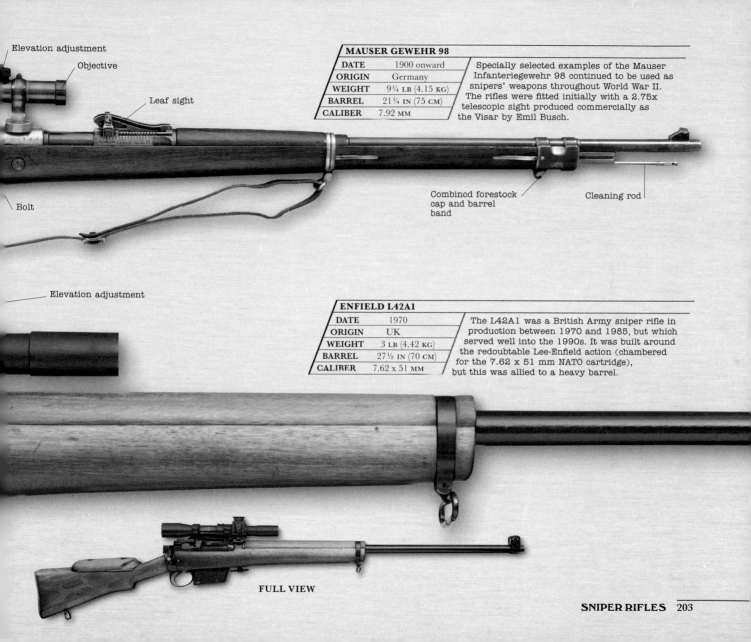

Elevation adjustment

Objective

Leaf sight

Bolt

Combined forestock
cap and barrel
band

Cleaning rod

MAUSER GEWEHR 98

DATE	1900 onward
ORIGIN	Germany
WEIGHT	9¼ LB (4.15 KG)
BARREL	21¼ IN (75 CM)
CALIBER	7.92 MM

Specially selected examples of the Mauser Infanteriegewehr 98 continued to be used as snipers' weapons throughout World War II. The rifles were fitted initially with a 2.75x telescopic sight produced commercially as the Visar by Emil Busch.

Elevation adjustment

ENFIELD L42A1

DATE	1970
ORIGIN	UK
WEIGHT	3 LB (4.42 KG)
BARREL	27½ IN (70 CM)
CALIBER	7.62 x 51 MM

The L42A1 was a British Army sniper rifle in production between 1970 and 1985, but which served well into the 1990s. It was built around the redoubtable Lee-Enfield action (chambered for the 7.62 x 51 mm NATO cartridge), but this was allied to a heavy barrel.

FULL VIEW

VASILY ZAITSEV

Although his number of confirmed kills varies according to the source—his story was heavily politicized in Russia—Vasily Zaitsev was undoubtedly one of WWII's greatest snipers. Born on March 23, 1915, Zaitsev grew up in the Urals, where he became an expert hunter.

With the onset of war, he joined the Red Army where his talents with a Mosin-Nagant rifle could be put to military use. It is reputed that in only his first 10 days of military service he shot and killed 40 Germans. Zaitsev achieved legendary status, however, during the battle of Stalingrad from August 1942 to February 1943. There he added another 142–242 kills to his credit, and was celebrated and decorated by his government. It was also in Stalingrad that he reputedly fought and won an epic battle with a German sniper, Major Konings, who had been dispatched from the sniper school at Zossen to kill Zaitsev. This duel was the subject of the book and film Enemy at the Gates (2001), but it is likely that it never actually happened. Nevertheless, Zaitsev's final WWII tally amounted to around 400 kills, but snipers he personally training killed another 3,000. Zaitsev died in 1991, a quiet hero.

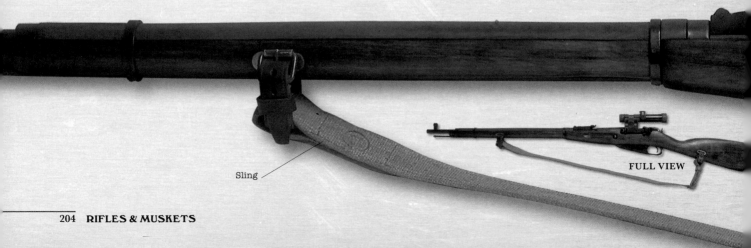

Sling

FULL VIEW

IT IS REPUTED THAT IN HIS FIRST 10 DAYS OF MILITARY SERVICE ZAITSEV SHOT AND KILLED 40 GERMANS.

MOSIN-NAGANT M1891/30PU

DATE	1941
ORIGIN	USSR
WEIGHT	11¼ LB (5.15 KG)
BARREL	28¾ IN (73 CM)
CALIBER	7.62 MM x 54R

In the 1930s the Red Army began issuing specially selected Model 1891/30 Mosin-Nagant rifles to its most accomplished marksmen. The sight was replaced with the 3.5-power PU and some 330,000 were produced during WWII.

3.5-power
PU sight

ENEMY AT THE GATES
Jude Law plays sniper Vasily Zaitsev in pursuit of his nemesis Major Konnings (played by Ed Harris) in the 2001 film 'Enemy at the Gates.'

Eyepiece

Elevation adjustment

Objective

Ejector port

Recoil pad

Bolt handle

Five-round
removable
box magazine

BARRETT MOD.90

DATE	1990–95
ORIGIN	US
WEIGHT	22 LB (10 KG)
BARREL	29 IN (73.7 CM)
CALIBER	.50 IN

In 1982, 20-year-old Ronnie Barrett designed a .50-caliber sniper rifle as a bet. The gas-operated Model 82 (adopted by the US Army as the M107) revolutionized the field, and was followed by the lighter, bolt-action, bullpup Model 90.

Polymer stock

Ten-round
removable box
magazine

Attachment point
for steadying sling

HECKLER & KOCH PSG-1

DATE	1985
ORIGIN	Germany
WEIGHT	17¼ LB (8.1 KG)
BARREL	25½ IN (65 CM)
CALIBER	7.62 MM

Intended as a police sniper rifle, the PSG-1 was essentially a heavily modified G3, as issued to the German Army, with the same roller-delayed blowback action. The most significant differences lie in the cold-forged, hexagonally rifled barrel and the Hensoldt 6x42 fixed-power sight, which has an illuminated reticle.

Hensoldt fixed-power telescopic sight

Polymer fore stock

Cheek pad

Five-round detachable box magazine

Pistol grip

Trigger is adjustable for weight of pull

Pommel locates the hand on the pistol grip

Fully floating stainless-steel barrel

Bipod in folded position

L96A1

DATE	1986 onward
ORIGIN	UK
WEIGHT	14 LB (6.5 KG)
BARREL	25¾ IN (65.5 CM)
CALIBER	7.62 MM NATO

The British Army's L96A1 sniper rifle, in service since 1986, was the first to be developed specifically for sniping: earlier versions had been based on various models of the Lee-Enfield. It has an aluminum frame to which its components are attached. Each rifle is individually fitted with a Schmidt & Bender 6x telescopic sight.

FULL VIEW

Rubber recoil pad

Optical sight

Bolt handle

Elevation
adjustment

Windage
adjustment

Magnification
selector, 2.5–
10x

Ejector port

Mounting clamp

WA 2000

WALTHER

Magazine
release catch

Six-round
detachable box
magazine

Semi-
shrouded
trigger

Thumb hole

Safety catch

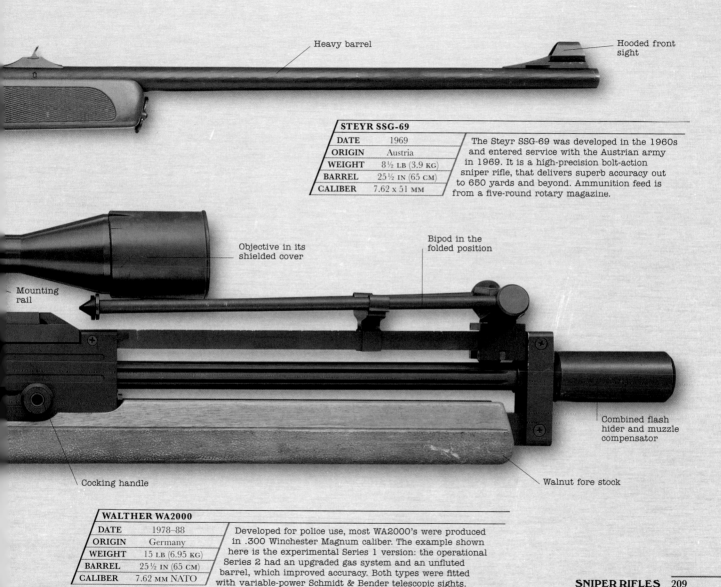

Heavy barrel

Hooded front sight

STEYR SSG-69

DATE	1969
ORIGIN	Austria
WEIGHT	8½ LB (3.9 KG)
BARREL	25½ IN (65 CM)
CALIBER	7.62 x 51 MM

The Steyr SSG-69 was developed in the 1960s and entered service with the Austrian army in 1969. It is a high-precision bolt-action sniper rifle, that delivers superb accuracy out to 650 yards and beyond. Ammunition feed is from a five-round rotary magazine.

Objective in its shielded cover

Bipod in the folded position

Mounting rail

Cocking handle

Combined flash hider and muzzle compensator

Walnut fore stock

WALTHER WA2000

DATE	1978–88
ORIGIN	Germany
WEIGHT	15 LB (6.95 KG)
BARREL	25½ IN (65 CM)
CALIBER	7.62 MM NATO

Developed for police use, most WA2000's were produced in .300 Winchester Magnum caliber. The example shown here is the experimental Series 1 version: the operational Series 2 had an upgraded gas system and an unfluted barrel, which improved accuracy. Both types were fitted with variable-power Schmidt & Bender telescopic sights.

SELF-LOADING RIFLES 1900–1945

Although there were many precursors, viable army-issue self-loading rifles did not emerge until the late 1920s. Before then automatic rifles had tended to be too expensive for production or too delicate for military use. The landmark firearm was the M1 Garand, a robust gas-operated .30 in rifle that was accepted for US Army service in 1936, and became the world's first standard issue self-loading rifle. Russia followed with its own semi-automatic rifles, such as the Tokarev SVT-40. During WWII Germany took the concept in a different direction with the Sturmgewehr 44, a weapon that used a shorter cartridge to produce lower recoil, but which still had effective killing power over a practical 450 yard (411 m) range. Hence was born the "assault rifle."

Rear sight

Cocking handle

FULL VIEW

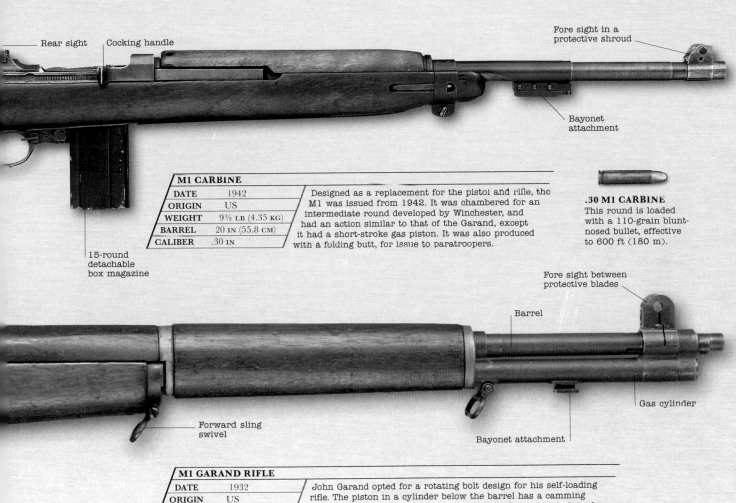

Rear sight   Cocking handle

Fore sight in a
protective shroud

Bayonet
attachment

15-round
detachable
box magazine

.30 M1 CARBINE
This round is loaded
with a 110-grain blunt-
nosed bullet, effective
to 600 ft (180 m).

Fore sight between
protective blades

Barrel

Gas cylinder

Forward sling
swivel

Bayonet attachment

M1 CARBINE

DATE	1942
ORIGIN	US
WEIGHT	9½ LB (4.35 KG)
BARREL	20 IN (55.8 CM)
CALIBER	.30 IN

Designed as a replacement for the pistol and rifle, the
M1 was issued from 1942. It was chambered for an
intermediate round developed by Winchester, and
had an action similar to that of the Garand, except
it had a short-stroke gas piston. It was also produced
with a folding butt, for issue to paratroopers.

M1 GARAND RIFLE

DATE	1932
ORIGIN	US
WEIGHT	9½ LB (4.35 KG)
BARREL	24 IN (61 CM)
CALIBER	.30-06 IN

John Garand opted for a rotating bolt design for his self-loading
rifle. The piston in a cylinder below the barrel has a camming
(spiraled) groove on its rear end, in which is located a stud on the
bolt. As the piston is driven back, it causes the bolt to rotate and
then drives it back against a spring that returns and relocks it,
having picked up a fresh round from the magazine on the way.

Ten-round detachable box magazine

Welded pressed-steel receiver

Rear sight

Rate-of-fire selector

Pistol grip

Perforated pressed-steel forestock

STURMGEWEHR 44	
DATE	1943
ORIGIN	Germany
WEIGHT	11¼ LB (5.1 KG)
BARREL	16½ IN (41.8 CM)
CALIBER	7.92 MM x 33

In 1940 work began on a selective-fire rifle chambered for a new intermediate 7.92 mm x 33 round. The result was a gas-operated weapon with a tipping bolt, which was put into production as the Maschinen Pistole 43 and later renamed the Sturmgewehr 44. Small numbers were fitted with the Krummlauf, a barrel extension that turned the bullet through 30°, for use by tank crews against infantry.

Muzzle
compensator

FULL VIEW

Fore sight

Gas cylinder cap

Forward sling
attachment

Rear sight

Cocking handle

Safety catch

Ten-round detachable
box magazine

Semi-pistol grip

TOKAREV SVT40

DATE	1910
ORIGIN	USSR
WEIGHT	8½ LB (3.9 KG)
BARREL	25 IN (61 CM)
CALIBER	7.62 MM x 54R

Fedor Tokarev designed a self-loading rifle with a tilting bolt locking into the floor of the receiver, and had it accepted by the Red Army in 1938. Two years later, he produced a more robust weapon that was cheaper and quicker to manufacture. The Samozaryadnaya Vintovka Tokarev 40 was issued to non-commissioned officers, though some were used as sniper rifles.

GEWEHR 43

DATE	1943
ORIGIN	Germany
WEIGHT	9½ LB (4.35 KG)
BARREL	20 IN (55.8 CM)
CALIBER	7.92 MM x 57

Soon after the start of World War II, the German army began demanding a self-loading rifle. Walther's original design employed a cup at the muzzle that unlocked the bolt and cycled the action. In 1943 a modified version, using the same action but with a conventional gas cylinder and piston mounted above the barrel, was introduced as the Gewehr 43.

BONNIE AND CLYDE

Bonnie Parker and Clyde Barrow, two of America's most notorious outlaws, roamed America's southern states in the early 1930s. Although know primarily as bank robbers, they also stole from convenience stores and gas stations.

Their exploits were broadcast nationwide and they became cult heroes as they continued to evade the police over a four-year period before meeting their end on May 23, 1934, on a desolate road near their hideout in Bienville Parish, Louisiana. Although they used a catalogue of firearms during their robberies, the couple's favorite weapon was the Browning Automatic Rifle (B.A.R.) M1918. This gun, stolen from an armory Clyde raided, weighed 16 pounds unloaded.

Ejector port

Trigger guard with
security lock in place

Rear sling
attachment

20-round detachable
box magazine

BROWNING AUTO RIFLE	
DATE	1918
ORIGIN	US
WEIGHT	16 LB (7.3 KG)
BARREL	24 IN (61 CM)
CALIBER	.30-60

John Browning set out to design a self-loading rifle, but it was soon obvious that the gun he produced was better suited to the role of light support weapon. It remained in military service until the mid-1950s.

Barrel

Gas tube

PARTNERS IN CRIME
Bonnie and Clyde pose for a photo in front of their prized Ford V8 getaway car. Shortly before his death, in 1934, Clyde wrote to Henry Ford full of praise for the vehicle. "For sustained speed and freedom from trouble the Ford has got every other car skinned," he said, "and even if my business hasn't been strictly legal it don't hurt anything to tell you what a fine car you got in the V8."

SELF-LOADING RIFLES 1945–

Post-war rifle development centered in many ways around an argument over caliber. On the one side were those who advocated retaining the full-power rifle round, preferring its long-range and penetration. This argument won out in the 1950s, leading to the adoption of the 7.62 x 51 mm as the standard NATO round, which in turn equipped weapons such as the US M14 and the Belgian FN FAL. From the 1960s, however, other voices advocated adopting the small, high-velocity 5.56 mm, pointing out that it was easier to control by the shooter, who could also carry more ammunition, and that the weapons firing it could be lighter. In the 1960s, the US switched to the 5.56 mm M16 rifle, and during the 1970s and 80s most other Western armies bought into the small-caliber concept as the 5.56 mm became a NATO standard, the 7.62 mm used more in machine guns and sniper rifles.

Rear sling swivel

Gas cylinder

Flash hider

STONER M63		
DATE	1962	
ORIGIN	US	
WEIGHT	7¾ LB (3.52 KG)	
BARREL	20 IN (50.8 CM)	
CALIBER	5.56 MM	

This M63 by Eugene Stoner is a modular design, and its 15 basic sub-assemblies can be put together in six different ways to produce a submachine gun, a carbine, an assault rifle (shown here), an automatic rifle, a light machine gun, and a general-purpose machine gun.

Rear sight

Cocking handle

Fore sight

Bayonet lug

Muzzle compensator

Forward sling attachment

Gas cylinder

Gas regulator

Magazine atch

20-round detachable magazine

M14	
DATE	1957
ORIGIN	US
WEIGHT	8½ LB (3.9 KG)
BARREL	22 IN (55.8 CM)
CALIBER	7.62 MM

In 1953, the North Atlantic Treaty Organization's (NATO) armies adopted a new full-power rifle cartridge, in 7.62 mm caliber. To accommodate it, the US developed a version of Garand's 20-year-old M1, endowed with a fully automatic fire capability and a larger magazine.

Shrouded rear sight

FULL VIEW

Cocking handle

30-round detachable box magazine

Cocking handle

Tubular butt
stock folds to
the left

Magazine catch

35-round
detachable box
magazine

GALIL ASSAULT RIFLE

DATE	1974
ORIGIN	Israel
WEIGHT	9½ LB (4.35 KG)
BARREL	18 IN (46 CM)
CALIBER	5.56 MM x 45

In 1968 Israeli Military Industries was
ordered to produce something similar to the
AK47. It chose a design by Israel Galil, a
near-copy of the Finnish Valmet M62, itself
an AK47 derivative, but opted for the
American 5.56 mm x 45 round.

FULL VIEW

Bipod
mounting point

Gas regulator

Carrying handle

High impact
plastic forestock

Fore sight

Flash hider

Cocking handle

Gas regulator

Ejection
port

Bolt
closing
device

High-impact
plastic butt
stock

STONER M16A1

DATE	1982
ORIGIN	US
WEIGHT	8 LB (3.6 KG)
BARREL	20 IN (50.8 CM)
CALIBER	5.56 MM x 45

Stoner's Armalite AR-15 was
accepted by the US Air Force in the
early 1960s, and subsequently taken
into service as the M16. The M16A1
was fitted with a bolt-closing device
and a revised flash hider.

Muzzle
compensator

Rear sling
attachment

Carrying handle

High-impact
plastic butt
stock

HECKLER & KOCH G41

DATE	1987
ORIGIN	Germany
WEIGHT	9 LB (4 KG)
BARREL	17½ IN (45 CM)
CALIBER	5.56 MM x 45

30-round
detachable
box magazine

The G41 was an updated version of the
G3, and shared its roller-delayed blowback
action. The modifications were necessary
to accommodate the 5.56 mm round, and
other standard NATO features such as the
universal sight mounting and magazine.

HECKLER & KOCH G3A3

The Heckler & Koch G3 ranks alongside the FN FAL and the M16 as a defining rifle type of the post-WWII world. It was developed by H&K in 1959 to chamber the 7.62 x 51 mm NATO cartridge, although it was actually based upon a Spanish CETME rifle that used the roller-delayed blowback system for which the G3 would be noted (this in turn had been spawned from a wartime Mauser design). The G3 is reliable, robust, simple to manufacture (it makes a heavy use of metal stampings and plastic fittings) and easy to use—qualities that resulted in its being adopted for use in 60 armies worldwide and license produced by 13 countries. The G3 blowback system has also led to numerous variants including sniper weapons (the G3SG/1, PSG-1, and MSG 90), submachine guns (MP5) and machine guns (HK21 and HK23).

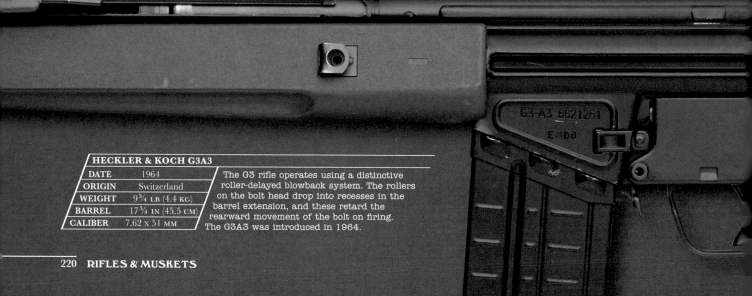

HECKLER & KOCH G3A3	
DATE	1964
ORIGIN	Switzerland
WEIGHT	9¾ LB (4.4 KG)
BARREL	17¾ IN (45.5 CM)
CALIBER	7.62 x 51 MM

The G3 rifle operates using a distinctive roller-delayed blowback system. The rollers on the bolt head drop into recesses in the barrel extension, and these retard the rearward movement of the bolt on firing. The G3A3 was introduced in 1964.

THE G3 IS RELIABLE, ROBUST AND SIMPLE TO MANUFACTURE.

FULL VIEW

Rear sight

Rate-of-fire selector

GERMAN ARMY'S ASSAULT RIFLE
A favorite of the German Army, the G3A3A1 is, in fact, an official German army designation, not a Heckler & Koch factory one.

5.56 MM NATO
The NATO-standard 5.56 mm
round has a steel-tipped projectile
weighing 62 grains.

SUSAT sight gives four-
power magnification and
has low-light capability

Eyepiece with protective
rubber shroud

Pistol grip with
high-impact
plastic molding

Large trigger guard
for gloved hand

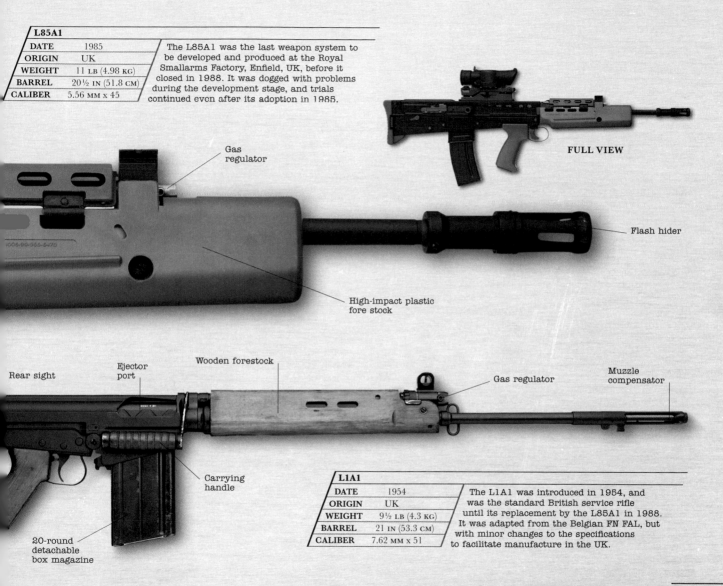

L85A1	
DATE	1985
ORIGIN	UK
WEIGHT	11 LB (4.98 KG)
BARREL	20½ IN (51.8 CM)
CALIBER	5.56 MM x 45

The L85A1 was the last weapon system to be developed and produced at the Royal Smallarms Factory, Enfield, UK, before it closed in 1988. It was dogged with problems during the development stage, and trials continued even after its adoption in 1985.

FULL VIEW

Gas regulator

Flash hider

High-impact plastic fore stock

Rear sight

Ejector port

Wooden forestock

Gas regulator

Muzzle compensator

Carrying handle

20-round detachable box magazine

L1A1	
DATE	1954
ORIGIN	UK
WEIGHT	9½ LB (4.3 KG)
BARREL	21 IN (53.3 CM)
CALIBER	7.62 MM x 51

The L1A1 was introduced in 1954, and was the standard British service rifle until its replacement by the L85A1 in 1988. It was adapted from the Belgian FN FAL, but with minor changes to the specifications to facilitate manufacture in the UK.

AK-47 ASSAULT RIFLE

More AK-type assault rifles have been manufactured than any other weapon in history—possibly up to 100 million units worldwide. Developed by Mikhail Timofeyevich Kalashnikov during WWII, the AK-47 was accepted as the Soviet army's standard rifle in 1949 and an improvement in manufacturing process resulted in the AKM gun from 1959, the most prolific type and the version directly copied in China's Type 56.

The massive success of the AK and its many variants is not due to its sophistication nor its firepower (the standard rifle has poor accuracy over a couple of hundred yards and is actually less powerful than many other 7.62 mm weapons), but its reliability. It is an incredibly robust 7.62 x 39 mm gas-operated rifle that needs minimal maintenance to keep functioning, regardless of the environmental conditions. Their durability means few AKs fall out of use, and combined with the illegal distribution of surplus ex-communist stocks it today fuels insurgencies and wars worldwide.

FULL VIEW

Change lever selects single-shot or automatic fire

Ejection port

Shoulder stock

Magazine catch

AK-47 ASSAULT RIFLE	
DATE	1951
ORIGIN	USSR
WEIGHT	9 ½ LB (4.3 KG)
BARREL	16 ¼ IN (41.5 CM)
CALIBER	7.62 MM x 39

Early AK-47s, made largely from welded components, suffered problems. From 1951, sturdier receivers machined from forged steel billets were introduced. The modified AKM was lighter than the original and had a reduced cyclic rate of full automatic fire.

Hand guard
(upper part)

READY TO FIGHT

Iraqi soldiers in Baghdad prepare for war in November 1998. The AK-47 and variants are among many small arms that are sold to governments, rebels, and criminals. This trade ensures a ready supply of weapons to a number of conflicts including the Balkans, Iraq, Afghanistan, and Somalia.

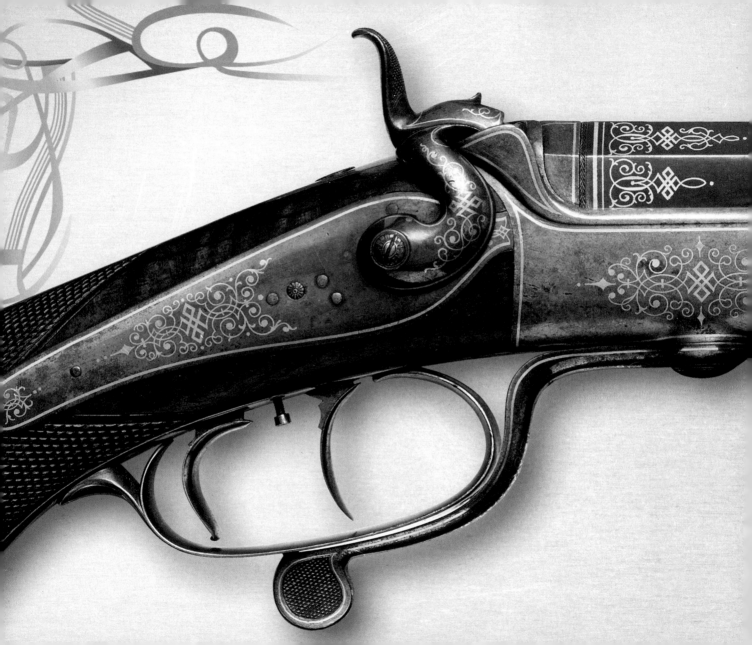

SPORT RIFLES & SHOTGUNS

Hunters have very different requirements from their firearms than soldiers. Most hunters want to eat what they kill—they do not want to obliterate the meat of the animal with excessive firepower. The hunter's ideal is to kill the prey instantly with a single shot that causes minimal disruption to the animal's edible parts. This consideration has been important in shaping the design of, and market, for sport rifles and shotguns.

※

As soon as guns were invented in the 14th century, they were turned to sport use. Hunters applied matchlock arquebuses, despite their limitations, to hunting difficult prey such as boar and wolf. Military shooting guilds also indulged in competitive target shooting from the 15th century—there is evidence of the first shooting club being set up in Lucerne, Switzerland, in 1466.

With the development of the flintlock, accurate sport shooting became even more viable (a flintlock was more reliable to shoot in damp field conditions). Early sport guns were also much more likely to be rifled than military versions. This is partly because civilian buyers could more likely afford the expense of a rifled gun, and also because a hunter wanted his first shot to be exactly on target—if prey was simply spooked there would be no time for a second shot. Muzzle-loading guns, both smoothbore and rifled, served the sport fraternities well until breechloading cartridge rifles took over in the 19th century.

The first breechloaders were single-shot weapons, but with bolt- and lever-action magazine rifles, such as the Winchester 1866 and the Mauser 1892, hunters could fire faster, and therefore kill much more prey. The late 19th and early 20th centuries consequently saw some of the most gratuitous environmental destruction in history, as hunters slaughtered a variety of wildlife on every continent with relatively inexpensive but powerful hunting guns.

※

From the beginning of the 20th century to the present day the preference of the hunting fraternity has remained fairly constant. Bolt-action and lever-action rifles still account for the bulk of hunting and target gun sales, being cheap, accurate, and available in calibers suited to every type of purpose. Many are still built upon venerable actions, particularly the Mauser bolt-action system.

Semi-auto rifles have had less dominance in the hunting world. Partly this is because many authorities frown on semi-auto fire for hunting, believing that it leads to dangerous multiple shots at a target rather than a one-shot kill. Furthermore, the potential firepower of a high-power semi-auto also makes it more difficult to own in many countries. In those countries with lighter legislation, semi-autos like the Armalite AR15 have been popular with those wanting a good home defense weapon.

❧

While rifled weapons have dominated accuracy sports, there is one smoothbore type that has prevailed to the present day—the shotgun. Shotguns fire a spread of shot rather than a single round, so rifling is inappropriate.

They are generally defined by their "gauge" (or bore) rather than the barrel's caliber dimension. The gauge is defined by the number of lead balls of the same diameter as the gun's bore that it would take to make 1 lb (0.45 kg) in weight. The range of a shotgun is limited when compared to a rifle—the effective range of a 12-gauge shotgun firing a load of No.7 shot is about 100 ft (32 m)—but the spread of shot enables more confident handling of flying or fast-moving targets.

Bird shooting with shotgun-type flintlock weapons, some double-barreled, was common from the 1600s, but, as with many other types of firearms, the shotgun was not perfected until the use of unitary cartridges established itself in the 19th century. During this period the double-barreled shotgun took on its classic form, mainly through the skill of English gunmakers such as Westley Richards, James Purdey, and Anson & Deeley, but also through US figures such as Daniel Myron LeFever.

While shotguns have found military use, they have been most successful for civilian markets, particularly with the enormous growth of clay-shooting sports. Double-barreled guns were mainly set in a side-by-side configuration until around 1914, but since then have been gradually outsold by shotguns with over-and-under barrels.

❧

Shotgunning remains today one of the world's most popular shooting sports, and one still steeped in very old traditions of sportsmanship and skill.

SPORT RIFLES & SHOTGUNS

EUROPEAN HUNTING GUNS

Early sport guns tend to be some of the finest examples of firearms from their respective periods, principally because only the rich could afford them. The matchlock was not an ideal sport weapon, but nonetheless 15th- and 16th-century wood carvings show hunters using them against everything from wild boar to camels. Target shooting also took off in the 16th century, with target guns utilizing rifled barrels for accuracy. Wheellocks were used extensively in hunting, but were too delicate for robust use. The invention of the snaphaunce lock in the 1530s, however, significantly increased the popularity and affordability of sport shooting.

Striking steel

Brass lock plate

Cock

Brass butt plate

Trigger guard

Jaw clamp screw

Cock

Striker/ pan cover

Mainspring

Rear sling swivel

ITALIAN MIQUELET SPORT GUN	
DATE	c.1775
ORIGIN	Italy
WEIGHT	8¼ LB (3.75 KG)
BARREL	31½ IN (80 CM)
CALIBER	.75 IN

The miquelet lock introduced the combined striker and pan cover, but used an external mainspring (unlike the later true flintlock, in which the mainspring was internal). This miquelet lock musket was manufactured in Naples by Pacifico in 1775.

SCOTTISH SNAPHAUNCE

DATE	1614
ORIGIN	Scotland
WEIGHT	7 LB (3.2 KG)
BARREL	38 IN (96½ CM)
CALIBER	.45 IN

The name snaphaunce derives from the Dutch schnapp-hahn, meaning "pecking hen," which it was thought to resemble. It was the first attempt to simplify the wheellock's method of striking sparks from a piece of iron pyrites. This superb example is attributed to Alison of Dundee, and was a gift from King James to Louis XIII of France.

Barrel band

Forward sling swivel

FULL VIEW

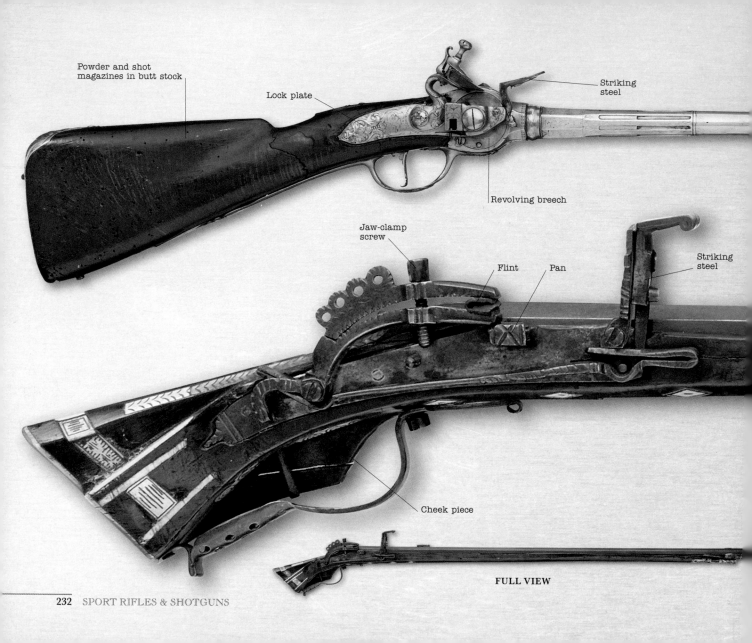

Powder and shot
magazines in butt stock

Lock plate

Striking
steel

Revolving breech

Jaw-clamp
screw

Flint

Pan

Striking
steel

Cheek piece

FULL VIEW

ITALIAN REPEATING FLINTLOCK

DATE	c.1690
ORIGIN	Italy
WEIGHT	8 ½ LB (3.95 KG)
BARREL	35 IN (89 CM)
CALIBER	.53 IN

Italian gun maker Michele Lorenzoni lived in Florence from 1683–1733, and invented an early form of repeating breech-loading flintlock. Paired magazines, one for powder and the other for shot, were located in the butt stock, and the breech block was rotated for charging by means of a lever on the left side of the gun.

SWEDISH "BALTIC" FLINTLOCK

DATE	c.1650
ORIGIN	Sweden
WEIGHT	7 ½ LB (3.28 KG)
BARREL	38 ½ IN (97.7 CM)
CALIBER	.4 IN

This early flintlock rifle, with a characteristic Baltic lock from the south of Sweden, has the distinctive "Goinge" type short butt stock reminiscent of weapons of a still earlier date. Compared with later examples, its simple lock is crudely made.

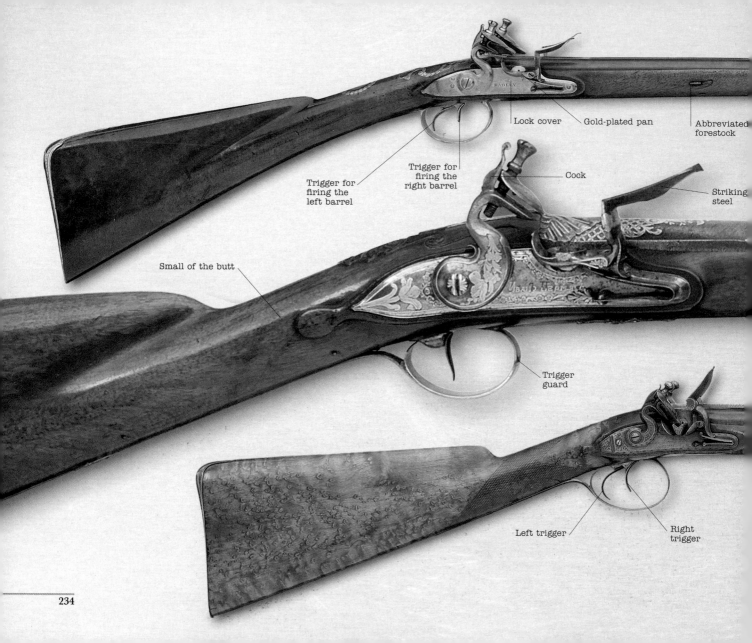

Lock cover

Gold-plated pan

Abbreviated forestock

Trigger for firing the right barrel

Cock

Striking steel

Trigger for firing the left barrel

Small of the butt

Trigger guard

Left trigger

Right trigger

DOUBLE-BARRELED FLINTLOCK SHOTGUN

DATE	c.1770
ORIGIN	England
WEIGHT	5 ½ LB (2.25 KG)
BARREL	35 ½ IN (90.2 CM)
CALIBER	.6 IN

This side-by-side double-barreled flintlock shotgun, attributed to Hadley, is typical of high-class fowling pieces of the latter part of the 18th century. Not only is its short stock silver mounted, but both its pans and its touch-holes are gold-plated to fend off corrosion.

FULL VIEW

RUSSIAN FLINTLOCK

DATE	1770
ORIGIN	Russia
WEIGHT	5 LB (2.2 KG)
BARREL	35 IN (89.8 CM)
CALIBER	.35 IN

This beautifully decorated smooth-bore flintlock gun was made by Ivan Permjakov, one of the most accomplished Russian gun makers. It is believed to have been recovered from the field after the battle of Alma River in 1854.

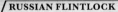

Ramrod-retaining barrel

SCOTTISH DOUBLE-BARRELED FLINTLOCK

DATE	1819
ORIGIN	Scotland
WEIGHT	7 ½ LB (3.4 KG)
BARREL	30 IN (76 CM)
CALIBER	.68 IN

By the beginning of the 19th century, the design of sport guns had already begun to diverge from that of military weapons, with shortened stocks becoming commonplace. This double-barreled piece is thought to have been made by Morris of Perth for Sir David Montcrieffe, a celebrated sportsman.

SPORT
RIFLES

The 19th century brought all the innovations of the percussion cap to hunting. Indeed, the invention of the first percussion lock by the Reverend Alexander Forsythe of Aberdeenshire, Scotland, patented in 1807, was specifically for the purpose of improving wildfowling shots. Percussion locks had a dramatic effect on shooting technique. The much faster ignition process meant that hunters did not have to give moving targets so much lead (the distance fired in front), and snapshooting at fast-flying birds yielded more reliable results. In addition, fewer kills were lost as the result of misfires. The introduction of unitary cartridges pushed sport shooting on further, giving the quick-reloading capability for large-volume shoots and improving range and accuracy through concomitant developments in bullet technology.

Nipple for priming pellet

Trigger

Grip extension

Straight "English style" stock

Flint clamping screw

Striking steel

Cock

Lock

Feather spring

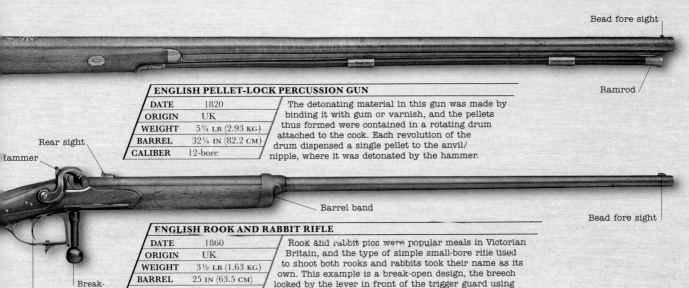

Bead fore sight

Ramrod

ENGLISH PELLET-LOCK PERCUSSION GUN

DATE	1820
ORIGIN	UK
WEIGHT	5¼ LB (2.93 KG)
BARREL	32¼ IN (82.2 CM)
CALIBER	12-bore

The detonating material in this gun was made by binding it with gum or varnish, and the pellets thus formed were contained in a rotating drum attached to the cock. Each revolution of the drum dispensed a single pellet to the anvil/ nipple, where it was detonated by the hammer.

Rear sight

Hammer

Barrel band

Bead fore sight

Trigger

Break-open lever

ENGLISH ROOK AND RABBIT RIFLE

DATE	1860
ORIGIN	UK
WEIGHT	3½ LB (1.63 KG)
BARREL	25 IN (63.5 CM)
CALIBER	.37 IN

Rook and rabbit pies were popular meals in Victorian Britain, and the type of simple small-bore rifle used to shoot both rooks and rabbits took their name as its own. This example is a break-open design, the breech locked by the lever in front of the trigger guard using a method patented by Frederick Prince in 1855.

ENGLISH HUNTING RIFLE

DATE	1700
ORIGIN	England
WEIGHT	12 LB (5.4 KG)
BARREL	55 IN (140 CM)
CALIBER	.75 IN

This fine English hunting rifle has a beautifully grained rosewood stock and an exceptionally long barrel, and would have been used for hunting deer or similar large game. The effective range from such a gun would have been in the region 200 yards.

Ramrod

FULL VIEW

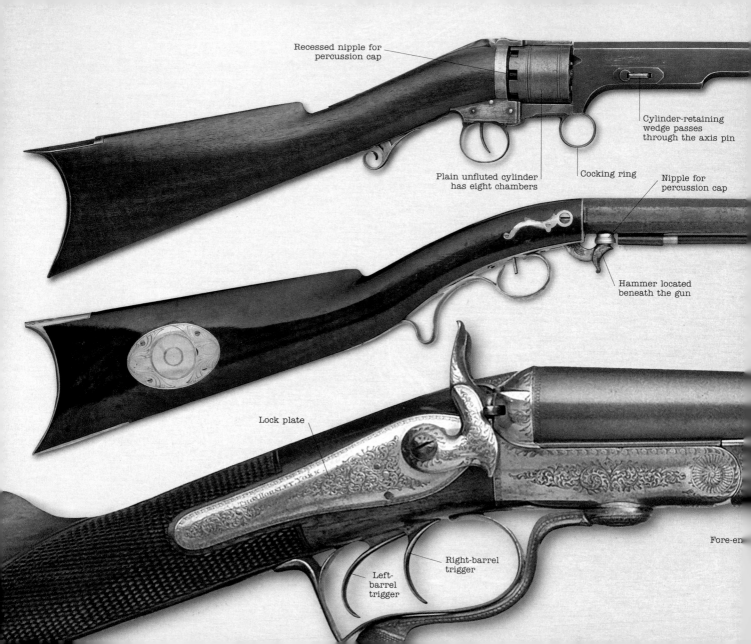

Recessed nipple for percussion cap

Cylinder-retaining wedge passes through the axis pin

Plain unfluted cylinder has eight chambers

Cocking ring

Nipple for percussion cap

Hammer located beneath the gun

Lock plate

Fore-en

Left-barrel trigger

Right-barrel trigger

COLT PATTERSON REVOLVING RIFLE

DATE	1837
ORIGIN	US
WEIGHT	8½ LB (3.9 KG)
BARREL	32 IN (81.3 CM)
CALIBER	.36 IN

Samuel Colt was awarded his first patent, for a six-shot revolver pistol, in London in October 1835, and set up his first factory, in Patterson, New Jersey. As well as pistols, he began turning out revolver rifles, but his facilities were limited and he soon went bankrupt. Patterson-built Colts, such as this first-pattern concealed-hammer eight-shot rifle, are extremely rare.

Rear sight

Ramrod

PERCUSSION UNDERHAMMER RIFLE

DATE	1835
ORIGIN	US
WEIGHT	Not known
BARREL	29½ IN (75 CM)
CALIBER	.44 IN

This underhammer rifle is by Vermont gunmaker, Nicanor Kendall. The stock is probably of American Cherry and the furniture is of a high nickel copper alloy which is cast and incised with decoration. The heavy octagonal barrel is fitted with four ramrod pipes, a leaf back sight, and a blade fore sight.

ENGLISH DOUBLE-BARRELED RIFLE

DATE	c1850
ORIGIN	England
WEIGHT	Not known
BARREL	Not known
CALIBER	Not known

Double-barreled rifles have traditionally been popular for heavy game taken quickly at short-ranges. This example has double exposed hammers, double triggers for quick barrel selection, and a break-open lever set beneath the trigger guard, rather than top mounted.

FULL VIEW

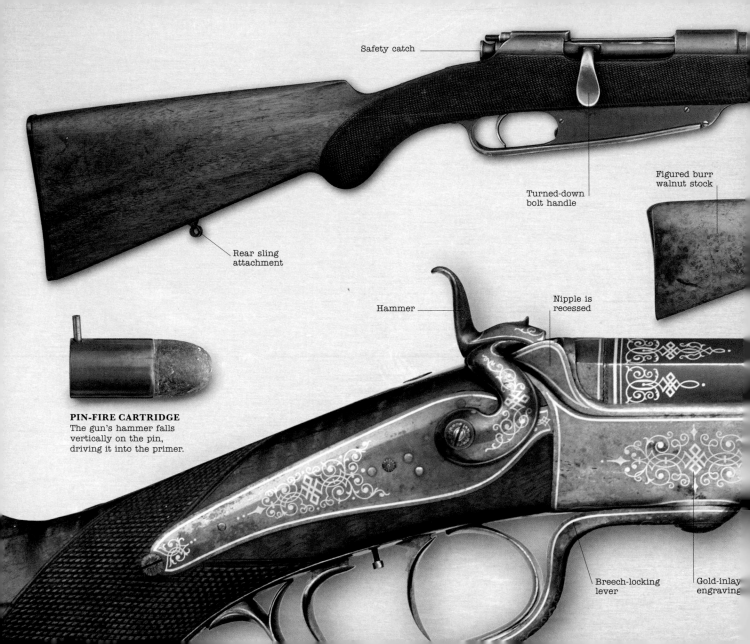

Safety catch

Turned-down
bolt handle

Figured burr
walnut stock

Rear sling
attachment

Hammer

Nipple is
recessed

PIN-FIRE CARTRIDGE
The gun's hammer falls
vertically on the pin,
driving it into the primer.

Breech-locking
lever

Gold-inlay
engraving

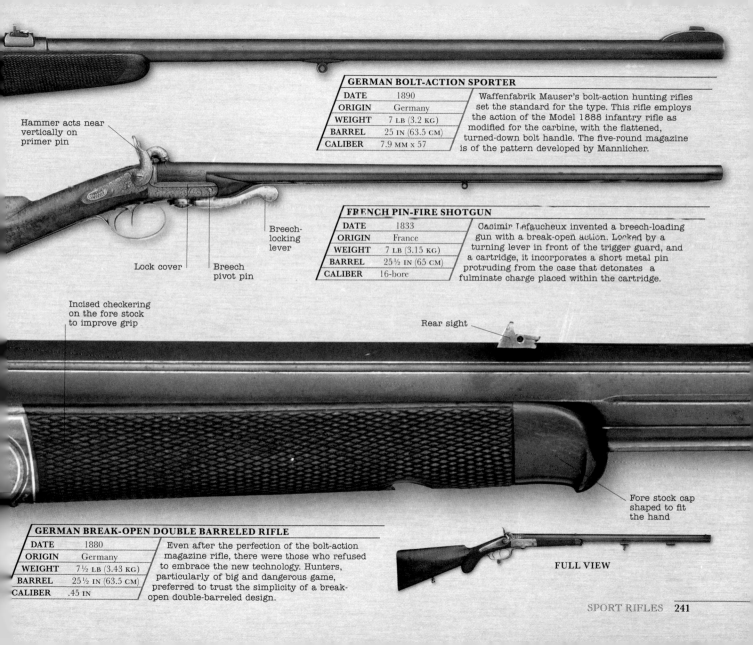

Hammer acts near vertically on primer pin

Lock cover

Breech pivot pin

Breech-locking lever

GERMAN BOLT-ACTION SPORTER

DATE	1890
ORIGIN	Germany
WEIGHT	7 LB (3.2 KG)
BARREL	25 IN (63.5 CM)
CALIBER	7.9 MM x 57

Waffenfabrik Mauser's bolt-action hunting rifles set the standard for the type. This rifle employs the action of the Model 1888 infantry rifle as modified for the carbine, with the flattened, turned-down bolt handle. The five-round magazine is of the pattern developed by Mannlicher.

FRENCH PIN-FIRE SHOTGUN

DATE	1833
ORIGIN	France
WEIGHT	7 LB (3.15 KG)
BARREL	25½ IN (65 CM)
CALIBER	16-bore

Casimir Lefaucheux invented a breech-loading gun with a break-open action. Locked by a turning lever in front of the trigger guard, and a cartridge, it incorporates a short metal pin protruding from the case that detonates a fulminate charge placed within the cartridge.

Incised checkering on the fore stock to improve grip

Rear sight

Fore stock cap shaped to fit the hand

GERMAN BREAK-OPEN DOUBLE BARRELED RIFLE

DATE	1880
ORIGIN	Germany
WEIGHT	7½ LB (3.43 KG)
BARREL	25½ IN (63.5 CM)
CALIBER	.45 IN

Even after the perfection of the bolt-action magazine rifle, there were those who refused to embrace the new technology. Hunters, particularly of big and dangerous game, preferred to trust the simplicity of a break-open double-barreled design.

FULL VIEW

FREDERICK C SELOUS

Frederick Selous (1851–1917) first traveled to southern Africa in 1870 and there spent the next 20 years hunting big game and also becoming intimately acquainted with Africa's wildlife and peoples. His familiarity with the region led, in 1890, to his appointment as a guide to commercial expeditions of the British South Africa Company, and his service resulted in the award of the Founder's Medal of the Royal Geographic Society. Selous subsequently became involved in several of Britain's wars in Africa, fighting in the Matabele War in 1893 and in the Rhodesian uprising of 1896.

In 1909, Selous led one of Africa's most famous safaris, when he took a party of 300 including Theodore Roosevelt on a hunting trip around British East Africa, the Congo, and Egypt.

Selous used a selection of powerful hunting guns throughout his career from producers such as Holland & Holland and Lee-Metford. These included a single-shot Farquharson acquired in 1893, a rifle with the penetration needed to bring down the largest African game (it fired a 215-grain bullet).

As an infantry officer in WWI, Selous was killed in East Africa on January 4, 1917, in a small action at Beho Beho.

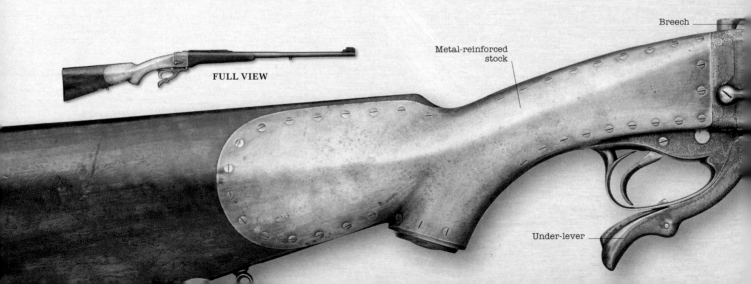

FULL VIEW

Breech

Metal-reinforced stock

Under-lever

"THE LAST OF THE MIGHTY HUNTERS
WHOSE EXPERIENCE LAY IN THE GREATEST HUNTING GROUND THE WORLD HAS EVER SEEN."

THEODORE ROOSEVELT, 1910

GIBBS-FARQUHARSON RIFLE

DATE	c.1890
ORIGIN	UK
WEIGHT	8¼ LB (4 KG)
BARREL	Not known
CALIBER	.450/.400

This rifle was made for F.C. Selous in .450/.400 caliber. The grip is fitted with steel plates, a customization requested by Selous to strengthen the gun. The original barrel has been replaced by one in .22 Hornet caliber.

Rear sight

Fore-end

HUNTER TURNED CONSERVATIONIST
Big-game hunter Frederick Courtney Selous poses with the head of a lion, circa 1895. During his life Selous became acutely aware of the evils associated with the mass slaughter of animals and, after his death, the Selous Game Reserve, Tanzania, was set up in his honor. The reserve was designated a UNESCO World Heritage Site in 1982 due to the diversity of its wildlife and undisturbed nature.

HUNTING GUNS

The refinement of brass cartridge weapons during the second half of the 19th century had important implications for sport shooters, particularly hunters. Unitary cartridges meant fast reloading, and this in turn meant that lone hunters could kill animals in greater volumes. On country estates in Britain, shooting parties not uncommonly clocked up "1,000 bird days" with their breech-loading shotguns. In Africa, large-bore bolt-action rifles could handle the heaviest of land animals. In the United States, the new breed of rifles led to one of the New World's greatest environmental catastrophes—the destruction of the American buffalo. A single shooter could kill 250 buffalo in a day, and by 1890, 60 million buffalo had been reduced to less than 1,000.

Hammer spur

Loading gate

Under-lever action

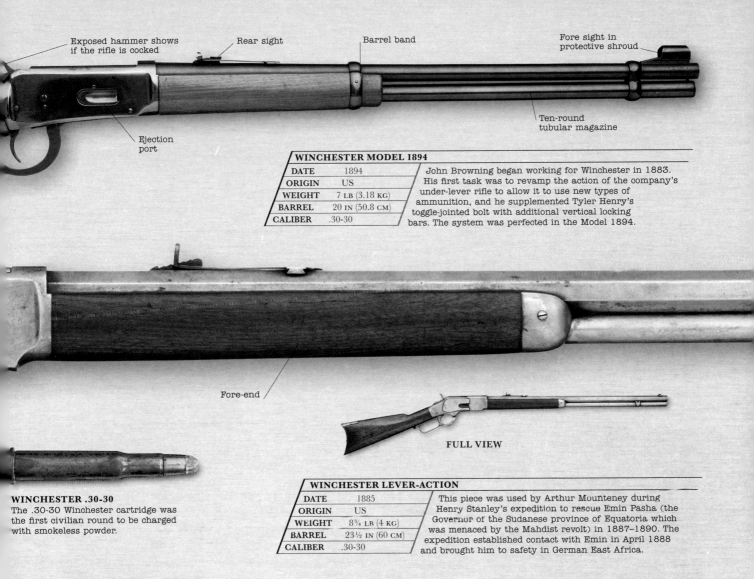

Exposed hammer shows
if the rifle is cocked

Rear sight

Barrel band

Fore sight in
protective shroud

Ejection
port

Ten-round
tubular magazine

WINCHESTER MODEL 1894

DATE	1894
ORIGIN	US
WEIGHT	7 LB (3.18 KG)
BARREL	20 IN (50.8 CM)
CALIBER	.30-30

John Browning began working for Winchester in 1883. His first task was to revamp the action of the company's under-lever rifle to allow it to use new types of ammunition, and he supplemented Tyler Henry's toggle-jointed bolt with additional vertical locking bars. The system was perfected in the Model 1894.

Fore-end

FULL VIEW

WINCHESTER .30-30
The .30-30 Winchester cartridge was the first civilian round to be charged with smokeless powder.

WINCHESTER LEVER-ACTION

DATE	1885
ORIGIN	US
WEIGHT	8¾ LB (4 KG)
BARREL	23½ IN (60 CM)
CALIBER	.30-30

This piece was used by Arthur Mounteney during Henry Stanley's expedition to rescue Emin Pasha (the Governor of the Sudanese province of Equatoria which was menaced by the Mahdist revolt) in 1887–1890. The expedition established contact with Emin in April 1888 and brought him to safety in German East Africa.

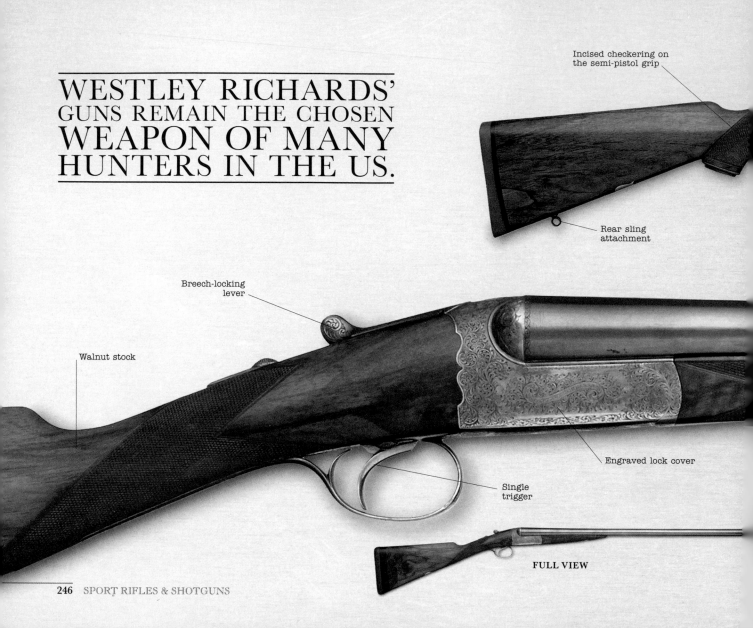

WESTLEY RICHARDS' GUNS REMAIN THE CHOSEN WEAPON OF MANY HUNTERS IN THE US.

Incised checkering on the semi-pistol grip

Rear sling attachment

Breech-locking lever

Walnut stock

Engraved lock cover

Single trigger

FULL VIEW

Bolt handle Bolt Rear sight

Forward sling
attachment

Internal five-round
box magazine

RIGBY MAUSER RIFLE

DATE	1925
ORIGIN	UK
WEIGHT	6¼ LB (2.8 KG)
BARREL	27½ IN (70 CM)
CALIBER	.375 IN

Rigby's began making guns in Dublin, Ireland, in the 18th century. In 1900, now in London, the company was appointed Mauser's UK agent, and began producing bolt-action rifles to its design in a variety of calibers. John Rigby, the company's head, oversaw the design of the British Army's bolt-action rifles.

Abbreviated forestock

WESTLEY RICHARDS HAMMERLESS EJECTOR GUN

DATE	c.1930
ORIGIN	UK
WEIGHT	6 LB (2.76 KG)
BARREL	26½ IN (67.5 CM)
CALIBER	12-bore

Master gunmakers Westley Richards produced various notable and highly innovative sport guns and rifles. This example of a double-barreled hammerless ejector gun has a patent one-striker mechanism and locks that can be detached by hand. A press button mechanism enables each barrel to be fired independently. Available in a choice of finishes, the gun could be tailored to suit the individual tastes of purchasers.

SURVIVAL GUNS 1945-

Survival guns are weapons designed to be transported easily in a backpack or stowed in a vehicle, and are purely for emergency use as basic hunting guns or for self-defense. The calibers of such weapons tend to be small, typically .22 LR or .410 gauge (larger calibers would require thicker, and therefore heavier, barrels) and the overall design strips the gun down to its most basic elements. Stocks are either skeleton or hollow to keep weight low, and all survival guns should either disassemble or fold down for convenient carriage. While survival weapons are popular among civilian survivalists, air force personnel tend to be the major military customers.

Hollow stock

Rear sight

Hammer

ITHACA GUN CO.

Stock/action hinge

Trigger

Skeleton stock

Rear aperture sight

Bolt

Barrel unit

Magazine

AR7 EXPLORER ARMALITE SURVIVAL RIFLE

DATE	1958
ORIGIN	US
WEIGHT	2½ LB (1.1 KG)
BARREL	16 IN (40 CM)
CALIBER	.22 LR

The AR7 was designed by Eugene Stoner in 1959 as a survival rifle for USAF aircrew. A semiautomatic .22 LR weapon, it ingeniously breaks down into four main parts, the barrel, action, and magazine then being stowed in the hollowed-out, water-resistant stock (which also floats if dropped in water).

DISASSEMBLED AR7 ARMALITE
The AR7 breaks down into its stock, action, magazine, and barrel. The hollow stock holds all the other components in a strong, waterproof container.

.22 LR barrel

FULL VIEW

DISASSEMBLED M6
The M6 hinges at a point just in front of the trigger, producing a folded length half that of the gun's extended length.

ITHACA M6 SURVIVAL RIFLE

DATE	1975
ORIGIN	US
WEIGHT	4 LB (1.82 KG)
BARREL	14 IN (36 CM)
CALIBER	.22 LR / .410

The Ithaca M6 survival rifle combines a rifled .22 LR upper barrel with a lower .410 shotgun barrel, the stock having storage capacity for 15 .22 cartridges and four shotgun shells. The gun originally had a folding design, while current models break down into two pieces.

EARLY COMBAT SHOTGUNS

Shotguns have a long history as combat weapons. During the American Revolutionary War, muskets were often loaded with a "buck and ball" combination to maximize the chances of a hit, and standard shotguns gave service in conflicts ranging from the US-Mexican War of 1846–48 to the Philippines insurrection of the early 1900s. During WWI, US infantrymen found that pump-action Winchester Model 1897s were superb weapons for close-quarters trench combat. In WWII shotguns were primarily used in the Pacific and other jungle-combat zones, where ranges were minimal, and for similar reasons shotguns found many applications in the post-war insurgency conflicts in Southeast Asia.

Cocking lever

Rear sling attachment

Exposed hammer shows if the weapon is cocked

Ejector port

Loading gate

Trigger

Semi pistol stock

FULL VIEW

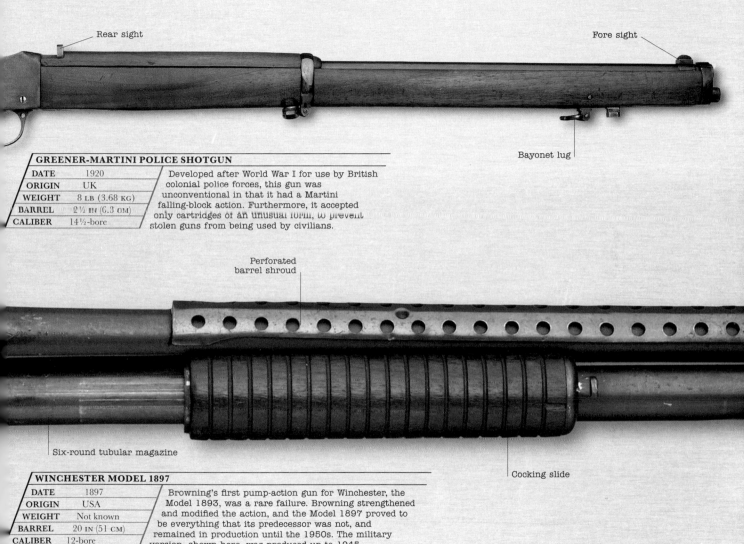

Rear sight

Fore sight

Bayonet lug

GREENER-MARTINI POLICE SHOTGUN

DATE	1920
ORIGIN	UK
WEIGHT	8 LB (3.68 KG)
BARREL	2½ IN (6.3 CM)
CALIBER	14½-bore

Developed after World War I for use by British colonial police forces, this gun was unconventional in that it had a Martini falling-block action. Furthermore, it accepted only cartridges of an unusual form, to prevent stolen guns from being used by civilians.

Perforated
barrel shroud

Six-round tubular magazine

Cocking slide

WINCHESTER MODEL 1897

DATE	1897
ORIGIN	USA
WEIGHT	Not known
BARREL	20 IN (51 CM)
CALIBER	12-bore

Browning's first pump-action gun for Winchester, the Model 1893, was a rare failure. Browning strengthened and modified the action, and the Model 1897 proved to be everything that its predecessor was not, and remained in production until the 1950s. The military version, shown here, was produced up to 1945.

COMBAT SHOTGUNS

Combat shotguns have a small but secure place in modern military arsenals, but a larger position in modern police and Special Forces units. At ranges of up to 100 ft (32 m), the shotgun is one of the most lethal firearms available, inflicting (with the right shot size) massive damage to the target. However, because shotguns are essentially short-range weapons, there is minimal risk to bystanders from the overflight of individual pellets. A modern combat shotgun, such as the Franchi SPAS-12, can also fire lock-busting, tear gas or less lethal beanbag rounds, making it a particularly versatile weapon.

Combined rear sight/carrying handle

Ejection port

FULL VIEW

AUTO

Fire mode selector switch

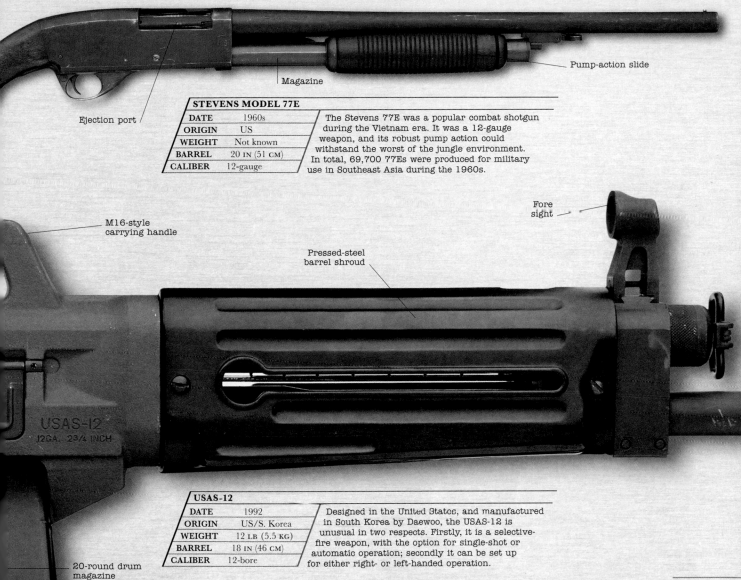

Magazine

Pump-action slide

Ejection port

STEVENS MODEL 77E

DATE	1960s
ORIGIN	US
WEIGHT	Not known
BARREL	20 IN (51 CM)
CALIBER	12-gauge

The Stevens 77E was a popular combat shotgun during the Vietnam era. It was a 12-gauge weapon, and its robust pump action could withstand the worst of the jungle environment. In total, 69,700 77Es were produced for military use in Southeast Asia during the 1960s.

M16-style carrying handle

Fore sight

Pressed-steel barrel shroud

USAS-12
12GA. 23/4 INCH

USAS-12

DATE	1992
ORIGIN	US/S. Korea
WEIGHT	12 LB (5.5 KG)
BARREL	18 IN (46 CM)
CALIBER	12-bore

Designed in the United States, and manufactured in South Korea by Daewoo, the USAS-12 is unusual in two respects. Firstly, it is a selective-fire weapon, with the option for single-shot or automatic operation; secondly it can be set up for either right- or left-handed operation.

20-round drum magazine

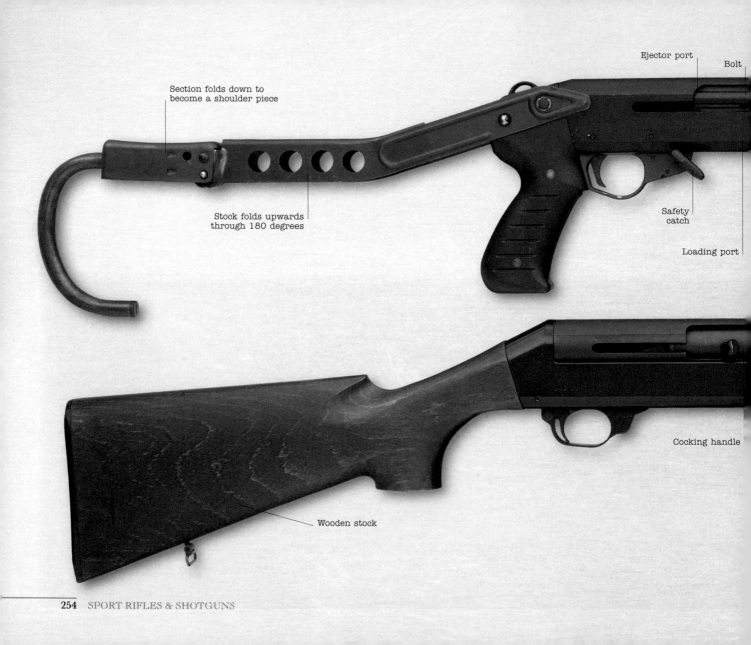

Ejector port

Bolt

Section folds down to
become a shoulder piece

Stock folds upwards
through 180 degrees

Safety
catch

Loading port

Cocking handle

Wooden stock

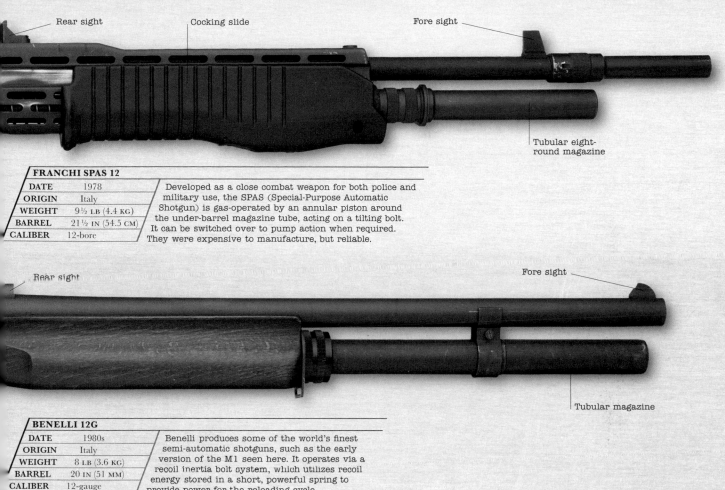

Rear sight

Cocking slide

Fore sight

Tubular eight-
round magazine

FRANCHI SPAS 12

DATE	1978
ORIGIN	Italy
WEIGHT	9½ LB (4.4 KG)
BARREL	21½ IN (54.5 CM)
CALIBER	12-bore

Developed as a close combat weapon for both police and military use, the SPAS (Special-Purpose Automatic Shotgun) is gas-operated by an annular piston around the under-barrel magazine tube, acting on a tilting bolt. It can be switched over to pump action when required. They were expensive to manufacture, but reliable.

Rear sight

Fore sight

Tubular magazine

BENELLI 12G

DATE	1980s
ORIGIN	Italy
WEIGHT	8 LB (3.6 KG)
BARREL	20 IN (51 MM)
CALIBER	12-gauge

Benelli produces some of the world's finest semi-automatic shotguns, such as the early version of the M1 seen here. It operates via a recoil inertia bolt system, which utilizes recoil energy stored in a short, powerful spring to provide power for the reloading cycle.

SPORT
SHOTGUNS

Modern sport shotguns break down into two main categories: double-barreled and single-barreled semi-auto. The former are subdivided into either over-and-under or side-by-side layouts (referring to the arrangement of the barrels on either the vertical or horizontal plane respectively). Twelve-gauge shotguns are the most popular type, being practical for most hunting uses. Sport shotguns have advanced in sophistication over the last decades of the 20th century. Interchangeable choke tubes (muzzle inserts that alter the spread of shot) are now standard on many guns, and stocks are frequently adjustable to custom-fit the shooter.

Decorated checkering
on the semi-pistol grip

Press-button
safety catch

External hammer

Walnut stock

Breech-opening
lever

Ejector port   Cocking handle

Ventilated barrel rib

Magazine cap

Loading port

Four-round
tubular magazine
located in the
fore stock

REMINGTON 1100 AUTOMATIC SHOTGUN

DATE	1985
ORIGIN	US
WEIGHT	8 LB (3.6 KG)
BARREL	28 IN (71 CM)
CALIBER	12-bore

John Browning produced the first design for a
gas-operated, self-loading shotgun while working for
Winchester, but it was not put into production. Modern
automatics can be either gas- or recoil-operated. This
Remington 1100 is gas-operated, and was produced in
a variety of barrel lengths and calibers.

Fore-end

Hinge pin

FULL VIEW

WILLIAM FORD "ECLIPSE"

DATE	c.1900
ORIGIN	UK
WEIGHT	Not known
BARREL	22 IN (55 CM)
CALIBER	10-gauge

William Ford was a Birmingham, UK, gunmaker
known for his sport weapons. This "Eclipse" 10-
bore shotgun is named after The Eclipse works that
produced the guns. It was probably intended for
crocodile hunting, as it has a powerful cartridge
but a short barrel for quick, close-range shooting.

BERETTA'S WIDE PRODUCT RANGE INCLUDES SHOTGUNS, RIFLES, PISTOLS, AND MACHINE GUNS.

Checkered straight-through grip

Breech-locking lever

Barrel pivot pin

Single trigger

Incised checkering on the semi-pistol grip

FULL VIEW

Abbreviated
forestock

Safety
catch

Twin
triggers

DARNE ROTARY-BREECH DOUBLE-BARREL SHOTGUN

DATE	1965
ORIGIN	France
WEIGHT	5¼ LB (2.4 KG)
BARREL	25½ IN (65 CM)
CALIBER	16-bore

Made by Darne, this shotgun has a patented breech action. Freed by means of the lever on top of the butt stock behind the breech, the entire lock rotates through a quarter turn to expose the chambers. Returning it to battery cocks the gun. The lever on the side of the breech-block is a cross-bolt safety.

Ventilated
barrel rib

BERETTA DOUBLE-BARRELED SHOTGUN

DATE	1982
ORIGIN	Italy
WEIGHT	6¾ LB (3.08 KG)
BARREL	28 IN (71 CM)
CALIBER	12-bore

Beretta's over-and-under double barreled shotguns, like this Model S-686, have been the most popular configuration for both hunting and trapshooting. Over-and-under guns have the advantage of a single sight line. Most are fitted with single-trigger locks.

HOLLAND & HOLLAND

Few names in the world of sport gun manufacture carry as much prestige as Holland & Holland. The firm was founded by Harris Holland, an accomplished sports shooter, in 1835 and in 1876 the company became Holland & Holland after Harris's nephew Henry Holland was made a partner. The company rapidly established a reputation for making rifles and shotguns of exquisite quality, and in 1883 H&H won all the rifle categories in trials ran by *The Field* magazine. Two years later the company was permitted to use the trade name "Royal" on its guns. The early 20th century saw H&H design influential new systems of sidelock shotgun mechanism and produce famous hunting cartridges such as the .375 H&H Magnum. H&H manufactured various military firearms during the two world wars, and since 1945 the company has maintained its focus on producing bespoke high-value sport guns or trading in collector's pieces. A pair of H&H shotguns can fetch upward of $175,000.

LOOKING DOWN THE BARREL
This Holland & Holland craftsman examines the production of a rifle barrel. The sheer number of tools required for his job is clear to see.

Breech opening lever

Recoil pad

IN 1883 HOLLAND & HOLLAND ENTERED THE TRIALS RUN BY THE MAGAZINE *THE FIELD*, AND COMPREHENSIVELY WON ALL THE RIFLE CATEGORIES.

Forward sling attachment

Semi-pistol grip

Rear sling attachment

DOUBLE-BARRELED RIFLE

DATE	1887
ORIGIN	England
WEIGHT	Not known
BARREL	Not known
CALIBER	4-bore

This double-barreled rifle has a short barrel and simple sights, both indicators that the gun would be best used for the hunting of fast, large game at close ranges. The gun is of a "boxlock" design, the operating mechanism being contained within a box-shaped housing.

Abbreviated fore stock

DOUBLE-BARRELED HAMMER GUN

DATE	1870s
ORIGIN	England
WEIGHT	Not known
BARREL	Not known
CALIBER	Not known

This fine H&H hammer gun has ornate scrollwork decorating the lock plates, double triggers for quick barrel selection and a splinter type fore-end characteristic of many English side-by-side guns. The stock has been fitted with a modern rubber recoil pad.

Smoothbore barrel

DOUBLE-BARRELED SHOTGUN

DATE	1878
ORIGIN	England
WEIGHT	6½ LB (3 KG)
BARREL	30 IN (76 CM)
CALIBER	12-bore

H&H are known for their superb quality of their bird guns. Here is an underlever-type shotgun with a classic English-style stock— it has no pistol grip. Shotguns are fired by accurate pointing rather than deliberate aiming, hence the lack of sights on this gun.

Double triggers

SPECIALIST
GUNS

G ENERALLY, SPECIALIST GUNS are produced with four main purposes: To increase destructive force; to suppress the noise of firing; to increase concealment (typically associated with assassination weapons); or to equip insurgency armies.

Before the era of breechloading cartridge weapons, attempts to increase destructive power centered around multi-barrel guns or, more rarely, single-barrel guns with hand-revolved multi-shot chambers. The "Pepperbox" pistols developed in the 1830s gave civilian users guns with rotating multiple chambers and barrels. Once practical revolvers were developed, however, such guns disappeared.

The two world wars accelerated innovation in specialist battlefield weapons. Anti-tank weapons emerged in 1917–18 to counter the appearance of armor on the Western Front, and during WWII dedicated anti-armor missile launchers were developed, including the US M1A1 Bazooka, the German Panzerfaust and the British Piat. Using shaped-charge warheads such weapons allowed an infantryman to destroy a tank at close range, and in the post-war period anti-armor missile launchers such as the RPG-7 and more sophisticated US launchers have become the greatest threat to armored vehicles on the battlefield. WWII also brought an attempt to increase a soldier's anti-tank and anti-personnel capabilities through grenade-launching adaptations for the standard rifle.

Rifle grenades gave a soldier an indirect-fire range of up to 820 ft (200 m), but they were generally tricky to set up. After the war, more success was had with standalone launchers, either hand-held such as the US M79 Blooper or tripod-mounted like the Russian AGS-17 Plamya.

The trend since the 1970s has been toward mounting grenade launchers on infantry rifles, usually in an underbarrel configuration, and in the US Army the M203 grenade launcher has become standard issue to at least one man in every four-man fireteam.

New systems are on the horizon. The US Objective Individual Combat Weapon (OICW) combines an assault rifle and 20 mm grenade launcher that fires range-programmable airburst munitions, giving the individual infantryman an unprecedented level of firepower.

Some of the most unusual firearms in history are not those designed for open battle, but for use in special operations. The growth of secret service agencies such as the Special

Operations Executive (SOE) and Office of Strategic Services (OSS) in the early 1940s generated enormous creativity in the field of spy weapons. Guns were disguised as belts, pens, cigars, pipes, or tubes of toothpaste.

Such innovations continued in the context of the Cold War, and in 1978 the Bulgarian dissident Georgi Markov was killed in London by means of a ricin-filled gas-propelled pellet shot from a specially designed umbrella gun. In the modern age assassinations tend to be carried out by precision air-launched munitions that have more certain outcomes than close-quarters devices.

One technology that has persisted, however, is the silencer—more properly termed a suppressor. Suppressors were invented around 1902, but did not enter military use for a further 30 years. WWII was again the spur to production of suppressed weapons, with pistols such as the Welrod, the Hi-Standard HD .22, the De Lisle, and a silenced version of the Sten machine gun being developed. Suppressed weapons, however, are by their very nature most effective with sub-sonic ammunition, so in military use they have usually been supplied only with pistol-caliber guns or with firearms adapted to special ammunition types, such as the .300 Whisper round.

Suppressed weapons are relatively sophisticated instruments. This chapter also looks at the other end of the scale—home-made guns and what might be termed "economy" guns. The former are those weapons crudely manufactured in home workshops, while the latter—the greatest example being the US Liberator pistol of WWII—were designed for production at a cost of a few dollars per unit for intended distribution to insurgency forces.

Both types of gun are typically very dangerous to the user, either through risk of malfunction or through the fact that they have to be used at point-blank range to be effective. In the post-war era, the huge illegal global distribution of firearms such as the AK assault rifle have resulted in home-made guns becoming more of a rarity.

SPECIALIST GUNS

COMBINATION WEAPONS

During the early centuries of gun development, the benefits of firearms over traditional forms of hand-held weapons were not immediately clear. Such considerations led some European armorers to combine firearms with edged weapons. Many of these weapons are highly decorated, suggesting more ornamental than practical purposes. However, examples of more viable combination weapons were later found in India in the 18th and 19th centuries.

DETAIL OF HAMMER
The paired cocks are more than just spring-loaded clamps to hold pieces of iron pyrites against the serrated edge of the striking wheels. They are exquisitely worked ornaments in their own right—gilded and chased with a floral pattern.

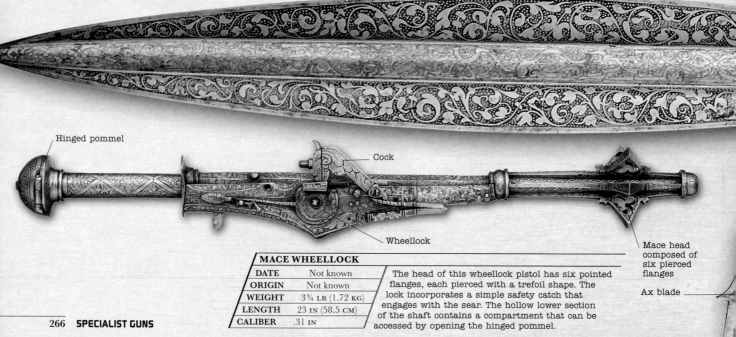

Hinged pommel

Cock

Wheellock

Mace head composed of six pierced flanges

Ax blade

MACE WHEELLOCK	
DATE	Not known
ORIGIN	Not known
WEIGHT	3¾ LB (1.72 KG)
LENGTH	23 IN (58.5 CM)
CALIBER	.31 IN

The head of this wheellock pistol has six pointed flanges, each pierced with a trefoil shape. The lock incorporates a simple safety catch that engages with the sear. The hollow lower section of the shaft contains a compartment that can be accessed by opening the hinged pommel.

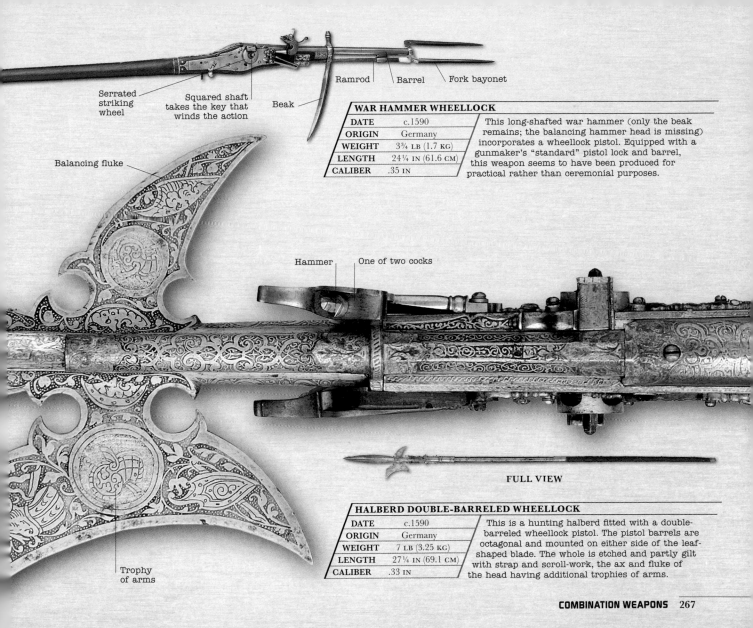

Ramrod   Barrel   Fork bayonet

Serrated
striking
wheel

Squared shaft
takes the key that
winds the action

Beak

Balancing fluke

WAR HAMMER WHEELLOCK

DATE	c.1590
ORIGIN	Germany
WEIGHT	3¾ LB (1.7 KG)
LENGTH	24¼ IN (61.6 CM)
CALIBER	.35 IN

This long-shafted war hammer (only the beak remains; the balancing hammer head is missing) incorporates a wheellock pistol. Equipped with a gunmaker's "standard" pistol lock and barrel, this weapon seems to have been produced for practical rather than ceremonial purposes.

Hammer   One of two cocks

Trophy
of arms

FULL VIEW

HALBERD DOUBLE-BARRELED WHEELLOCK

DATE	c.1590
ORIGIN	Germany
WEIGHT	7 LB (3.25 KG)
LENGTH	27¼ IN (69.1 CM)
CALIBER	.33 IN

This is a hunting halberd fitted with a double-barreled wheellock pistol. The pistol barrels are octagonal and mounted on either side of the leaf-shaped blade. The whole is etched and partly gilt with strap and scroll-work, the ax and fluke of the head having additional trophies of arms.

THE LETHAL QUALITY
OF COMBINATION WEAPONS
AT CLOSE QUARTERS
IS PLAIN TO SEE.

Balancing fluke

Dog lock

FULL VIEW

CARBINE AX	
DATE	c.1720
ORIGIN	Denmark
WEIGHT	3½ LB (1.55 KG)
LENGTH	32½ IN (82.5 CM)
CALIBER	.58 IN

The butt of this fully stocked, dog-lock carbine is reduced so that it can be gripped in the hand. The axhead is shaped to double-up as a rudimentary bayonet, and its balancing fluke as the beak of a war hammer. The head, retained by a spring catch, can be easily removed.

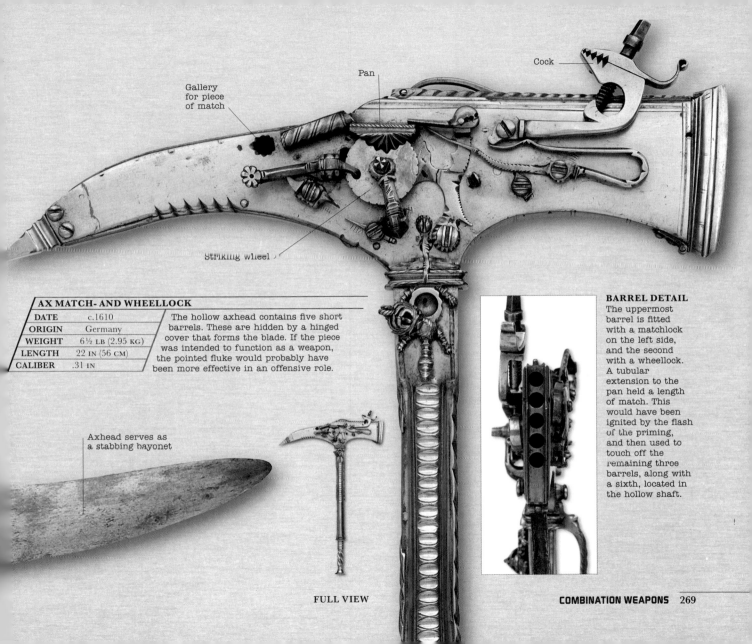

Gallery
for piece
of match

Pan

Cock

Striking wheel

AX MATCH- AND WHEELLOCK

DATE	c.1610
ORIGIN	Germany
WEIGHT	6½ LB (2.95 KG)
LENGTH	22 IN (56 CM)
CALIBER	.31 IN

The hollow axhead contains five short barrels. These are hidden by a hinged cover that forms the blade. If the piece was intended to function as a weapon, the pointed fluke would probably have been more effective in an offensive role.

Axhead serves as
a stabbing bayonet

BARREL DETAIL
The uppermost barrel is fitted with a matchlock on the left side, and the second with a wheellock. A tubular extension to the pan held a length of match. This would have been ignited by the flash of the priming, and then used to touch off the remaining three barrels, along with a sixth, located in the hollow shaft.

FULL VIEW

EARLY MULTI-SHOT FIREARMS

Even in trained hands a flintlock musket was only capable of up to four shots per minute. Options for mechanically improving the rate of fire prior to breech-loading centered around either increasing the number of barrels or introducing a cylinder to increase the number of chambers that could be loaded. The former weapons are found as far back as the late 14th century, with examples of multi-barrel "hand-gonnes," each barrel with its own touch-hole. In later wheellock or flintlock-type designs, barrels were arranged so that they could be rotated in turn to sit under a single cock. Cylinder-type firearms were more commonly seen in the development of revolver-type pistols, but flintlock revolving rifles make appearances from the 17th century onward.

ENCLOSED LOCK DETAIL
The flintlock sport gun often misfired, either because the flint had broken or the primer had become damp. When it did fire successfully, the flash and smoke from the pan could obscure the target from view or frighten the game.

Striking steel

Cock

Revolving chambers

Stock inlaid with silver

FULL VIEW

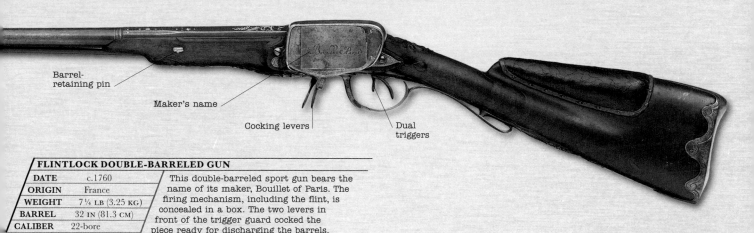

Barrel-
retaining pin

Maker's name

Cocking levers

Dual
triggers

FLINTLOCK DOUBLE-BARRELED GUN

DATE	c.1760
ORIGIN	France
WEIGHT	7 ¼ LB (3.25 KG)
BARREL	32 IN (81.3 CM)
CALIBER	22-bore

This double-barreled sport gun bears the name of its maker, Bouillet of Paris. The firing mechanism, including the flint, is concealed in a box. The two levers in front of the trigger guard cocked the piece ready for discharging the barrels.

FLINTLOCK REVOLVING RIFLE

DATE	c.1670
ORIGIN	France
WEIGHT	7 ½ LB (3.37 KG)
BARREL	31 ¼ IN (79.5 CM)
CALIBER	22-bore

French gunmakers produced some of the finest sport guns of the 17th century. This example has three revolving chambers, each fitted with its own striker and spring. This type of multi-shot weapon risked a dangerous chain reaction, in which firing one chamber set off all of the others.

> **"**
> THE CARBINE IS TO BE FIRED AT
> ## ABOUT A TWELVE FOOT
> DISTANCE AND LEVELLED AT THE KNEES OF YOUR ENEMIE'S HORSE.
> **INSTRUCTIONS TO CAVALRY, 1672**
> **"**

MULTI-SHOT FIREARMS

Multi-shot weapons have a long tradition in volley guns—multibarrel weapons designed to discharge their barrels either simultaneously or in sequence. Matchlock "organ" guns were arranged in batteries on wooden trailers or carriages from the 1400s, and multi-barreled weapons are seen in all subsequent centuries. In the 18th century, the British navy took a particular interest in volley guns, and purchased over 600 seven-barreled rifles made by John Nock, based on a design by one James Wilson. These formidable pieces were designed to deliver devastating fire against enemy crews during boarding actions, or to fight off enemy boarding tenders.

Nipple for a
percussion cap

Stock is made
of walnut

Small of stock has
incised checkering

Trigger

Hammer

Disc is bored
with seven
radial chambers

FULL VIEW

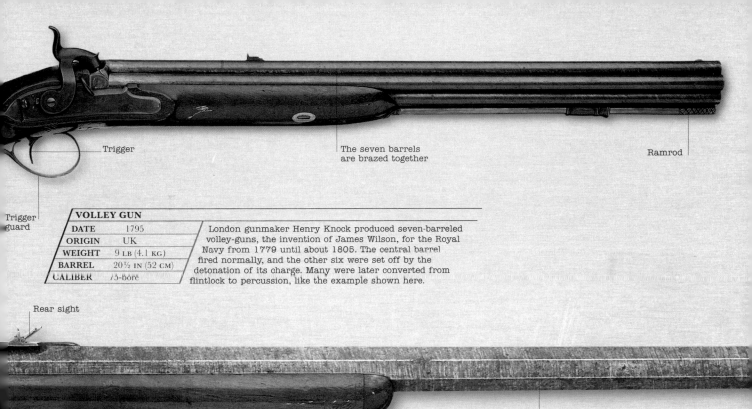

Trigger

The seven barrels
are brazed together

Ramrod

Trigger
guard

VOLLEY GUN

DATE	1795
ORIGIN	UK
WEIGHT	9 LB (4.1 KG)
BARREL	20½ IN (52 CM)
CALIBER	75-bore

London gunmaker Henry Knock produced seven-barreled volley-guns, the invention of James Wilson, for the Royal Navy from 1779 until about 1805. The central barrel fired normally, and the other six were set off by the detonation of its charge. Many were later converted from flintlock to percussion, like the example shown here.

Rear sight

Octagonal barrel

UNDER-HAMMER TURRET RIFLE

DATE	1839
ORIGIN	UK
WEIGHT	9 LB (4.07 KG)
BARREL	29 IN (73.7 CM)
CALIBER	14-bore

The so-called turret gun, an attempt to evade Colt's patent, appeared in the 1830s. Examples also exist in which the wheel of cylinders is set vertically. It soon became apparent that if flash-over from one cylinder to another occurred, the result would most likely be catastrophic to any bystanders, or even the shooter himself.

ANTI-TANK WEAPONS

The first dedicated anti-tank rifle was the Mauser T-gewehr, a bolt-action 13 mm weapon which could penetrate up to 0.8 in (20 mm) of armor. As armor became more of a feature of modern warfare, many other countries designed their own anti-tank rifles and applied them in WWII. Most were huge weapons with extremely long barrels, heavy calibers of up to 20 mm, and hefty recoil control. Although impressive to fire, their effect on the new types of armor appearing in WWII was minimal, and they essentially disappeared from practical use by the end of the war.

Barrel recoils into receiver

Left hand pulls stock tightly to shoulder

Box magazine holds five rounds

Bolt handle

Left-hand grip

Pistol grip

Fore sight

PTRD ANTI-TANK RIFLE

DATE	1941
ORIGIN	USSR
WEIGHT	38¼ LB (17.3 KG)
BARREL	48¼ IN (123 CM)
CALIBER	14.5 MM

The PTRD was a more complicated weapon than it appeared. It had a barrel that recoiled into the stock and unlocked the bolt in the process; this was held back when the barrel returned to battery, opening the breech and ejecting the spent round. A fresh round was then introduced and the bolt closed by hand.

FULL VIEW

BOYS ANTI-TANK RIFLE

DATE	1936
ORIGIN	UK
WEIGHT	36 LB (16.3 KG)
BARREL	36 IN (91.5 CM)
CALIBER	.55 IN

Birmingham Small Arms produced the Boys rifles in the mid-1930s. They were bolt-action weapons firing a heavy tungsten-steel round. Even though the barrel recoiled into the stock, the effect on the firer was fearsome and it was abandoned as ineffective in 1941.

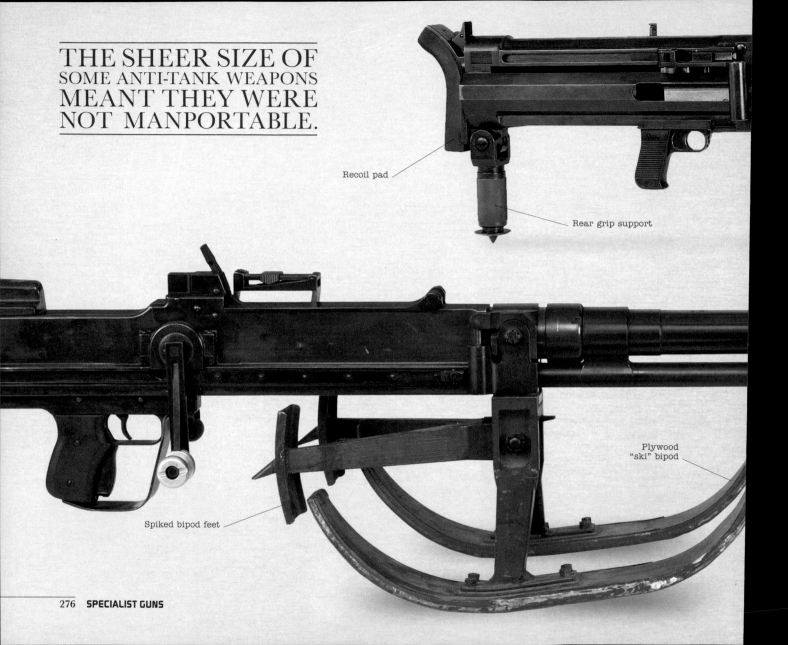

THE SHEER SIZE OF
SOME ANTI-TANK WEAPONS
MEANT THEY WERE
NOT MANPORTABLE.

Recoil pad

Rear grip support

Plywood
"ski" bipod

Spiked bipod feet

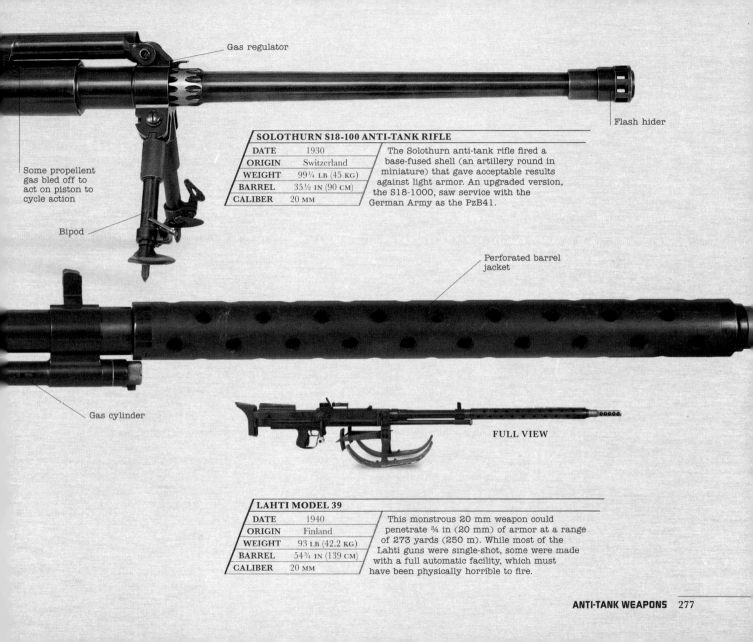

Gas regulator

Flash hider

Some propellent gas bled off to act on piston to cycle action

Bipod

SOLOTHURN S18-100 ANTI-TANK RIFLE

DATE	1930
ORIGIN	Switzerland
WEIGHT	99¼ LB (45 KG)
BARREL	35½ IN (90 CM)
CALIBER	20 MM

The Solothurn anti-tank rifle fired a base-fused shell (an artillery round in miniature) that gave acceptable results against light armor. An upgraded version, the S18-1000, saw service with the German Army as the PzB41.

Perforated barrel jacket

Gas cylinder

FULL VIEW

LAHTI MODEL 39

DATE	1940
ORIGIN	Finland
WEIGHT	93 LB (42.2 KG)
BARREL	54¾ IN (139 CM)
CALIBER	20 MM

This monstrous 20 mm weapon could penetrate ¾ in (20 mm) of armor at a range of 273 yards (250 m). While most of the Lahti guns were single-shot, some were made with a full automatic facility, which must have been physically horrible to fire.

TASER GUN

For modern police forces, the increasing threat of litigation arising from the use of firearms has led to the adoption of several less-than-lethal weapons, including the Taser gun. The name is an acronym of "Thomas A. Swift's Electric Rifle" after a science-fiction character known by the weapon's US designer, Jack Cover.

———◆———

Cover helped perfect the weapon in association with the Air Taser company in 1993, and today over 9,500 law-enforcement agencies worldwide use Taser products. The basic firearm consists of a handgun that fires electrodes out to a distance of 35 ft (10 m). These hit the assailant then, via wires still connected to the gun, deliver an incapacitating electric shock. Although early models had darts on the ends of the electrodes, which embedded in the assailant's skin, the latest versions apply an electrical pulse that does not need skin penetration. There is no doubt that Tasers have led to a reduction in firearms-related deaths in many police forces.

4-mode light selector

Trigger

Textured grip

TASER M26	
DATE	1998
ORIGIN	US
WEIGHT	1 LB (0.5 KG)
LENGTH	7 IN (18 CM)
CALIBER	Fires electrodes

The Taser M26 was developed in 1998 aimed at achieving more efficient incapacitation. Its electrodes—which can be fired up to 35 ft (10 m)—deliver 18–26 watt electrical signals, generating massive muscle constrictions in the victim that drop him or her to the floor.

THE TASER CAN GENERATE MORE
STOPPING POWER
THAN BEING HIT WITH A
.357 MAGNUM BULLET.

Electrode
cavity

Heavy-duty
plastic casing

SHOCK TACTICS
An English police officer
demonstrates the power
of the Taser gun. This
example features a
connecting wire but
Taser also manufacture
a wireless option.

RIFLE-MOUNTED GRENADE LAUNCHERS

Rifle grenades came to the fore during WWII as an attempt to give infantrymen a better direct and indirect fire capability against personnel and even armored targets. Modern rifle-mounted grenade launchers are part of the "modular" trend in weaponry that began in the 1970s, whereby a soldier could call on different types of fire from a single weapon platform. Most rifle-mounted grenade launchers fire 40mm grenades, and have a maximum indirect-fire range of around 450 yards (410 m). The latest generation of weapons have integral laser range-finders that give the precise distance to the target.

Receiver

Cocking handle

Ten-round magazine

Bolt handle

Ten-round magazine

NO. 4 RIFLE WITH AT-GRENADE LAUNCHER	
DATE	1940s
ORIGIN	UK
GRENADE	Anti-tank
CALIBER	.303 IN
RANGE	330 FT (100 M)

With the introduction of the No. 4 Rifle, with its exposed muzzle, the British Army was able to develop a new style of tubular launcher. Mounted over the muzzle on the bayonet lugs, the No. 4 launched a fin-stabilized anti-tank grenade. This example is fitted with a later model L1A1 practice grenade.

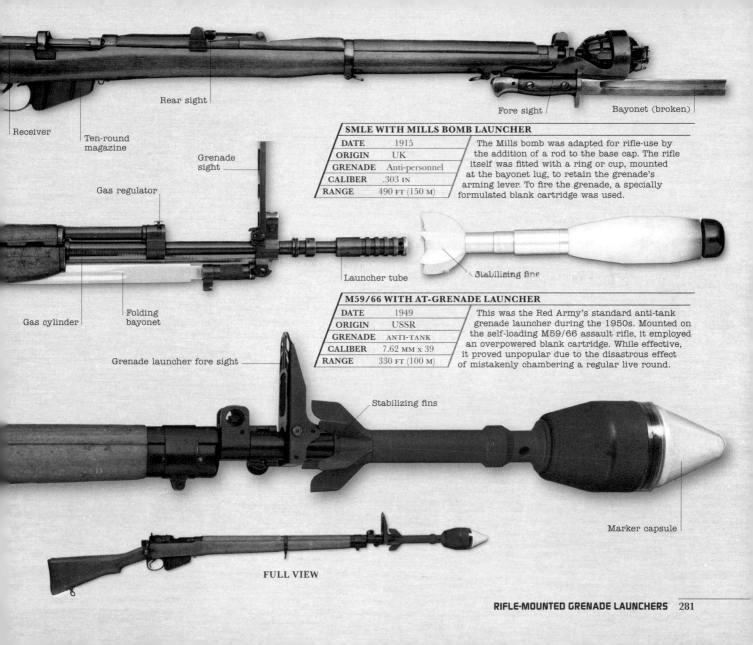

Rear sight

Fore sight

Bayonet (broken)

Receiver

Ten-round magazine

Grenade sight

Gas regulator

Gas cylinder

Folding bayonet

Launcher tube

Stabilising fins

Grenade launcher fore sight

Stabilizing fins

Marker capsule

FULL VIEW

SMLE WITH MILLS BOMB LAUNCHER

DATE	1915
ORIGIN	UK
GRENADE	Anti-personnel
CALIBER	.303 IN
RANGE	490 FT (150 M)

The Mills bomb was adapted for rifle-use by the addition of a rod to the base cap. The rifle itself was fitted with a ring or cup, mounted at the bayonet lug, to retain the grenade's arming lever. To fire the grenade, a specially formulated blank cartridge was used.

M59/66 WITH AT-GRENADE LAUNCHER

DATE	1949
ORIGIN	USSR
GRENADE	ANTI-TANK
CALIBER	7.62 MM x 39
RANGE	330 FT (100 M)

This was the Red Army's standard anti-tank grenade launcher during the 1950s. Mounted on the self-loading M59/66 assault rifle, it employed an overpowered blank cartridge. While effective, it proved unpopular due to the disastrous effect of mistakenly chambering a regular live round.

A MODERN RIFLE GRENADE
CAN HAVE A FLAT
TRAJECTORY OF OVER
110 YARDS (100 M).

Butt stock

Folded rear sight for
grenade launcher

Rifle
cocking
handle

M16A1 WITH M203

DATE	1972
ORIGIN	US
GRENADE	ANTI-PERSONNEL
CALIBER	40 MM
RANGE	490 FT (150 M)

The US Army's version of the assault rifle-
mounted grenade launcher, the M203,
employs a grenade mated to a cartridge case
containing the propellant charge. The empty
case remains in the chamber after the round
has been fired and needs to be ejected.

Rifle
trigger

Gas
cylinder

Muzzle
compensator

40 mm anti-
personnel
grenade

Grenade launcher tube is rifled

Pistol
grip

Grenade
launcher
trigger

30-round
magazine

БГ15NA51429

AK74 WITH GP25

DATE	1978
ORIGIN	USSR
GRENADE	ANTI-PERSONNEL
CALIBER	40 MM
RANGE	490 FT (150 M)

The barrel-mounted grenade launcher was slow to use. The answer was to fit the grenade with its own propellant charge and so the Red Army adopted one with the charge in the body of the grenade. This AK74 lacks the recoil pad that is normally fitted to grenade launcher rifles.

FULL VIEW

Launcher fore sight in
the folded position

Rifle fore
sight

Launcher mounts
onto fore stock

STAND-ALONE GRENADE LAUNCHERS

It was in the second half of the 20th century that stand-alone grenade launchers became truly practical systems. Modern launchers vary from single-shot shoulder-fired weapons like the M79 "Blooper," through to belt-fed, tripod-mounted automatic guns such as the new US XM307 Advanced Crew Served Weapon (ACSW). Both can take a variety of lethal and non-lethal roles, from anti-armor attacks through to CS gas dispensing in riot situations. Many of the larger specimens are also taking over from mortars on the battlefield. The ACSW, for example, can fire 25 mm high-explosive, high-explosive anti-tank (HEAT), or thermobarbic warheads in airbursting mode to ranges of up to 2200 yards (2000 m) and at rates of 260 rpm.

FULL VIEW

Laser designator

Rifle barrel has cooling fins

Skeleton butt stock can be folded forward

Fore grip can be loosened to rotate around barrel

MECHEM/MILKOR MGL MK 1	
DATE	1990
ORIGIN	South Africa
WEIGHT	12 LB (5.6 KG)
BARREL	12 IN (30.5 CM)
CALIBER	40 MM

A scaled-up version of a shotgun of similar design, the MGL MK 1 is a six-shot revolver grenade launcher. Its maximum range is around 1,150 ft (350 m).

Cylinder holds six 40 mm grenades

Non-disintegrating belt emerges here

AGS-17 "PLAMYA"

DATE	1975
ORIGIN	USSR
WEIGHT	48¼ LB (22 KG)
BARREL	11¾ IN (30 CM)
CALIBER	30 MM

The Soviet equivalent of the American 40 mm M19 that was first used in the Vietnam war. It is a belt-fed, blowback-operated launcher with a maximum range of 1 mile (1.61 km). Such weapons are commonly mounted in ground vehicles, boats, and hovercraft.

Elevating quadrant

Drum contains 29 30 mm grenades in non-disintegrating belt

MISSILE LAUNCHERS

The most important first step in the development of missile launchers was the invention in the 1940s of the shaped-charge warhead, designed to create a lethal jet of molten steel that, even in its early development, could cut through 4 in (10 cm) of plate armor. Since the war, manportable anti-tank weapons have increased in lethality and proliferation. Modern systems such as the FGM-148 Javelin can destroy any Main Battle Tank (MBT), while the RPG-7 has become one of the world's greatest insurgency threats.

Optical sights graduated to 1,650 ft (500 m)

Muzzle, where projectile is loaded

Trigger

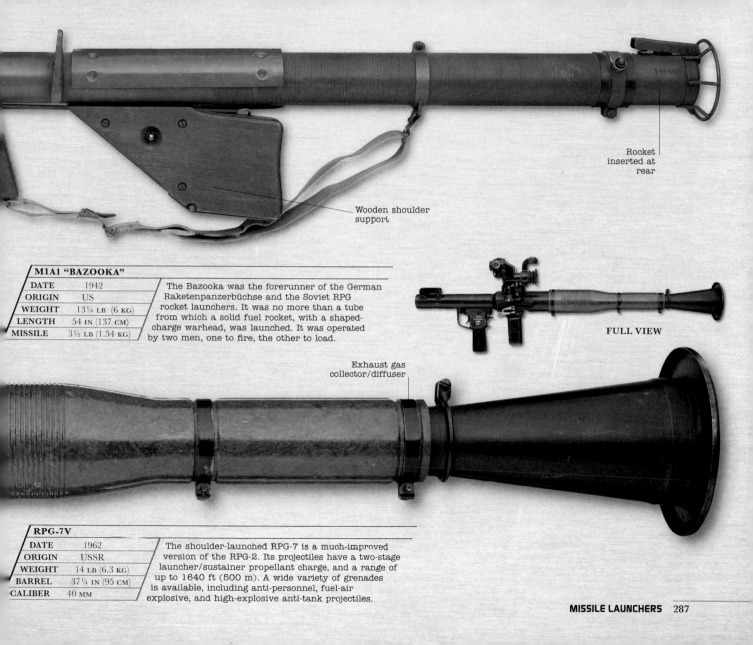

Rocket
inserted at
rear

Wooden shoulder
support

M1A1 "BAZOOKA"

DATE	1942
ORIGIN	US
WEIGHT	13¼ LB (6 KG)
LENGTH	54 IN (137 CM)
MISSILE	3½ LB (1.54 KG)

The Bazooka was the forerunner of the German
Raketenpanzerbüchse and the Soviet RPG
rocket launchers. It was no more than a tube
from which a solid fuel rocket, with a shaped-
charge warhead, was launched. It was operated
by two men, one to fire, the other to load.

FULL VIEW

Exhaust gas
collector/diffuser

RPG-7V

DATE	1962
ORIGIN	USSR
WEIGHT	14 LB (6.3 KG)
BARREL	37¼ IN (95 CM)
CALIBER	40 MM

The shoulder-launched RPG-7 is a much-improved
version of the RPG-2. Its projectiles have a two-stage
launcher/sustainer propellant charge, and a range of
up to 1640 ft (500 m). A wide variety of grenades
is available, including anti-personnel, fuel-air
explosive, and high-explosive anti-tank projectiles.

MECHANICAL-ELECTRICAL GUNS

The post-war years saw the firepower of the machine gun taken to its practical extreme. In 1945 in the United States, Johnson Automatics Inc. was commissioned to reinvigorate Gatling's now antique Gatling Gun design. The Johnson company's solution was to take the same multi-barreled rotary configuration, but power the whole system by electrical motor rather than hand crank to produce a cyclical rate of fire of 5800 rpm. Over time "Project Vulcan," as it was known, spawned a whole new generation of electrically powered Gatling-type weapons, all with devastating firepower offsetting their bulk and weight. Most of these weapons found applications in aircraft, although today variants are also found on armored vehicles and even as a prototype infantry machine gun, the 5.56 mm XM-214 Six-Pac.

Bolt handle

Electric motor

Mour

Ammunition feed

GATLING MINIGUN M134	
DATE	1960s
ORIGIN	US
WEIGHT	35 LB (16 KG)
BARREL	22 IN (56 CM)
CALIBER	7.62 x 51 MM

The M134 is a Gatling-type rotary weapon that is powered by electric motor to achieve extremely high rates of fire—up to 6000 rpm, although typically the rate is limited to around 4000 rpm. The weight and bulk of the external power source means that the gun is usually used in helicopters, on armored vehicles, or boats.

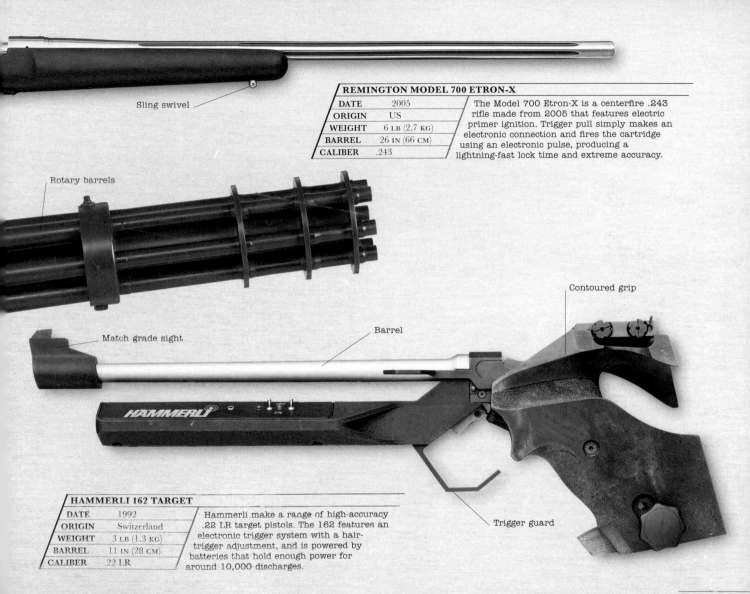

Sling swivel

REMINGTON MODEL 700 ETRON-X

DATE	2005
ORIGIN	US
WEIGHT	6 LB (2.7 KG)
BARREL	26 IN (66 CM)
CALIBER	.243

The Model 700 Etron-X is a centerfire .243 rifle made from 2005 that features electric primer ignition. Trigger pull simply makes an electronic connection and fires the cartridge using an electronic pulse, producing a lightning-fast lock time and extreme accuracy.

Rotary barrels

Contoured grip

Match grade sight

Barrel

Trigger guard

HAMMERLI 162 TARGET

DATE	1992
ORIGIN	Switzerland
WEIGHT	3 LB (1.3 KG)
BARREL	11 IN (28 CM)
CALIBER	.22 LR

Hammerli make a range of high-accuracy .22 LR target pistols. The 162 features an electronic trigger system with a hair-trigger adjustment, and is powered by batteries that hold enough power for around 10,000 discharges.

SPECIAL OPERATIONS EXECUTIVE (SOE)

The Special Operations Executive (SOE) was formed in July 1940 in Britain with the mission of conducting, or supporting, irregular warfare throughout German-occupied Europe. Over the subsequent four years its agents were to be found across Europe from Norway to Greece, and from 1942 SOE even conducted operations in South-East Asia. Specializing in covert warfare, SOE naturally gravitated toward commissioning or developing specialist firearms (although SOE was not a

gunmaker *per se*). A large array of disguised weapons came from SOE's Inter Services Research Bureau (ISRB) near Welwyn, Wales, including .22 guns disguised as pens, smoking pipes and cigars, and pistols that fitted around the wrist or were set into belts. SOE also used many silenced guns, including the SOE-developed Welrod pistol, the De Lisle Carbine, and silenced versions of the Sten submachine gun. Many of the designs were innovative but impractical, and SOE had more influence supplying partisan forces with conventional weaponry.

9 MM PARABELLUM
The 9 mm Parabellum, or Luger, is the most common cartridge in the world.

‚ Trigger

TOP SECRET
A range of recently declassified documents from the SOE, including a plot to assassinate Hitler.

LUGER P08 WITH SILENCER	
DATE	1940s
ORIGIN	Germany
WEIGHT	2¾ LB (1.2 KG)
BARREL	11¼ IN (28 CM)
CALIBER	9 MM Parabellum

This Luger was a firearm used by the SOE during WWII, and is here fitted with a silencer for use as an assassination weapon. In many ways, the Luger was best suited to covert, police and security work, as its mechanical system was vulnerable to the dirt of battlefield use.

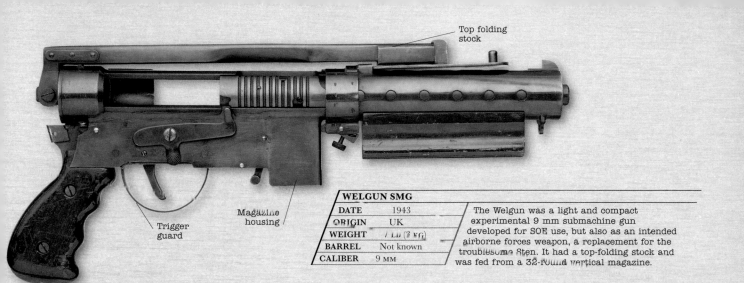

Top folding stock

Trigger guard

Magazine housing

WELGUN SMG	
DATE	1943
ORIGIN	UK
WEIGHT	7 LB (3 KG)
BARREL	Not known
CALIBER	9 MM

The Welgun was a light and compact experimental 9 mm submachine gun developed for SOE use, but also as an intended airborne forces weapon, a replacement for the troublesome Sten. It had a top-folding stock and was fed from a 32-round vertical magazine.

THE SOE'S RANGE OF SPECIALIST WEAPONS WAS INTEGRAL TO THE WAR EFFORT.

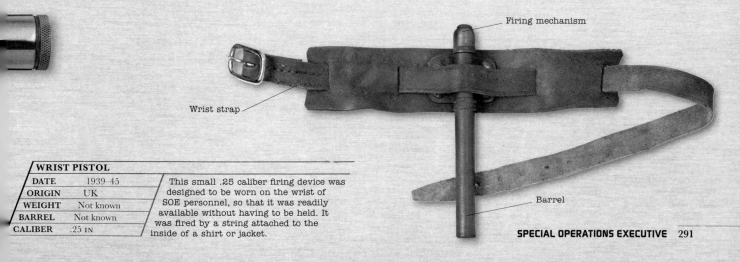

Firing mechanism

Wrist strap

Barrel

WRIST PISTOL	
DATE	1939–45
ORIGIN	UK
WEIGHT	Not known
BARREL	Not known
CALIBER	.25 IN

This small .25 caliber firing device was designed to be worn on the wrist of SOE personnel, so that it was readily available without having to be held. It was fired by a string attached to the inside of a shirt or jacket.

GENTRY GUNS

The category "gentry guns" denotes firearms contained within accoutrements such as canes and umbrellas. Their purpose is somewhat ambiguous, as they are impractical for hunting and, usually, are of limited power for self defense. Perhaps their overall rationale is simply to provide the user with some basic emergency firepower, for purposes of the user's choosing. Caliber in such weapons tends to be small—often .410 for smoothbore barrels and .22 for rifled barrels.

Chamber

Trigger

Chamber

Trigger

BULGARIAN DEFECTOR GEORGI MARKOV WAS KILLED IN 1978 ON WATERLOO BRIDGE IN LONDON BY A RICIN-FILLED PELLET FIRED FROM A GAS-POWERED UMBRELLA GUN.

Barrel in
shaft of
cane

WILSON CANE GUN

DATE	1984
ORIGIN	UK
WEIGHT	Not known
BARREL	Not known
CALIBER	.410

The cane gun here is produced by the same gunmaker as that behind the umbrella gun (below), and shares the .410 gauge. Being able to fire the .410 cartridge makes the cane gun suitable for use against small game at ranges of up to 25 yards.

Muzzle

WILSON UMBRELLA GUN

DATE	1985
ORIGIN	UK
WEIGHT	Not known
BARREL	Not known
CALIBER	.410

Umbrellas lend themselves well to concealed firearms. This example, however, is more of a sporting weapon, having a centerfire mechanism around a .410 gauge barrel.

COVERT FORCES GUNS

Guns are in many way obtrusive pieces of technology. They can be bulky, heavy, expensive to make, and deliver a highly conspicuous report when fired. With the development of Special Forces and secret service government agencies during the 20th century, attempts were made to obviate many of these problems and produce guns configured for covert use. Hiram Maxim patented a working sound suppressor device in 1908, and suppressors were first issued to the Office of Strategic Services (OSS) in WWII for their High Standard .22 pistols. Other projects saw the production of extreme low-budget guns such as the Liberator, designed to be dropped in their thousands into war zones to fuel friendly insurgencies. Such projects and technologies, while interesting, did not always balance innovation with practicality.

AROUND ONE MILLION LIBERATOR PISTOLS WERE MANUFACTURED IN JUST THREE MONTHS, MUCH OF THE WEAPON SIMPLY BEING STAMPED FROM SHEET STEEL.

Optical sight

Cocking handle

Ejection port

Sight

Hand-operated
breech block

Trigger guard

Pressed
steel body

LIBERATOR

DATE	1942
ORIGIN	US
WEIGHT	1 LB (0.45 KG)
BARREL	4 IN (10 CM)
CALIBER	.45 ACP

The Liberator was designed from an OSS commission as the cheapest possible handgun. It was intended to drop hundreds of thousands of Liberators to resistance groups, and each gun was supplied with 10 rounds of .45 ACP and visual instructions on use.

Suppressor

Sling swivel

FULL VIEW

RUGER MODEL 10/22

DATE	1980s
ORIGIN	US
WEIGHT	6.2 LB (2.8 KG)
BARREL	18½ IN (47 CM)
CALIBER	.22 LR

The Ruger 10/22 is an extremely popular .22 LR autoloading rifle, with a long history of use in sport shooting. Suppressed versions have also entered military service. Israeli special forces, for example, used them on rioters during the Palestinian Intifada of 1987.

SILENCED GUNS

Although silencers, or "suppressors" as they are otherwise known, do reduce the report of a gun considerably—some by as much as 90 per cent—they do not obliterate the sound entirely. The first effective suppressors emerged at the beginning of the 20th century, Hiram Maxim leading the way with his "Maxim Silencer" of c.1902. Since then most suppressors have worked on similar principles. The most popular type involves a bulbous chamber containing a series of baffles fitted to the end of the muzzle, this serving to contain and dampen the gas expansion from the muzzle when the gun is fired. Silenced weapons typically require use with subsonic cartridges, as supersonic rounds create much of their noise when they break the sound barrier.

Hammer

Ejection port

Slide

Rear sight

Integral silencer

Magazine inserted into grip

TYPE 67		
DATE	1980s	The Type 67 was a development of the Type 64, both being 7.62 x 17 mm blowback pistols with integral silencers. It featured a manual slide locking system, which stopped ejection after firing, giving the shooter the chance to find somewhere quieter to unload.
ORIGIN	China	
WEIGHT	2¼ LB (1.02 KG)	
BARREL	3½ IN (89 MM)	
CALIBER	7.62 x 17 MM	

External silencer

M20 SILENCED

DATE	1950s
ORIGIN	China
WEIGHT	1¾ LB (0.83 KG)
BARREL	9¼ IN (23 CM)
CALIBER	7.62 x 25 MM

The M20 was a Chinese copy of the Soviet 7.62 x 25 mm Tokarev TT-33. There is almost nothing to distinguish between the two guns (apart from the Chinese gun having more slide grip cuts), both being short-recoil operated and utilizing Browning's swinging link breech lock. The gun here features a silencer.

Ejection port

Trigger

FULL VIEW

VZ27

DATE	1927
ORIGIN	Czechoslovakia
WEIGHT	1½ LB (0.7 KG)
BARREL	4 IN (10 CM)
CALIBER	7.65 x 17 MM

The VZ27 was a redesign of the 9 mm VZ24. Instead of the latter's short-recoil operation, the VZ27 had a much simpler blowback mechanism and its caliber was taken down to 7.65 x 17 mm. The VZ27 also had a longer barrel. This popular gun stayed in production until the 1950s.

Hammer spur

Rear sight

PROPERTY OF U.S.

Slide grips

Barrel

Trigger guard

Blade front sight

Suppressor

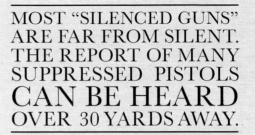

MOST "SILENCED GUNS"
ARE FAR FROM SILENT.
THE REPORT OF MANY
SUPPRESSED PISTOLS
CAN BE HEARD
OVER 30 YARDS AWAY.

HI-STANDARD MODEL B

DATE	1932
ORIGIN	US
WEIGHT	2¾ LB (1.3 KG)
BARREL	9¼ IN (23 CM)
CALIBER	.22 LR

One of High Standard's first guns was the Model B, a highly accurate .22 handgun designed for casual target shooting, but which also found military applications. Unlike the Model A target pistol, which was similar but had adjustable sights, the Model B had fixed sights. This gun was used by OSS forces in WWII.

External suppressor

FULL VIEW

WEBLEY & SCOTT 1907

DATE	1907
ORIGIN	UK
WEIGHT	2 LB (0.9 KG)
BARREL	9¼ IN (23 CM)
CALIBER	7.65 MM

The Webley & Scott 1907 was one of several automatic pistols manufactured by Webley in the first decades of the 20th century (the Webley & Scott name distinguished automatics made by Webley from its revolvers). This gun is fitted with a silencer, and equipped British SOE agents in WWII.

CONCEALED SPY GUNS

There is a long history of disguising guns as other objects. For example, an elaborate German walking staff dated from 1600 hides both a sword and an attached wheellock pistol that runs up the side of the blade. Apart from long cane guns, most disguised weapons tend to reduce into small, easily concealed formats, from lipsticks to pens. Such guns have severe limitations. Their very short barrels mean they have to be used at point blank range. As a result, if the bullet fails to achieve its desired result, the assassin can all too easily become the victim.

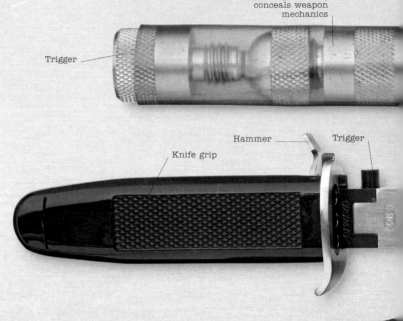

Trigger

Flashlight casing conceals weapon mechanics

Hammer

Trigger

Knife grip

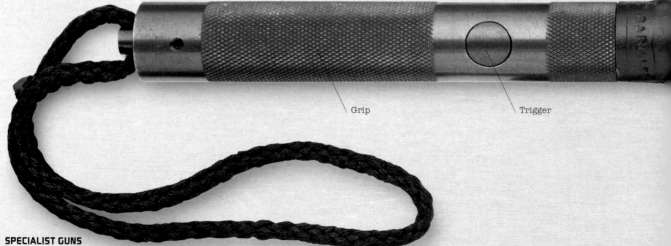

Grip

Trigger

Bullet fires
through front
of flashlight

FLASHLIGHT STINGER

DATE	1980s
ORIGIN	US
WEIGHT	1¼ LB (0.8 KG)
BARREL	2 IN (5 CM)
CALIBER	.22 LR

This covert weapon is disguised as a flashlight, and actually contains a .22 LR single-shot firearm. The bullet is loaded behind the flashlight's bulb section, and is fired by depressing the light switch. The gun was developed in the US during the post-war period.

KNIFE PISTOL

DATE	2000s
ORIGIN	China
WEIGHT	¾ LB (0.31 KG)
BARREL	1 IN (2.5 CM)
CALIBER	.22 LR

This modern weapon originated in China in the 2000s, and would be intended for criminal or covert use. It features a folding knife integrated with a three-shot pistol firing .22 LR ammunition. The .22 LR round is ideal for small weapons such as this, having negligible recoil.

Muzzle

Truncheon head

BARRILET TRUNCHEON PISTOL

DATE	Not known
ORIGIN	France
WEIGHT	1¼ lb (0.58 KG)
BARREL	14 IN (36 CM)
CALIBER	Not known

This French weapon is a fusion of a pistol and truncheon, the whole device weighing 1¼ lb (0.58 kg). The gun barrel runs up inside the flared truncheon head, and the gun is fired via a button on the grip shaft.

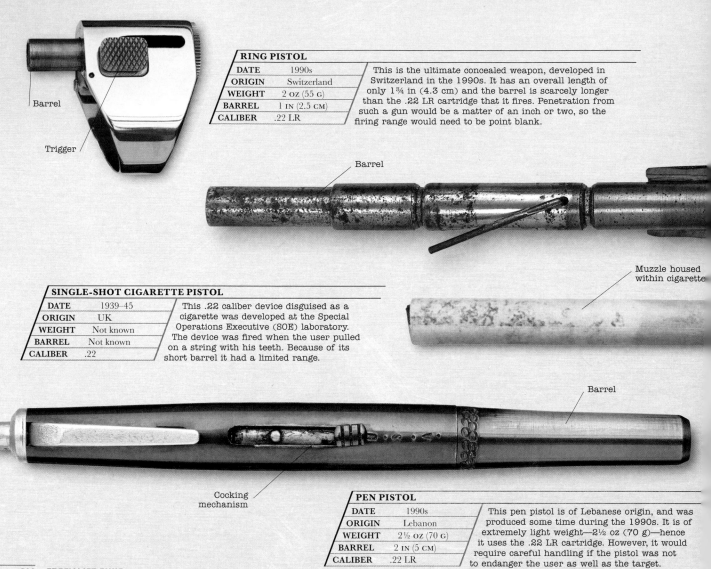

Barrel

Trigger

RING PISTOL

DATE	1990s
ORIGIN	Switzerland
WEIGHT	2 oz (55 g)
BARREL	1 in (2.5 cm)
CALIBER	.22 LR

This is the ultimate concealed weapon, developed in Switzerland in the 1990s. It has an overall length of only 1¾ in (4.3 cm) and the barrel is scarcely longer than the .22 LR cartridge that it fires. Penetration from such a gun would be a matter of an inch or two, so the firing range would need to be point blank.

Barrel

Muzzle housed within cigarette

SINGLE-SHOT CIGARETTE PISTOL

DATE	1939–45
ORIGIN	UK
WEIGHT	Not known
BARREL	Not known
CALIBER	.22

This .22 caliber device disguised as a cigarette was developed at the Special Operations Executive (SOE) laboratory. The device was fired when the user pulled on a string with his teeth. Because of its short barrel it had a limited range.

Barrel

Cocking mechanism

PEN PISTOL

DATE	1990s
ORIGIN	Lebanon
WEIGHT	2½ oz (70 g)
BARREL	2 in (5 cm)
CALIBER	.22 LR

This pen pistol is of Lebanese origin, and was produced some time during the 1990s. It is of extremely light weight—2½ oz (70 g)—hence it uses the .22 LR cartridge. However, it would require careful handling if the pistol was not to endanger the user as well as the target.

PIPE PISTOL

DATE	1939–45
ORIGIN	UK
WEIGHT	Not known
BARREL	Not known
CALIBER	Not known

Common items carried on the person were capable of being transformed into lethal firing devices. This World War II device was designed for use by SOE personnel. It was fired by removing the mouthpiece and twisting the bowl while grasping the barrel.

LIPSTICK PISTOL

DATE	1939–45
ORIGIN	Russia
WEIGHT	Not known
BARREL	Not known
CALIBER	Not known

This Russian KGB 4.5 mm single-shot firing device was found in the purse of an East German spy arrested in West Berlin during World War II. The female spy using this weapon would have deployed it on the unsuspecting victim at very close quarters.

Firing string

Trigger

Muzzle

Firing mechanism
housed within casing

CIGARETTE LIGHTER PISTOL

DATE	1970s
ORIGIN	Not known
WEIGHT	3 oz (85 g)
BARREL	1½ in (4 cm)
CALIBER	.22 LR

What appears to be a cigarette lighter actually contains a single-shot .22 LR pistol, firing from a 1½ in (4 cm) barrel. The trigger is of a clasp type and runs up the side of the "gun" body. It is not known which country produced this firearm, but it was originated in the 1970s.

IMPROVISED GUNS

Improvised firearms vary enormously in their build-quality and performance. At the more sophisticated end of the scale, we see examples of submachine guns constructed in home workshops that feature selector and safety switches and detachable magazines. At the opposite end there are guns that consist of nothing more than a piece of pipe and a spring-loaded nail for a firing pin. In insurgency or terrorist contexts—the principal environments in which improvised guns are produced—most home-made weapons have proved as dangerous to the user as the victim. The poor quality of metals used, the inability to form gas-tight seals around the chamber, and incorrect calibration cause many improvised guns to explode when fired.

Trigger

Stock reminiscent of a Lee-Enfield

Muzzle

Perforated barrel shroud serves as the fore grip

MAU-MAU CARBINE

DATE	1950s
ORIGIN	Kenya
WEIGHT	3½ LB (1.6 KG)
BARREL	20¼ IN (51.2 CM)
CALIBER	.303 IN

This short-barreled, bolt-action, single shot carbine was made in Kenya during the time of the "Mau-Mau" insurrection against British rule in the 1950s. Most of the improvised weapons made by the rebels exploded when they were fired.

LOYALIST SUBMACHINE GUN

DATE	1970s
ORIGIN	UK
WEIGHT	5¾ LB (2.6 KG)
BARREL	7¾ IN (20 CM)
CALIBER	9 MM

This homemade machine pistol was produced by Loyalist paramilitaries in Northern Ireland. The barrel shroud and receiver have been fashioned from square-framed tubing, while the magazine appears to be that of an L2 Stirling SMG.

Unrifled barrel

Fore sight

Barrel band
and rear
sight

Bolt
handle

Cartridge case from 20 mm
cannon shell serves as barrel

Hole used to ignite charge

Roughly
carved
wooden grip

Wire wrapping secures
barrel to stock

Sling

Magazine
release
catch

EOKA PISTOL

DATE	1950s
ORIGIN	Cyprus
WEIGHT	½ LB (.23 KG)
BARREL	4¼ IN (11 CM)
CALIBER	Not known

This "gun" is so crudely fashioned that it barely
qualifies for the name. The barrel is a spent 20
mm-caliber cartridge case, secured to the rough-
hewn wooden frame. The "muzzle" would have
needed to be virtually in contact with the
victim's body before the gun was discharged.

Square-section
receiver

FULL VIEW

Pistol grip

34-round box
magazine from
Sterling SMG

Safety
catch

Trigger

PROTOTYPE GUNS

Prototype firearms have an important role in the development of guns. Although many trials weapons never actually reached production, the data collected has helped refine everything from operating systems to ammunition. The prototype phase became especially important during the late 19th and 20th centuries, when prototypes had to establish the groundwork for mass production models. Sometimes the development phases have felt undue political influence—the rush to produce an indigenous replacement for the British Army's SLR rifle in the 1980s resulted in disastrous deficiencies in the adopted SA80A1. However, when the process is politically impartial, prototypes have proved extremely influential.

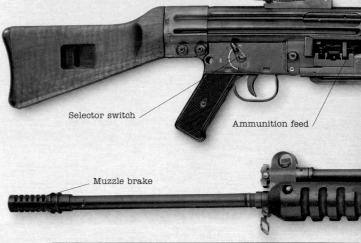

Rear sight

Selector switch

Ammunition feed

Muzzle brake

FN FAL TRIALS MODEL		
DATE	1950	Although the FN FAL would be most famous in its 7.62 x 51 mm NATO chambering, it was first designed in 1948 around the German 7.92 x 33 mm Kurz intermediate round.
ORIGIN	Belgium	
WEIGHT	9¼ LB (4.2 KG)	
BARREL	23¾ IN (60 CM)	
CALIBER	7.92 x 33 MM	

Ejection port

Cocking handle

Folding stock

Magazine release

Gas tap-off point

MAUSER-CETME LMG

DATE	1960s
ORIGIN	Spain/Germany
WEIGHT	18 LB (8 KG)
BARREL	23¼ IN (59 CM)
CALIBER	7.62 x 51 MM

The Mauser-CETME light machine gun (LMG) was a joint German-Spanish development of the German MG42, although chambered for the 7.62 x 51 mm NATO round. The gun was not a success in this chambering, but CETME later achieved a good workable design in its 5.56 x 45 mm NATO Ameli machine gun.

Box magazine

Fire selector switch

Vented housing

Flash hider

STERLING LIGHT AUTO RIFLE

DATE	1970s
ORIGIN	UK
WEIGHT	9 LB (4.1 KG)
BARREL	19¾ IN (50 CM)
CALIBER	5.56 x 45 MM

Sterling produced this light automatic rifle in the 1970s, by which time the 5.56 x 45 mm NATO round was becoming established as a standard cartridge. The Sterling gun was also 5.56 mm, and featured a patent folding butt to improve the gun's portability.

FULL VIEW

MACHINE GUNS & SUBMACHINE GUNS

THE DESIRE TO PRODUCE a fully automatic firearm goes back a long way. In 1718 James Puckle of London patented his "Puckle Gun," a single-barrel flintlock gun fed from a hand-cranked revolving cylinder consisting of nine chambers, all of which could be discharged in less than a minute. In the 1860s, Puckle's invention inspired Dr. Richard Gatling to design the Gatling Gun and so began the true era of mechanized firepower.

The Gatling took rates of fire up to 250 rpm, and in the second half of the 19th century gave genuinely solid combat service in the United States and Europe. Soon the Gatling was joined by the 1879 Gardner machine gun, another hand-cranked gun but one with a slighter faster rate of fire than the Gatling (around 370 rpm).

The Gardner and the Gatling and a handful of others took hand-cranked guns to the limits of their performance. It was Hiram Maxim who took the next step.

His 1883 Maxim gun had only a single barrel, but utilizing the force of recoil as an automatic reloading system, and feeding from a long belt of ammunition, the gun could achieve up to 500 rpm. The military implications of the Maxim were enormous—a small team of three or four people (although only one gunner) could generate firepower equivalent to 30 rifle-armed infantrymen. The years between Maxim's invention and the onset of WWI saw the heavy machine gun type perfected in several influential firearms designs, including improved Maxims, the British .303 Vickers, and the Browning M1917, and a new-generation of gas-operated machine guns such as the Hotchkiss Mle 1914.

The use of machine guns during WWI proved their efficiency—a huge percentage of the British Army's 59,000 casualties on the first day of the Battle of the Somme in 1916 were due to the hammering of Maxims.

WWI also saw the expansion of the machine gun into different roles and formats. In an attempt to improve the portability of automatic firepower, a new class of weapon termed the light machine gun (LMG) was introduced, these being machine guns that could be easily transported around the battlefield, usually by two-man teams, and so provide a transferable base of suppressive fire.

In addition to LMGs, submachine guns also made their inaugural appearance in WWI. Led by the Italian Vilar-Perosa and the German Bergmann MP18, these guns transferred full-auto fire into a pistol-caliber weaponry. The choice of ammunition meant that the submachine gun was an intrinsically short-range weapon, but it was ideal for close-quarters trench conditions.

By the outbreak of WWII, world infantry forces had integrated machine guns into the heart of their tactics. Heavy machine guns like the M2HB handled long-range suppressive fire, and were also adapted to vehicle mounts and as anti-aircraft weapons.

Medium machine guns—crew-served guns of calibers below .50 in, such as the M1917, which could be fired from a carriage or tripod—were used in general support-fire roles. LMGs such as the British Bren or the Japanese Type 96 gave tactical fire at a maneuver level. The submachine guns provided automatic fire across ranges of around 150 yards (137 m), their high rate of fire compensating for other soldiers' restrictive rate of rifle fire.

Another type also emerged—the General Purpose Machine Gun (GPMG). This was a manportable machine gun that could suit both light roles and, with the correct mount, sustained-fire medium roles suited to heavier weapons. The Germans, in particular, mastered this format in the superb MG34 and MG42 weapons, both of which imposed heavy Allied losses on all fronts of the war.

Following WWII, and running forward to the present day, the composition of full-auto firearms has changed little. The most significant shift is that by the 1960s submachine guns had become increasingly relegated to Special Forces and security use, as full-auto assault rifles took over the role of standard infantry weapons.

All the other types have persisted and have familiar tactical remits. In the US forces, for example, the M249 Squad Automatic Weapon (SAW, based on the FN Minimi) occupies the light role, the M240 (derived from the FN MAG) and the M60 take the general-purpose tasks, while the M2HB takes the heavy-duty firepower. Properly distributed throughout a military force, machine guns remain the major force in light infantry tactics.

MACHINE GUNS & SUBMACHINE GUNS

EARLY BATTERY & MACHINE GUNS

The first machine guns, developed in Europe and the United States in the 1850s and 1860s, were mechanical weapons—they were powered by the operator, typically via a hand-turned crank. Numerous designs emerged, some more effective than others. The French army's 25-barrel Montigny Mitrailleuse, for example, could deliver about 250 rpm of fire. It was Richard Gatling's infamous Gatling Gun, however, that defined machine guns as tactically effective weapons and spurred other hand-cranked designs, including the Lowell gun, famed for having fired 50,000 rounds in two days in 1875. Yet it was Hiram Maxim who created the first true machine gun, the gun's cycle powered by the forces of recoil generated on firing.

"Ladder" type rear sight

Ejection port

Water coolant jacket

Trigger

Elevation/traverse controls

Elevation adjustment

MAXIM EARLY PATTERN MACHINE GUN

DATE	1885
ORIGIN	Germany/UK
WEIGHT	40 LB (18 KG)
BARREL	28 IN (72 CM)
CALIBER	.45 IN

Hiram Maxim demonstrated his first machine gun by 1884. At first, orders were hampered by the Maxim's clouds of black-powder smoke, but once it was allied to smokeless powders it became a truly significant battlefield weapon.

COLT-BROWNING M1895 "POTATO DIGGER"

DATE	1895
ORIGIN	US
WEIGHT	40 LB (18 KG)
BARREL	28 IN (71 CM)
CALIBER	.30–40 KRAG

The Colt M1895 was the creation of John Browning, and was nicknamed the "Potato Digger" on account of its innovative mechanics. Gas tapped off from near the muzzle was used to drive an arm through a 170-degree action. Through a linkage the arm in turn powered the opening and closing of the breech.

Gas-powered driving arm

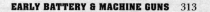

FULL VIEW

GATLING GUN

Invented by Dr. Richard Gatling and patented in 1862, the Gatling Gun was a revolution in infantry firepower. It was a rotary hand-cranked weapon, with 10 barrels arranged around a central axis. Turning the crank rotated the barrels, into which were fed cartridges from a cartridge container set above the gun. Each barrel fired and ejected its cartridge once during a full rotation of the barrel group, the advantage not only being the rate of fire but also that barrel overheating could be controlled.

The Gatling Gun averaged a practical rate of fire of around 280 rpm. It was soon combat proven, particularly in the Spanish-American War of 1898 and in various Anglo-Zulu battles in Africa. It was only rendered obsolete by the advent of Maxim's recoil-operated machine gun.

Barrels

Pivot for revolving mechanism

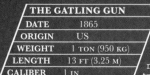

THE GATLING GUN	
DATE	1865
ORIGIN	US
WEIGHT	1 TON (950 KG)
LENGTH	13 FT (3.25 M)
CALIBER	1 IN

Early versions of the Gatling Gun were mounted on carriages, just like conventional field guns. It was not until lighter versions could be mounted on tripods that their true potential could be realized.

Shackle for attaching rope, to help move gun over difficult terrain

FIRING ABOUT 400 ROUNDS A MINUTE, IT WAS DEVASTATINGLY EFFECTIVE.

ZULU WAR
British soldiers crew a Gatling Gun during the 1879 Zulu War. The gun increased the Europeans' advantage against natives in colonial wars.

Elevating gear

Trail stabilized gun and allowed it to be towed

RECOIL-OPERATED MACHINE GUNS

By the beginning of WWI, a variety of different mechanisms were powering the world's machine guns, with two types dominant—recoil operation and gas operation. The former was perfected in types such as the British Vickers and the US Browning, and in the updated versions of the Maxim gun. These weapons offered firepower on a truly industrial scale and with impressive reliability. During one trial of the Browning

M1917, a single gun fired 40,000 rounds and suffered only two jams, both the fault of the ammunition. Development from 1918–45 saw many machine guns adopt air cooling, and superb general-purpose machine guns such as the German MG42 gave enormous manportable firepower for both attack and defense.

Fore sight

Ammunition belt feedway

Rear sight

Water jacket

Pistol grip

FULL VIEW

BROWNING M1917	
DATE	1912
ORIGIN	US
WEIGHT	24 IN (61 CM)
LENGTH	38½ IN (58 CM)
CALIBER	.30-06 IN

John Browning came up with a simpler method of locking breech-block and barrel than Maxim had used. His new gun was adopted by the US Army as the M1917 and soon became the air-cooled M1919. It remained in service in that form until the 1960s.

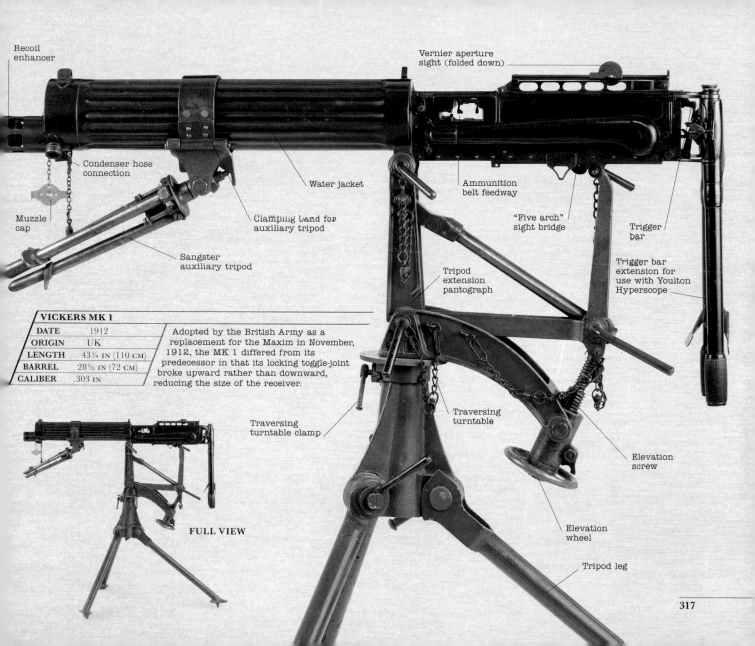

Recoil
enhancer

Vernier aperture
sight (folded down)

Condenser hose
connection

Water jacket

Ammunition
belt feedway

Muzzle
cap

Clamping band for
auxiliary tripod

"Five arch"
sight bridge

Trigger
bar

Sangster
auxiliary tripod

Tripod
extension
pantograph

Trigger bar
extension for
use with Youlton
Hyperscope

VICKERS MK 1	
DATE	1912
ORIGIN	UK
LENGTH	43¼ in (110 cm)
BARREL	28½ in (72 cm)
CALIBER	.303 in

Adopted by the British Army as a
replacement for the Maxim in November,
1912, the MK 1 differed from its
predecessor in that its locking toggle-joint
broke upward rather than downward,
reducing the size of the receiver.

Traversing
turntable clamp

Traversing
turntable

Elevation
screw

FULL VIEW

Elevation
wheel

Tripod leg

AN EXPERT MG42 TEAM COULD CHANGE BARRELS IN AROUND FIVE SECONDS, GIVING ONLY A TINY WINDOW OF OPPORTUNITY FOR ENEMY ATTACKERS.

Flash hider

Belt feed mechanism

Triggers

Barrel-change handle

Firing lever

Heavy barrel

Amunition box

Tripod mount

.5/12.7 MM M2
Developed for the M2 machine gun and adopted as a rifle round, the M2 has a 710-grain (46 g) bullet and a muzzle velocity of 2,800 fps.

BROWNING M2 HB		The US Army was pleased with Browning's
DATE	1936
ORIGIN	US
LENGTH	64½ IN (164 CM)
BARREL	45 IN (114 CM)
CALIBER	.5 IN (12.7 MM)

The US Army was pleased with Browning's M1917, but wanted a heavier weapon too, and Browning obliged with the water-cooled M1921. Like the rifle-caliber gun, its water jacket was later removed, and it meta-morphosed into the M2.

Ventilated
barrel
shroud

21 in
(53.3 cm)
barrel

Recoil
transmission
bar

Pistol
grip

Recoil-actuated
automatic
traverse
mechanism

Bracing bar

Pad for ease
of carrying

7.92 mm x 57 MAUSER
The cartridge was loaded with a
steel-jacketed 177-grain (11.5 g)
boat-tailed bullet that left the
muzzle at 2,745 fps.

MG42	
DATE	1943
ORIGIN	Germany
LENGTH	48 IN (122 CM)
BARREL	21 IN (53 CM)
CALIBER	7.92 MM

In 1934 the Maschinengewehr 34 was
officially adopted as the MG08's
replacement. It was light, yet robust
enough to deliver sustained fire at 900
rpm, but it was expensive to produce,
and was superseded by the MG42.

FULL VIEW

GAS-OPERATED MACHINE GUNS

Gas-operated machine guns evolved in the 1880s and '90s, the first claim to a working design being the Colt-Browning "Potato Digger" of 1890. In 1893, Austrian cavalryman Baron Odkolek von Augezd designed a more sophisticated weapon, sold it to the French Hotchkiss company, and in turn this became the hugely successful Hotchkiss machine gun. Since then gas-operated systems have proliferated and are one of the major systems of machine gun. Gas-operation is reliable and guns using the system tend to be light and easily controlled (the gas piston and springs inside a gas-operated gun absorb much of the recoil). For these reasons many light and medium machine guns have been gas-operated.

Flash hider   Fore sight   Gas port

26.7 in (67.8 cm) barrel   Cooling fins   Ammunition belt feedway

ZB 53 (VZ/37 OR BESA)	
DATE	1937
ORIGIN	Czechoslovakia
WEIGHT	Not known
BARREL	26¾ IN (67.8 CM)
CALIBER	7.92 MM

Machine gun designer Vaclav Holek was one of the stars of the 1930s. He used similar locking methods on both the Bren gun and the ZB 53. The latter was known as the VZ/37 by the Czechs and Besa by the British, who used it in their tanks.

HOTCHKISS MLE 1914

DATE	1914
ORIGIN	France
LENGTH	50 IN (127 CM)
BARREL	30½ IN (77 CM)
CALIBER	8 MM Lebel

The original design Baron von Augezd sold to Hotchkiss in 1893 was robust and simple. Its major weakness was a tendency to overheat. Between 1897 and 1914, it underwent a series of modifications aimed at correcting this fault, and also to make it cheaper to produce and to improve its feed mechanism, which employed metallic strips holding 24 rounds.

Gas cylinder

Cooling fins

Rear sight

Ammunition strip feedway

Optical sight

Elevation gear

Shoulder brace

Trigger

Steadying grip

Pistol grip

Elevation wheel

Traversing turntable

FULL VIEW

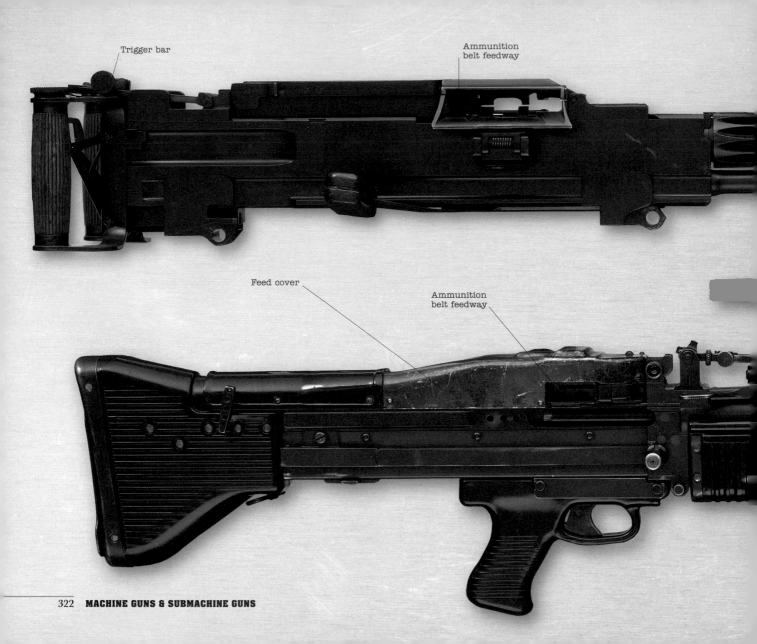

Trigger bar

Ammunition
belt feedway

Feed cover

Ammunition
belt feedway

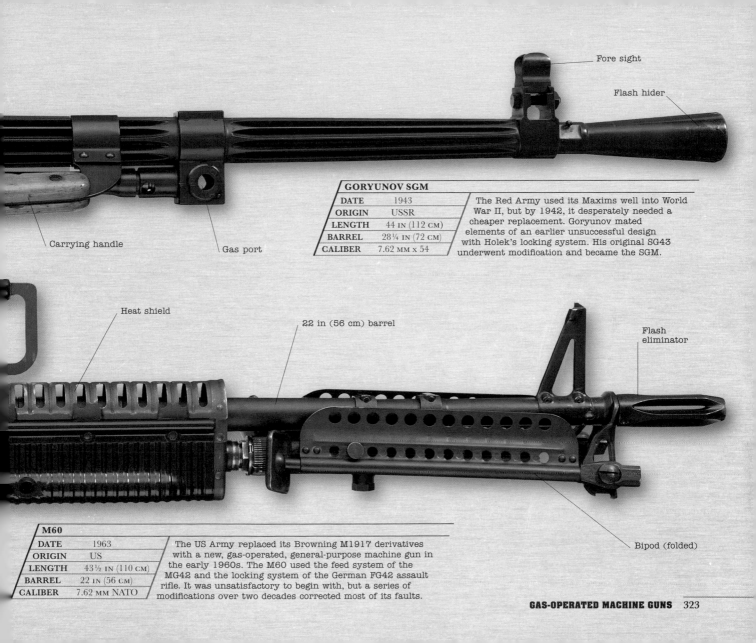

Fore sight

Flash hider

Carrying handle

Gas port

GORYUNOV SGM

DATE	1943
ORIGIN	USSR
LENGTH	44 IN (112 CM)
BARREL	28¼ IN (72 CM)
CALIBER	7.62 MM x 54

The Red Army used its Maxims well into World War II, but by 1942, it desperately needed a cheaper replacement. Goryunov mated elements of an earlier unsuccessful design with Holek's locking system. His original SG43 underwent modification and became the SGM.

Heat shield

22 in (56 cm) barrel

Flash eliminator

Bipod (folded)

M60

DATE	1963
ORIGIN	US
LENGTH	43½ IN (110 CM)
BARREL	22 IN (56 CM)
CALIBER	7.62 MM NATO

The US Army replaced its Browning M1917 derivatives with a new, gas-operated, general-purpose machine gun in the early 1960s. The M60 used the feed system of the MG42 and the locking system of the German FG42 assault rifle. It was unsatisfactory to begin with, but a series of modifications over two decades corrected most of its faults.

THE IMPACTS FROM A TRIPOD-MOUNTED 7.62 MM MACHINE GUN WILL CREATE A LETHAL "BEATEN ZONE" OUT BEYOND 2,000 YARDS.

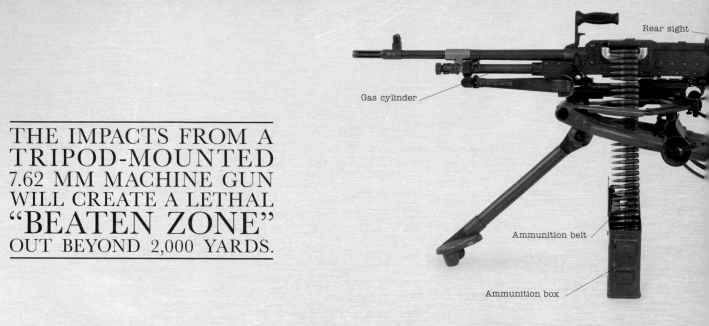

Rear sight

Gas cylinder

Ammunition belt

Ammunition box

Barrel can be changed quickly

MG43	
DATE	2001
ORIGIN	Germany
WEIGHT	19 LB (8.5 KG)
BARREL	19 IN (48 CM)
CALIBER	5.56 MM

The MG43 is light enough to be handled in the light machine gun (LMG) role and rugged enough to function as a sustained-fire weapon. The barrel can be changed in seconds, its handle folding to lie along the receiver just in front of the cocking handle.

FN MAG (GPMG)

DATE	1958
ORIGIN	Belgium
LENGTH	40½ in (104 cm)
BARREL	21½ in (55 cm)
CALIBER	7.62 mm NATO

The MAG (Mitrailleuse à Gaz), produced by FN, used a modified form of the locking system developed by John Browning for his Automatic Rifle; this was mated to the feed mechanism of the MG42. The gun was adopted by the British Army as the General-Purpose Machine Gun.

SUSAT sight with four-power magnification and low-light capability

FULL VIEW

Picatinny rail accepts standard sighting units

Barrel handle attachment point

Barrel locking catch

HK MG 43   Kal. 5.56mm x 45

AC   96-000015

F

S

Bipod folded beneath gas tube

Trigger

STEYR-MANNLICHER

Steyr-Mannlicher was born in the Austrian town of Steyr in 1853, when Joseph Werndl took over his father's gunmaking factory. By 1890 the company, now named Österreichische Waffenfabriks-Gesselschaft (OWG), was producing approximately 11,000 rifles every week. A dip in commercial fortunes in the early 20th century was remedied by the mobilization for war in 1913–14, and in total OWG made over 10 million arms between 1914 and 1918. The tough inter-war years brought structural changes, first with the creation of Steyr-Werke AG in 1922 then an amalgamation into Steyr-Daimler-Puch in 1934. WWII galavanized production again, and since 1950 Steyr-Mannlicher GmbH, as it became in 1963, has returned to being a world force in firearms manufacture, producing submachine guns, assault rifles (the excellent Steyr AUG), sniper rifles and sport guns.

STEYR FACTORY
A large part of the gunmaking process is still done by hand at Steyr's Austrian factory.

Bipod

Front grip

STEYR AUG LMG	
DATE	1980
ORIGIN	Austria
WEIGHT	10¾ LB (4.9 KG)
BARREL	25½ IN (62 CM)
CALIBER	5.56 x 45 MM

By fitting a bipod and a heavy barrel Steyr produced a light machine gun from its AUG assault rifle. It can be fitted either with the AUG's standard optical sight/carrying handle combination or without the handle to allow fitting of a different sight on a rail.

Ejector port

Flash hider

Magazine in
pistol grip

STEYR SPP

DATE	1993
ORIGIN	Austria
WEIGHT	3 LB (1.3 KG)
BARREL	5 IN (13 CM)
CALIBER	9 MM

The SPP—Special Purpose Pistol—is a pistol version of
Steyr's TMP submachine gun. Working on a delayed
blowback principle, the gun is semi-auto only and can take
either 15- or 30-round magazines of 9 mm Parabellum
ammunition. The whole gun is very compact, with a total
length of a fraction over 11 in (28 cm).

Telescoping
stock

Ejector port

Sling

Magazine

Magazine catch

See-through
plastic magazine

STEYR MPI 81

DATE	1990s
ORIGIN	Austria
WEIGHT	6¾ LB (3 KG)
BARREL	10¼ IN (26 CM)
CALIBER	9 MM

The MPi 81 is essentially an MPi 69 with
a conventional cocking handle. Both guns
are 9 mm blowback weapons with fire
selection via trigger pressure—light
pressure fires single shots while heavy
pressure produces automatic fire.

LIGHT MACHINE GUNS 1900-1945

Many of the early machine guns were good performers from static positions, but their excessive weight prevented their use in mobile tactics. The light machine gun (LMG) was designed to give assault troops portable heavy firepower, the machine gunner providing a moveable base of fire to other infantry during maneuvers. The first LMG was the Danish 8 mm Madsen, at 20 lb (9 kg) convenient enough to take forward in an assault. By 1911 the LMG was also faithfully realized in the superb .303 Lewis gun, and many other designs emerged between the two world wars. Some LMGs, such as the Bren, dealt with the problem of barrel overheating by utilizing quick-change barrels, while others used fixed barrels for simplicity.

Wooden butt stock

FULL VIEW

Rear sight

Gunner's left hand grips stock here

Trigger

Ejector port

Cocking handle

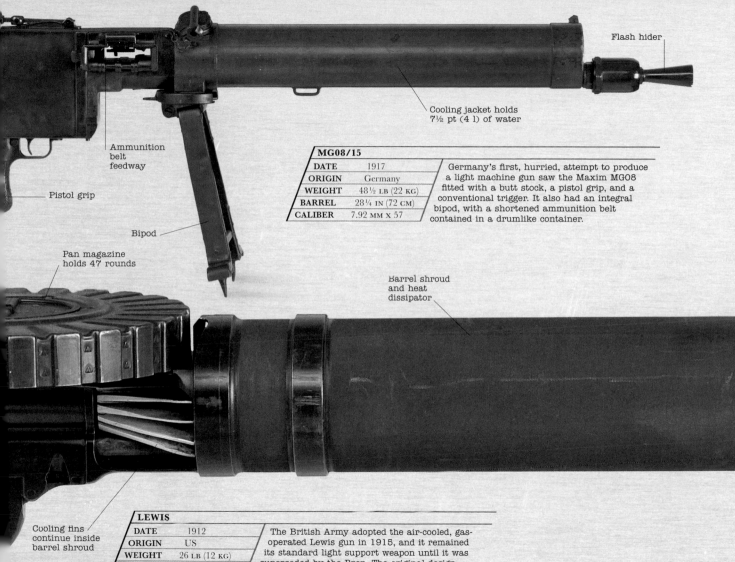

Flash hider

Cooling jacket holds
7½ pt (4 l) of water

Ammunition
belt
feedway

Pistol grip

Bipod

Pan magazine
holds 47 rounds

Barrel shroud
and heat
dissipator

Cooling fins
continue inside
barrel shroud

MG08/15

DATE	1917
ORIGIN	Germany
WEIGHT	48½ LB (22 KG)
BARREL	28¼ IN (72 CM)
CALIBER	7.92 MM X 57

Germany's first, hurried, attempt to produce a light machine gun saw the Maxim MG08 fitted with a butt stock, a pistol grip, and a conventional trigger. It also had an integral bipod, with a shortened ammunition belt contained in a drumlike container.

LEWIS

DATE	1912
ORIGIN	US
WEIGHT	26 LB (12 KG)
BARREL	26¼ IN (66.5 CM)
CALIBER	.303 IN

The British Army adopted the air-cooled, gas-operated Lewis gun in 1915, and it remained its standard light support weapon until it was superseded by the Bren. The original design was the work of Samuel MacLean, but it was modified by Colonel Isaac Lewis of the US Army.

Top-mounted
magazine

Laminated wooden
butt stock

Recoil spring
housing

Rear sight

Ejection port

Rate-of-fire
selector and
safety catch

Single shot
trigger

Automatic
fire trigger

Wooden fore-end

Barrel

Flash hider

Ammunition
belt feedway

Ejector

Gas tube

Bipod

DEGTYAREV RP46

DATE	1946
ORIGIN	USSR
WEIGHT	28¾ LB (13 KG)
BARREL	23¾ IN (60.5 CM)
CALIBER	7.62 MM x 54 R

The Red Army adopted the Degtyarev RP in 1928. It was modified in 1945, and the following year, it received a heavier barrel and was adapted to take belts as well as drum magazines. It was still not entirely satisfactory, however, and was soon replaced by the RPD.

Barrel

Bipod

Gas cylinder

FULL VIEW

CHÂTELLERAULT MODÈLE 1924/29

DATE	1929
ORIGIN	France
WEIGHT	20¼ LB (9 KG)
BARREL	19¾ IN (50 CM)
CALIBER	7.5 x 54 MM

The Mle 1924 was designed as a light machine gun replacement for the terrible WWI-era Chauchat, but was let down by poor ammunition. The cartridge was redesigned along with parts of the gun to produce the Mle 1924/29, which served through WWII and into the 1950s.

LIGHT MACHINE GUNS 1945-

Since 1945 light machine guns (LMGs) have retained, if not increased, their influence within small-unit tactical thinking. Many light machine guns—such as the RPK74 and L86A1—are little more than standard infantry rifles with extended barrels and, sometimes, an increased ammunition capacity. These guns typically have fixed barrels, meaning that they are not suited to sustained-fire modes, but they offer extended range over the squad's rifles. However, many armies have turned to belt-fed light machine guns to soup up squad firepower, the FN Minimi and its variants being a particular favorite in this regard. These are capable of delivering sustained fire at 750 rpm and beyond, and have a quick-change barrel facility.

Cocking handle

STANAG 30-round detachable magazine

Rear sight

Rate-of-fire selector and safety catch

FULL VIEW

Plastic
forestock

Barrel support

L86A1 LIGHT SUPPORT WEAPON

DATE	1986
ORIGIN	UK
WEIGHT	12 LB (5.4 KG)
BARREL	25 ½ IN (64.5 CM)
CALIBER	5.56 MM

The L86A1, which replaced the L484 Bren gun in the light support role, has a heavier and larger barrel than the L85A1, and a rear grip to aid sustained firing. There is no quick-change barrel, so the gun must be fired in short, controlled bursts to prevent overheating.

Cocking
handle

Carrying handle

Fore sight

Muzzle
compensator

Ejector port

FN MINIMI

DATE	1975
ORIGIN	Belgium
WEIGHT	15 LB (6.83 KG)
BARREL	18 ½ IN (46.5 CM)
CALIBER	5.56 MM x 45

FN's gas-operated, air-cooled Minimi accepts the NATO STANAG magazine or disintegrating-link belts, without modification. The Minimi was adopted by the US Army as its M249 Squad Automatic Weapon, and also by the British Army as the L108A1.

BREN GUN

The Bren Gun is a textbook lesson in superb gun design. This .303 in machine gun was produced from 1937, but its origin actually lay several years further back in the fine Czech 7.92 mm ZB30. During the 1930s the British commissioned the Ceskoslvenska Zbrojovka company to redesign the ZB30 as a .303 in weapon, with a view to replacing the British Army's venerable Lewis Guns.

The result, the ZB33, was accepted and was renamed the Bren Gun (the name derives from Brno, the Czech town where the ZB30 was designed and made, fused with Enfield, where British production began). The Bren was an infantryman's dream weapon. It was easy to operate and simple to strip down for cleaning. Properly maintained its gas-operated system rarely went wrong, and it was also extremely accurate. The Bren's virtues kept it in British Army service in variant forms until the 1970s, the last in the series being the 7.62 mm L4.

BREN	
DATE	1937
ORIGIN	Czechoslovakia
WEIGHT	22½ LB (10 KG)
BARREL	25 IN (63.5 CM)
CALIBER	.303 IN

The Bren gun was the British Army's principle light support weapon from its introduction until the 1970s. If it had a deficiency, it lay in its rimmed ammunition, not the gun itself.

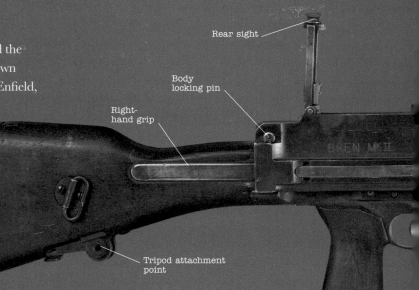

Rear sight

Body locking pin

Right-hand grip

Tripod attachment point

THE BREN WAS AN INFANTRYMAN'S DREAM WEAPON.

30-round detachable
box magazine

FULL VIEW

Carrying handle

Magazine
port cover

Gas cylinder

JUNGLE PATROL
With Bren gun at the ready, a
soldier of the New Zealand 22nd
Squadron Air Service, patrols a
river and surrounding swamps
in the Malayan jungle in 1957.

Rear sight

Skeleton light-alloy butt stock

Cocking handle

Optical sight

THE LIGHT MACHINE GUN, WITH ITS 500–1,000 RPM RATE OF FIRE, IS AT THE CENTER OF THE INFANTRY FIRE TEAM.

Fore sight

Barrel

FULL VIEW

Bipod folded
under gas
cylinder

NEGEV

DATE	1988
ORIGIN	Israel
WEIGHT	15¾ LB (7.2 KG)
BARREL	18 IN (46 CM)
CALIBER	5.56 MM

Israel Military Industries' Negev is one of the breed of
lightweight automatic weapons that has blurred the
distinction between LMG and General Purpose
Machine Gun (GPMG). Chambered for the SS109 NATO
round in 5.56 mm caliber, it can deliver automatic fire
at 700 or 900 rounds per minute (rpm).

Gas tube

Gas regulator   Folded bipod

RPK74

DATE	1976
ORIGIN	USSR
WEIGHT	11 LB (5 KG)
BARREL	23¼ IN (59 CM)
CALIBER	5.45 MM x 39

The RPK74 was developed from the successful
AKM assault rifle, and many parts are
interchangeable with those of other Kalashnikov
weapons. It entered service in the early 1960s,
and replaced the RPD as the standard light
machine gun of the Soviet infantry.

SUBMACHINE GUNS

Submachine guns (SMGs) were developed in the context of WWI, as armies sought to improve short-range infantry firepower for trench combat and patroling. The Bergmann Musquete, designed in 1916 but later christened the MP18, inaugurated the true submachine era. During WWII most armies had a portion of their infantry armed with cheap, effective submachine gun types. After 1945, the assault rifle undermined the rationale behind the submachine gun in military service (although Israel's Uzi resisted this change for some years) and today submachine guns tend to be consigned to Special Forces and police counter-terrorist units.

WITHIN A TRENCH OR BUILDING, THE SUBMACHINE GUN WAS DEVASTATING AGAINST GROUP TARGETS.

Magazine catch

Front sling attachment

Barrel shroud

VILLAR PEROSA

DATE	1920s
ORIGIN	Italy
WEIGHT	6¾ LB (3 KG)
BARREL	11 IN (28 CM)
CALIBER	9 MM Glisenti

The first SMG was manufactured in 1915 as a double gun, paired in a simple mounting and fitted with spade grips, a single trigger bar, and a bipod. Later, these were revamped as carbines, with butt stocks and conventional triggers.

Noise/flash suppressor

Fore grip insulated against heat

FULL VIEW

STEN MARK 2 (SILENCED)

DATE	1941
ORIGIN	UK
WEIGHT	7½ LB (3.4 KG)
BARREL	35¾ IN (91 CM)
CALIBER	9 MM Parabellum

The Sten was very cheap to buy, and naturally had its faults, but it was an effective way of putting devastating short-range firepower into the hands of inexperienced combatants. This version had an integrated noise- and flash-suppressor.

Fore sight

Cocking handle

Skeleton butt stock (folded)

Pistol grip

MP40

DATE	1940
ORIGIN	Germany
WEIGHT	9 LB (4 KG)
BARREL	9¾ IN (25 CM)
CALIBER	9 MM Parabellum

In 1938, the German Army adopted a new, handier design for a SMG, but it was still uneconomical to produce. Two years later, it was re-engineered to replace expensive machining with pressed and welded construction.

32-round magazine

Cocking sleeve

Burst-fire trigger

Single-shot trigger

Wooden butt stock

Rear sight

Fixed skeleton butt

Pressed and stamped steel body

PPSH41

As the Germans experienced with the MP38, so the Russians acknowledged that their PPD40 submachine gun was not ideally suited to the conditions of fast production during the early years of WWII. A new design program resulted in the 7.62 mm PPSh41, a crude weapon produced from stamped steel, welding, and pinning, and which used Mosin-Nagant rifle barrels that were cut in half.

The barrel jacket ran ahead of the barrel itself and so acted as a rudimentary muzzle brake to control muzzle climb when firing fully automatic. The operating system was simple blowback, and the gun had a 900 rpm rate of fire—extremely fast when compared to the 500–700 rpm of the MP38/40. To cope with its ammunition demand, the PPSh41 had a 71-round drum magazine, although later in the war 35-round box magazines were also

introduced. Around five million PPSh41s were produced during WWII, and they added considerable firepower to Russian infantry formations, particularly in the close-range fighting preferred by Soviet tacticians.

FULL VIEW

BY SPRING 1942, PPSH FACTORIES WERE PRODUCING 3,000 UNITS PER DAY.

PPSH41	
DATE	1944
ORIGIN	USSR
WEIGHT	7¾ LB (3.5 KG)
BARREL	10½ IN (27 CM)
CALIBER	7.62 MM SOVIET

Shpagin's "Peh-Peh-Sheh," reliable and simple both to manufacture and to maintain, became the mainstay of the Red Army after it stopped the German advance into the Soviet Union. At least five million had been produced by 1945.

Body locking pin

Magazine port

Rate-of-fire selector

RED ARMY'S MACHINE GUN
A Red Army soldier, armed with a PPSh41, guards German prisoners during World War II.

THE M3 EARNED ITS
NICKNAME BECAUSE OF ITS
CLOSE RESEMBLANCE
TO AUTOMOTIVE
GREASE GUNS OF THE PERIOD.

Peforated
barrel shroud

Cocking-handle cover
acts as safety catch

Cocking handle

Magazine port   Graduated rear sight

32-round "snail"
drum magazine

BERGMANN MP18/I

DATE	1918
ORIGIN	US
WEIGHT	11½ LB (5.25 KG)
BARREL	7¾ IN (19.6 CM)
CALIBER	9 MM Parabellum

The Hugo Schmeisser-designed MP18/I can lay claim to being the first effective submachine gun. It was produced in response to a request from the German Army's storm troopers for a handier weapon than the heavy, cut-down MG08/15s they were using when assaulting defended positions.

Barrel locking nut

Flash suppressor

M3/M3A1 ("GREASE GUN")

DATE	1940s
ORIGIN	US
WEIGHT	8 LB (3.5 KG)
BARREL	8 IN (20 CM)
CALIBER	.45 IN ACP

Designed specifically as a low-cost substitute for the Thompson submachine gun, the Grease Gun entered service in December 1942. It was cheap to produce and simple to strip, clean, and maintain. It fired the same heavy round as the Colt automatic pistol.

FULL VIEW

Pivoting magazine
housing doubles as fore grip

32-round detachable
box magazine

Rear
pistol
grip

MAT 49		
DATE	1950s	
ORIGIN	France	
WEIGHT	7¾ LB (3.5 KG)	
BARREL	9 IN (29 CM)	
CALIBER	9 MM	

The MAT 49's distinctive feature is its
pivoting magazine housing; as well as making
the weapon easier to conceal, it's a very
positive safety device. The gun saw wide-
spread combat use during the Indo-China and
Algeria wars, as well as the 1956 Suez Crisis.

MANY SUBMACHINE GUNS ARE INACCURATE —THEY ARE OFTEN AIMED BY WATCHING THE BULLETS IMPACT AND THEN GUIDING THESE ONTO THE TARGET.

FULL VIEW

Optical sight

Transparent plastic
50-round detachable
box magazine

7x28

FN P90

DATE	1990s
ORIGIN	Belgium
WEIGHT	6 LB (2.7 KG)
BARREL	11¾ IN (30 CM)
CALIBER	5.7 MM

The P90 uses a "miniature" caliber round designed with damage limitation in mind. All its non-mechanical components are molded from plastic, and its unique horizontal ammunition feed mechanism allows the magazine to be incorporated into the receiver.

Fabrique Nationale Herstal BELGIUM

Trigger

AL CAPONE

Alphonse (Al) "Scarface" Capone (1899–1947) is the defining American gangster. He joined Johnny Torrio's criminal fraternity in New York at the age of 14, and later became his partner in bootlegging and brothel operations in Chicago.

Torrio retired in 1925, and Capone stood up as the new head of the Chicago crime family. Capone was never shy about using firepower. The infamous Valentine's Day massacre on February 14, 1929, in which seven members of the "Bugs" Moran gang died in a hail of Thompson SMG and shotgun fire, was sanctioned and partly organized by Capone. Capone, along with gangsters such as John Dillinger and "Baby Face" Nelson, is forever associated with the Thompson M1921. Thompsons came into their own for the high-risk raid, used against massed police o for targets situated in automobiles. Several of Capone's associates who lived by the Thompson died by it, but Capone was finally brought down in 1931 on charges of income tax evasion.

Fore sight

FULL VIEW

Forward pistol grip

AMERICA'S MOST WANTED
Despite his violent tendencies and the many rival gangsters who were either killed by him, or put to death on his orders, Al Capone was ultimately convicted in 1931 on the relatively minor charge of income tax evasion.

THOMPSON M1921	
DATE	1921
ORIGIN	US
WEIGHT	10¾ LB (4.9 KG)
BARREL	10½ IN (26.7 CM)
CALIBER	.45 ACP

By 1919, John Tagliaferro Thompson had produced an early version of what would be widely known as the Tommy Gun. The M1921 was the first to come to the market, and it quickly became a firm favorite among America's criminal fraternity.

Receiver machined from solid steel

MODEL OF 1921
NO. 487

THOMPSON SUBMACHINE GUN,
CALIBRE 45 AUTOMATIC COLT CARTRIDGE
MANUFACTURED BY
COLT'S PATENT FIRE ARMS MFG CO.
HARTFORD, CONN., U.S.A.

FIRE

Advanced
collimator
sight

Optional noise/
flash suppressor

FULL VIEW

Retractable
buttstock

Mounting rail

EOTech

Ambidextrous
controls

Magazine

Cocking handle

Skeleton stock both
retracts and hinges to
lie over the receiver

Wrist strap

Combined pistol
grip and magazine
housing

INGRAM MAC-10

DATE	1970s
ORIGIN	US
WEIGHT	7 ½ LB (3.4 KG)
BARREL	5¾ IN (14.5 CM)
CALIBER	9 MM Parabellum

A telescoping bolt and a magazine incorporated into the pistol grip allowed Ingram to reduce the overall size of the MAC-10 to that of an automatic pistol. With a cyclical rate of fire of well over a thousand rounds per minute, it can empty its 32-round magazine in little more than a second.

SOME MAC-10s ARE STILL USED BY THE US ARMY'S SPECIAL UNIT, DELTA FORCE.

Folding
vertical
foregrip

HECKLER & KOCH MP7

DATE	2001
ORIGIN	Germany
WEIGHT	4 LB (1.8 KG)
BARREL	7 IN (18 CM)
CALIBER	4.6 x 30 MM

The MP7 is a personal defense weapon designed to provide greater penetration against body armor than conventional submachine guns offer. It uses the same action as the H&K G36, but fires a high-velocity 4.6 x 30 mm round.

Fore sight
in protective
shroud

Cocking handle

Barrel-locking nut

Replaceable
barrel

Molded-plastic
fore grip

Forward
sling swivel

Cocking
handle

Replaceable
barrel

Safety catch/rate-
of-fire selector

Retractable
skeleton stock

Pistol grip

20-round
detachable
box magazine

VZ/68 SKORPION MOD 83	
DATE	1960s
ORIGIN	Czechoslovakia
WEIGHT	3 LB (1.3 KG)
BARREL	4½ IN (11.5 CM)
CALIBER	9 MM Parabellum

The Skorpion was designed as a close-protection
weapon that could be carried in a holster and
used with one hand. Its unlocked blowback action
and lightweight moving parts would give a very
high rate of fire, but a clever counterweight
mechanism in the butt reduces the rate.

Pressed-steel receiver

Rear sight in
protective shroud

Rate-of-fire
selector

UZI	
DATE	1950s
ORIGIN	Israel
WEIGHT	8 LB (3.6 KG)
BARREL	10¼ IN (26 CM)
CALIBER	9 MM Parabellum

The secret of the Uzi's legendary stability lies
in its bolt being wrapped around its barrel;
this brings the center of gravity forward, and
helps to cure the tendency for the barrel to
rise during automatic fire. Heavy moving parts
keep its rate of fire to a manageable level.

FULL VIEW

32-round
detachable
box magazine

HECKLER & KOCH MP5

The MP5 has achieved superb international sales since it entered production in 1966, particularly among Special Forces and law-enforcement agencies. Its initial name was actually HK54, but the West German police and border guard relabeled it Maschinenpistole 5 (MP5) upon adoption.

The MP5 uses the same roller-delayed blowback mechanism found in the H&K G3 rifle, and also fires from a closed bolt. The latter feature makes the MP5 superbly accurate even when firing full auto; many submachine guns fire from an open bolt position, meaning the bolt must transfer its whole mass forward when the trigger is pulled, the shift in weight disrupting accuracy. MP5s have been produced in nearly 30 variants, including with a telescoping metal stock (MP5A3), a compact version (MP5K), and with an integral suppressor (MP5SD).

Cocking handle

GRENADE
The MP5 can fire a range of 40 mm grenades over distances of several hundred yards.

HECKLER & KOCH MP5	
DATE	1966
ORIGIN	Germany
WEIGHT	6¼ LB (2.8 KG)
BARREL	8¾ IN (22.5 CM)
CALIBER	9 MM

The MP5 is also available with a rigid plastic stock. The trigger group (this example has safe/single/three-round/full-auto options) is also from the HK33, but it can be exchanged for one of a different configuration. A version with an integral silencer is also available.

THE MP5 WAS USED BY THE SAS DURING THE 1980 IRANIAN EMBASSY SIEGE.

Rear sight

Butt locking pin

Magazine release catch

Rate-of-fire icons: single-shot, three round burst (above), and automatic (top)

NAVY SEALs
These US Navy SEALs are equipped with MP5N variants. They are standard MP5s with a fully ambidextrous Navy trigger group, a retractable stock, and a threaded barrel for mounting steel suppressors.

GLOSSARY

ACTION The method of loading and/or firing a gun.

AUTOMATIC A firearm that will continue to load and fire while the trigger is pressed.

BATTERY The state of a gun's action when it is ready to fire.

BENT A notch on the cock, hammer or striker in which the sear engages, to hold it off.

BELT FEED A way of supplying ammunition to the breech of an automatic weapon.

BLOWBACK A way of operating an automatic or semi-automatic weapon in which the breech is not locked, but held closed by a spring or by inertia.

BOLT The part of the weapon that closes and seals the breech. It may also load and extract cartridges and carry the firing pin.

BOLT ACTION A firearm relying on a turning bolt to lock its breech closed.

BORE The number of shot of a given size which can be cast from 1 lb of lead; the diameter of a barrel.

BOX-LOCK A flintlock in which the action is contained within a central box behind the breech.

BREECH The closed rear end of a gun's barrel.

BREECH-BLOCK Analogous to the bolt.

BULLET The projectile a weapon fires. It may be spherical, cylindro-conical (a cylinder with a cone-shaped point) or cylindro-ogival (a cylinder with a rounded point), or even hollow-pointed.

BULLPUP A rifle that has its mechanism set well back in the shoulder stock, allowing a normal barrel length in an abbreviated weapon.

BUTT The stock between shoulder and trigger; the part of a pistol held in the hand.

CALIBER The internal diameter of the barrel.

CARBINE A short-barreled rifle or musket.

CARTRIDGE CASE The container for the propellant, primer and projectile.

CHARGER A frame that holds cartridges, allowing them to be loaded into a magazine.

CLIP See charger.

CLOSED BOLT A configuration found in automatic and semi-automatic weapons in which battery is with the bolt in the closed position, with a cartridge chambered; see also open bolt.

COCK The clamp that holds the flint in a flintlock weapon; the act of pulling back a hammer, bolt or cock to ready a weapon for firing.

COMPENSATOR A device that reduces the muzzle's tendency to lift or swing.

CYCLE The series of operations necessary to fire a round and return the gun to battery.

CYCLIC RATE The notional rate of fire of an automatic weapon.

DELAYED BLOWBACK A type of blowback action in which the bolt is briefly delayed to allow chamber pressure to drop to a safe level.

DOUBLE-ACTION A pistol in which the act of pulling the trigger first cocks, then releases, the action.

EJECTOR A device that throws a spent cartridge case clear after it has been extracted from the chamber.

EXTRACTOR A device that grips the cartridge case and pulls it clear of the chamber.

FLASH ELIMINATOR An attachment at the muzzle that cools the propellant gas below its flash point.

GAS OPERATION A weapon in which the cycle is effected by the propellant gas.

GENERAL-PURPOSE MACHINE GUN (GPMG) A machine gun that can be used as a light machine gun or in the sustained-fire role.

GRIP SAFETY A device that keeps the weapon from being fired unless held correctly.

GROOVES The parallel spirals cut into the barrel that give spin to the bullet.

GUNPOWDER A mixture of saltpeter, charcoal, and sulfur.

HEAD The closed end of a cartridge case, where the primer is located.

HEAVY MACHINE GUN
A machine gun chambered for a round of larger-than-rifle caliber, usually 12.7 mm.

HINGED FRAME A pistol in which the barrel can be hinged down to expose the chamber or chambers.

HOLD-OPEN DEVICE A catch that holds the bolt back if there is no cartridge to be chambered; a catch that holds the slide of a self-loading pistol back so that the weapon may be dismantled.

HOLLOW-POINT A bullet with a chamber or a recess at its point, which causes it to expand or even fragment when it hits its target.

LANDS The inner surfaces of a barrel, between the grooves.

LIGHT MACHINE GUN (**LMG**) A machine gun, usually fitted with a bipod, chambered for rifle-caliber ammunition, but not capable of sustained fire.

LOCKED BREECH A weapon in which the breech-block is physically locked to the barrel during firing.

MACHINE GUN A weapon that uses gas or recoil to cycle its action and thus give continuous fire.

MACHINE-PISTOL See submachine gun.

MAGAZINE A holder for cartridges that delivers them, usually by means of spring pressure, to the action.

MEDIUM MACHINE GUN
A machine gun chambered for rifle-caliber ammunition, which is capable of sustained fire.

MUZZLE The open front end of the barrel.

MUZZLE BRAKE See compensator.

OPEN BOLT A weapon in which the bolt is held back until the trigger is pulled, allowing the chamber to cool; see also closed bolt.

PARABELLUM The 9 mm x 19 cartridge developed by Georg Luger for his self-loading pistol.

PRIMER
Fine gunpowder used to initiate the firing sequence; a percussion cap set into a cartridge case.

RECOIL The rearward movement of the barrel (or weapon) in reaction to the forward motion of the bullet.

RECOIL INTENSIFIER
A device attached to the muzzle that increases the recoil of a recoil-operated automatic weapon.

RECOIL OPERATION
A weapon in which the cycle is effected by the recoil of the barrel or breech-block.

REVOLVER A weapon in which the ammunition is carried in a rotating cylinder.

RIFLING The spiral grooves cut into the barrel that induce spin on the bullet.

RIMLESS A type of cartridge case that has a recessed groove, rather than a rim, around its head, to allow the extractor to grip it.

RIMMED A cartridge case with a rimmed head to allow the extractor to grip it.

SEAR Part of the firing mechanism that connects the trigger to the cock, hammer, or striker by engaging a bent in it.

SELECTIVE FIRE A weapon that can fire single rounds or automatically.

SELF-LOADING A weapon in which the act of firing a round recocks it, having chambered a fresh cartridge.

SILENCER A device at the muzzle that slows the propellant gas, by diverting it through baffles, and also slows the bullet to below the speed of sound.

SUBMACHINE GUN A hand-held automatic weapon firing pistol-caliber rounds.

TRIGGER The short lever that trips the sear out of the bent on the cock, hammer, etc. to initiate the firing sequence.

WINDAGE The adjustment of a sight to compensate for the effect of a cross-wind upon the bullet.

ZEROING Adjusting a weapon's sights so that the point of aim and the point of impact are the same.

INDEX

S

ACKNOWLEDGMENTS

Dorling Kindersley would like to thank Philip Abbott and Mark Murray-Flutter at the Royal Armouries for their assistance; Jane Parker for the index; Gary Ombler for photography; and Myriam Megharbi for picture research.

Picture Credits

The publisher would like to thank the following for their kind permission to reproduce their photographs:

(Key: a-above; b-below/bottom; c-center; l-left; r-right; t-top)

12-13 DK Images: The Board of Trustees of the Armouries. **13 Alamy Images:** Mary Evans Picture Library (r). **18-19 DK Images:** The Board of Trustees of the Armouries. **19 Mary Evans Picture Library:** Bruce Castle Museum (r). **24-25 DK Images:** By kind permission of the Trustees of the Wallace Collection. **26-27 DK Images:** The Board of Trustees of the Armouries. **28-29 DK Images:** The Board of Trustees of the Armouries (c). **29 Corbis:** Bettmann (r). **34 Corbis:** Andrew Lichtenstein / Sygma (bl). **DK Images:** The Board of Trustees of the Armouries (br). **35 DK Images:** The Board of Trustees of the Armouries. **44-45 DK Images:** The Board of Trustees of the Armouries. **45 The Bridgeman Art Library:** Private Collection / Peter Newark Western Americana (r). **50-51 DK Images:** The Board of Trustees of the Armouries. **51 National Archives and Records Administration, USA:** (r) (photo no. 111-SC-94129). **62 DK Images:** The Board of Trustees of the Armouries (br). **Getty Images:** Time &

Life Pictures (bl). **63 DK Images:** The Board of Trustees of the Armouries. **68-69 DK Images:** The Board of Trustees of the Armouries. **69 The Kobal Collection:** Columbia (r). **78 Corbis:** Gianni Giansanti / Sygma (bl). **DK Images:** The Board of Trustees of the Armouries (br). **79 DK Images:** The Board of Trustees of the Armouries. **86-87 DK Images:** The Board of Trustees of the Armouries. **87 Getty Images:** Scott Olson / Staff (r). **92-93 DK Images:** The Board of Trustees of the Armouries. **93 The Kobal Collection:** Warner Bros (r). **98-99 DK Images:** The Board of Trustees of the Armouries. **99 Getty Images:** Hulton Archive (r). **104-105 DK Images:** The Board of Trustees of the Armouries (c). **105 The Kobal Collection:** Danjaq / Eon / UA (r). **120-121 DK Images:** The Board of Trustees of the Armouries. **121 The Bridgeman Art Library:** Private Collection / The Stapleton Collection. **122-123 DK Images:** The Board of Trustees of the Armouries. **124-125 DK Images:** The Board of Trustees of the Armouries. **132-133 DK Images:** The Board of Trustees of the Armouries. **133 Schoharie County Historical Society, Schoharie, NY:** (r). **142-143 DK Images:** The Board of Trustees of the Armouries. **143 Getty Images:** Time & Life Pictures. **144-145 DK Images:** By kind permission of the Trustees of the Wallace Collection (c) (b). **145 DK Images:** By kind permission of the Trustees of the Wallace Collection (t). **146-147 DK Images:** The Board of Trustees of the Armouries. **148-149 The Board of Trustees of the Armouries:** (b). **DK Images:** The Board of Trustees of the Armouries (t).

149 DK Images: The Board of Trustees of the Armouries (cra). **150-151 The Board of Trustees of the Armouries:** (b). **DK Images:** The Board of Trustees of the Armouries (t). **152-153 DK Images:** The Board of Trustees of the Armouries. **153 The Bridgeman Art Library:** Private Collection / Topham Picturepoint (r). **160-161 DK Images:** The Board of Trustees of the Armouries. **161 Getty Images:** Hulton Archive (r). **168-169 DK Images:** The Board of Trustees of the Armouries. **169 akg-images:** (r). **174 Corbis:** Bettmann (bl). **174-175 DK Images:** The Board of Trustees of the Armouries. **175 DK Images:** The Board of Trustees of the Armouries (t) (b). **184-185 DK Images:** The Board of Trustees of the Armouries. **185 Corbis:** Bettmann (r). **194-195 DK Images:** The Board of Trustees of the Armouries. **195 TRH Pictures:** (r). **204-205 DK Images:** Imperial War Museum, London. **205 akg-images:** Tri Star Pictures / Alex Bailey (r). **214-215 DK Images:** The Board of Trustees of the Armouries (c). **215 Getty Images:** Hulton Archive (r). **220-221 DK Images:** The Board of Trustees of the Armouries. **221 TRH Pictures:** (r). **224-225 DK Images:** The Board of Trustees of the Armouries. **225 Getty Images:** Scott Peterson (r). **242-243 DK Images:** By kind permission of the Trustees of the Wallace Collection (b). **243 Getty Images:** Time Life Pictures / Stringer (r). **260 Holland & Holland Limited:** (bl). **260-261 DK Images:** The Board of Trustees of the Armouries (c) (b). **261 DK Images:** The Board of Trustees of the Armouries (t). **278-279 DK**

Images: The Board of Trustees of the Armouries. **279 Alamy Images:** Les Gibbon (r). **290 DK Images:** The Board of Trustees of the Armouries (br). **Empics Ltd:** (bl). **291 DK Images:** The Board of Trustees of the Armouries (tl); H. Keith Melton Collection (br). **296 DK Images:** The Board of Trustees of the Armouries (bl). **296-297 DK Images:** The Board of Trustees of the Armouries (t). **297 DK Images:** H. Keith Melton Collection (b) (crb). **304 DK Images:** H. Keith Melton Collection (cr) (tr). **305 DK Images:** H. Keith Melton Collection (c). **314-315 DK Images:** Museum of Artillery, The Rotunda, Woolwich, London. **315 The Art Archive:** (b). **326 Steyr Mannlicher GmbH & Co KG:** (tr). **326-327 DK Images:** The Board of Trustees of the Armouries (cb). **327 DK Images:** The Board of Trustees of the Armouries (tl) (cr). **334-335 DK Images:** The Board of Trustees of the Armouries. **335 Getty Images:** Horace Abrahams / Stringer (r). **340-341 DK Images:** The Board of Trustees of the Armouries. **341 TRH Pictures. 346-347 DK Images:** The Board of Trustees of the Armouries (b). **347 Corbis:** Bettmann (r). **352-353 DK Images:** The Board of Trustees of the Armouries. **353 Getty Images:** Time & Life Pictures

All other images © Dorling Kindersley

For further information see:
www.dkimages.com